ONE VILLAGE, ONE WAR, 1914-1945

ONE VILLAGE, ONE WAR, 1914-1945

A Thinking About The Literature of Stone

By Douglas How

LANCELOT PRESS
Hantsport, Nova Scotia

*To my children
and their own*

Copyright © Douglas How 1995

ISBN 0-88999-563-X

Published 1995

ALL RIGHTS RESERVED. No part of this book may be reproduced in any form without written permission of the publisher except brief quotations embodied in critical articles or reviews.

LANCELOT PRESS LIMITED, Hantsport, Nova Scotia.
Office and production facilities situated on Highway No. 1, 1/2 mile east of Hantsport.

MAILING ADDRESS:
P.O. Box 425, Hantsport, N.S. B0P 1P0

ACKNOWLEDGEMENT: This book has been published with the assistance of the Canada Council and the Nova Scotia Department of Education, Cultural Affairs Division.

Contents

Preface	7
Chapter One	9
Chapter Two	23
Chapter Three	71
Chapter Four	101
Chapter Five	133
Chapter Six	159
Chapter Seven	198
Chapter Eight	231
Chapter Nine	256
Chapter Ten	279
Chapter Eleven	310
Chapter Twelve	345
Chapter Thirteen	361
Appendix	373

In every generation, Canadians have had to rework the miracle of their political existence.
        Historian A.R.M. Lower in Colony to Nation, 1946

This is a story of two generations and how they reworked Canada in ways she may have lost.

It is becoming hard not to feel sometimes that both sides are the victims of a common terror, that everybody's guns are against everybody ultimately.
        Donald Pearce in Journal of a War,
    a magnificent and largely forgotten book about being a
            frontline lieutenant with the North Nova Scotia
                    Highlanders in 1944-45

This is the story of a village that had soldiers on both sides.

Preface

On a November 11 in the late 1940s, I was covering the annual Remembrance Day service at the national war memorial in Ottawa. The ceremony was just over. The prime minister and other dignitaries were leaving. A mother who had lost two sons in battle was leaving. A band was playing quietly and the veterans were marching off. I was about to go too when I saw a woman and a boy of six or seven, and a reporter's impulse made me follow them. They went up to a cenotaph banked deep with wreaths bright with the red of the poppies in them. The two of them stood there, silent, just looking, and then the boy asked a question, and I'll never forget the question and I'll never forget the mother's answer.

"Why are they there?" the boy said of the poppies and the wreaths, and at first the mother said nothing. She thought. Then in three words she caught the mystery of man and war.

"No one knows," she said.

Chapter One

THERE IS THIS PICTURE Ina Brien had taken in 1925 when Adolf Hitler was 36 and had learned what he could do with words, and she was teaching grades one and two in the five-room village school. There she is at the rear and there are her students in front of her, three rows of us sitting or standing in long grass that bends as though the Fundy winds decreed it. When she sent me a copy in the l960s, I was so pleased that I sent others off to everyone in it I could find. It was only later that it told me other things:

That those kids would be 25 or so years of age before they'd be conscious of living in a world dominated by neither economic depression nor war. That these would be the things they'd remember like the weights and anchors of existence. That they were members of the only Canadian generation to grow up among the veterans of one world war and produce the veterans of another. That, so far as I know, every boy in that snapshot would go to war or try to, and at least one would die in it, and a number of the girls would marry men who'd go. That behind them in school there soon would be boys who would reach the milestone years of 1939 and 1940 at the milestone age of 18 at which, militarists say, boys combine those qualities of innocence, energy, zest and physical endurance which fit them best for war. That what made this macabre was that the same thing had happened so recently and was never supposed to happen again. In fact, all these things took place in such a relatively short period that what once was known as the Great War of 1914-18 has become known as World War I and what happened between 1939 and 1945 as World War II. That is to say, there has been a rearrangement of brute, unlovely facts that comes close to agreeing with those who argue that there were not two great wars but one with a pause in between long enough to grow another generation of soldiers; one two-phase war which started in 1914 and ended in 1945. One 31-year war associated above all with the Adolf Hitler who by 1925 had already revealed in a book what his plans were and would become a compass, a calendar and a curse in the lives of Miss Brien's students and many millions more in doing what he'd said he'd do.

This book is about a typical Canadian village and the 31-year war, what it did there, what it meant to Ina Brien's students. What it meant to have in their midst a German boy who believed the lies that Hitler told, and how the war made people feel they belonged to a Canada that was more than the sum of its parts, and why to this day there are people to whom both the beginning and the end are like scarlet towers on the highways of their lives:

August 4, 1914. Lawyer Mariner George Teed, K.C., and wife Madge are ensconced in the great stone Georgian house built by a Father of Confederation at the top of the two-tiered hill in Dorchester, New Brunswick, shiretown of Westmorland County, population roughly 800. It was their home until Mariner re-established his practice in Saint John some years back in keeping with trends that are turning a rural country into an increasingly urban one. Now the great stone house is their summer home and it is always a village event when they arrive with possessions which take up half a railway boxcar and include both the horse Bonnie and a flock of hens, Rhode Island Reds from their city henhouse, not to mention linen and dishes and the many packages of vegetable and flower seeds Mrs. Teed has spent weeks selecting from catalogues for her annual liaison with the soil. This is why their village-born sons Hugh and Lionel are here this August day. They have both attended the Royal Military College in Kingston, Ont., and, at 22, Hugh has become a robustly good-looking engineer. Lionel is nearly 21 and still a student, thinner than Hugh, rather ascetic in appearance. They both have about them the indefineable touch of social rank, even though there are those who say/gossip that the late former Premier and Judge Daniel "Roaring Dan" Hanington and his wife were not terribly pleased when daughter Madge married a Teed, and others who say that's just the way families are.

On this fine August day, the two young men and some friends have gone downshore to picnic and swim at Coles Point. Many years later no one will remember just what friends, but the chances are they include Joe and/or Jack Hickman and maybe one of the Foster boys or one of the Landry boys. The weekly Sackville *Tribune's* social notes have kept recording their summer activities such as the one from which they are now returning. They are travelling by horse and carriage, and they are noisy and laughing and then they see Mr. and Mrs. Teed and others waiting on the lawn of the great house the way people wait when they have a purpose in waiting. They know tensions have been mounting over that seemingly eternal cause of tension, The Situation in Europe. Someone of monarchical importance was recently assassinated in the Balkans, and on July 28 Austro-Hungary declared war on Serbia and on August 1 Germany declared war on Russia and now the Germans are surging through Belgium to get at France, and the British have been saying they shouldn't, they mustn't, or else. Just yesterday the *Tribune* carried a large front-page advertisement by Eastern Hay and Feed Co. Ltd. warning that WAR "will send the price of flour and sugar soaring." So when the young, laughing people reach those on the lawn it is more of a shock than a surprise when they are told England has declared war on Germany.

First there is a hush. Then a gasp from young ladies. Then six-year-old Constance Teed sees the young men break into cheers. Their faces are bright and shining, and they are exultant. They are happy not so much about the war, Connie Teed will think years later, but about this momentous thing England has done. At six, she is by no means certain what a war consists of but she has no doubt her brothers will go to whatever it is. As an editorial in the ardently Liberal *Tribune* said just yesterday, former Prime Minister Sir Wilfrid Laurier, "that grand old Liberal chieftain," had proclaimed that "When Britain is at war Canada is at war" and, it added, this "will prove true if the Mother Country is drawn into war."

Now she is drawn in and it doesn't matter whether you call her Great Britain or the Mother Country or the Old Country or the British Empire or England, and it doesn't matter whether you are Conservative as the Teeds are or Liberal as the Hickmans are, on that lawn it is accepted, emotionally, spontaneously and certainly legally accepted, that Canada is drawn in too. Young as she is, Connie Teed senses that, senses that if England has a war Canada will have one too. The same one. For that's the way things are. "It was England, you know," she'll say in old age, England that made those young men cheer.

Chapter One

May 7, 1945: Eight-year-old Ruthie Lewis is walking home from school. Her parents, Elmer and Lavinia (Vinnie) Lewis, run a garage and small store on the far side of town, one of those places where people gather to gossip and pass the time of day and, in this case, to play cards. As far back as she can remember, there have been boys and men playing cards in the evening in the kitchen back of the store, and most of them wearing uniforms because there has been a war on as far back as she can remember too. But what matters at the moment is that she is walking the two or so miles home. She walks through the village square at the foot of the hill with the stone house on whose lawn the young men cheered. She walks past the stores and the courthouse and the hotel and the monument with the 25 names chiselled into granite, which means that they are dead in a sad and special way. Three of the names are those of people named Hugh and Lionel Teed and Jack Hickman, but neither these nor any of the others involve the one supreme sacrifice she knows much of anything about.

He went away when she was four, and there is a story that he and two pals left about the same time and that one of them said he didn't expect to come back, and that he didn't. None of the three did. None of their names is on the monument yet, but people say they will be because they died for a "cause," just like the Teed boys, only years later. He seemed, this special one, to attach importance to the fact that they both liked animals and were born on the 23rd of June. In June 1942 and again in June 1943, he sent messages to wish her a happy birthday, and her parents have kept them for her till she knows more. Her parents also sent him parcels, but they don't do that anymore and there was no message from him in 1944 and there will be none next month because he got it or he bought it, people say. He died as a Canadian in a British unit and amid a great irony, namely that Britain-the Mother Country-the

British Empire-England will lose a 19th century empire by winning 20th century wars.

At eight, of course, such elaborate thoughts are beyond Ruthie Lewis as she walks down the hill below the square, walks along the long stretch where the wind comes in from Fundy, and sees the penitentiary, the pen, like some fortress on its hill, and then, below, the row of white wooden houses where guard families live, and this is where it happens. Doors burst open and people burst out, laughing and shouting and waving flags and embracing. She's never seen anything like it, but every indication is that it's a good thing. The official celebration of VE (Victory in Europe) Day won't come till tomorrow, but the news is already out. It's on the radio. "It's over," the people are shouting. "The war in Europe is over." There is a war with Japan to be finished too, and it will last another three months and then end in a way that will change the world. But it's the one in Europe that matters most, and it's over. This time it really is.

The veterans of 1914-18 are nearly all gone now and the veterans of 1939-45 are dead or just about as old as most people get. Books without number have been written to try to explain what happened and why, and still they come. But, even as I get deep into my 70s, I sense that those vivid and tragic times will never be totally explained. Perhaps it's this way because age increases your sense of the mystery of human life. Perhaps it isn't. All I know is that I used to think of Canada's part in the 31-year war in relatively simple terms and that I no longer do. That for all the books about it, the most eloquent yet baffling testimonial is that of the war memorials from one end of this country to the other. For they were erected as obelisks of sorrow and pride, of a deep and defining grief, a unifying grief because they bespoke not something small and local but something that had to do with a profound sense of belonging together. They are a literature of stone that says things we have never otherwise been able to say and, I suspect, have never fully grasped. Things that enter into the confounding character of Canadians themselves, things that have a mystery of their own, and which is in one sense a peculiarly Canadian mystery. Things corroborated by tens of thousands of graves across the seas.

So there is to me something haunting about those memorials, and this is a belated attempt to understand what it is. To understand by trying to find a focus small enough and perhaps deep enough to help tell the story of what the war or wars did and meant to a country by telling what it or they did and meant to one small village in it: the village of my childhood, the village that still stirs lyric memories in the aging of my mind. I can even identify the moment the thought first came to me.

It is a Remembrance Day in the mid-1970s, and for the first time I am back home to march to the war memorial with the village veterans. We form up on the school grounds and on feet trying to remember how to march properly, we proceed to the square, to the monument. There must be 25 of us and I'd guess that fewer than half a dozen were there the day the monument was unveiled half a century earlier.

There are only a limited number of things that reveal what a nation is and how it got that way, and there we are for one of them. A stone soldier watches as we do what hundreds of thousands will do this day from coast to coast. We sing hymns. We hear a clergyman link those we honor with God Almighty. We observe two minutes of silence. We hear Frank L. Dobson trumpet "The Last Post," that immemorial lament that could make granite eyes shed tears, and we pledge that we will remember those whose names this granite contains:

> They shall grow not old ,
>   as we that are left grow old;
> Age shall not weary them,
>   nor the years condemn,
> At the going down of the sun
>   and in the morning
> We will remember them

There are 41 names now, 16 more than there used to be, but the monument also says things the names themselves don't say. Its arithmetic is strikingly similar to the statistics for the entire country: the loss of lives in 1914-18 was roughly 50% greater than it was in 1939-45 when the national population was twice as large. Moreover, the village has done what many communities have: it has, in a sense, accepted that there were not two wars but one, has put the names of the fallen of 1939-45 on the memorial to the fallen of 1914-18. Many cities and towns have dedicated parks and libraries and rinks as memorials of a more practical kind, but something has happened to the theology of monuments; some scepticism or bewilderment in the 20th century mind seems to have numbed the urge to erect memorials to human beings, perhaps as part of a doubt in man about man himself.

So the names of the 16 dead of my generation stare at me, and I remember most of them. Their faces come to me, young again, surprisingly vivid, laughing with the radiance of youth, haunting with the age they've been denied. But when the service is over I look at the original 25 names, and I recognize family names but no faces come to me. For they are the names of men who died before I was born. In the evening at the Legion banquet, I speak of the village dead of my own generation and suddenly realize that most of the men in the room have never known them either. I remember that amid the incandescence of the '60s there arose among the young a feeling that since war is bad something less than honor is due to those who wage it; that at a recent Remembrance Day service at nearby Mount Allison University virtually the only students who showed up were those assigned a role in the ceremony.

That's when it strikes me that that lyric pledge to remember the war dead is valid only in a limited and symbolic way, that it will not be long before all 41 names on that memorial mean nothing specifically to anyone. It may not matter, but it seems to matter. It makes me start thinking about whatever it is this book becomes, eventually makes me set out on a quest for the story of what put those names where they are and made their generations what they were and do what they felt they ought to do. It turned out to be a quest that would go on sporadically for years, bring me into touch with families I had had no contact with for decades, stimulate a blizzard of correspondence, unearth letters, snapshots, scrapbooks and medals long since tucked away, take me to the war cemeteries of Italy and Western Europe, lead to conversations that could go on for hours, bring me face to face with psychological hurts and wounds that refuse to die. It took me to the village's own Keillor House Museum. To the National Archives in Ottawa and its hundreds of thousands of personnel files. To the Royal Canadian Military Institute in Toronto where thousands of books crowd one another, and all are about war. It led to dead ends and surprising discoveries. It amazed me to find how much of two massive national efforts could be told through what the people of one village and area did. It even took me to Germany because that German boy who believed

Hitler's lies helped fight Hitler's war.

It started out as a sort of salute to my village, to people and families I remember with warmth and affection, to honor others I never knew. It went beyond that. It made me see our war memorials as something beyond what they ostensibly signify, as monuments to the other side of sacrifice, to the irony of what war did for and to this country. It left me with that vague sense that something that had once seemed simple wasn't simple at all. It left me wondering what our literature of stone had said to the nation, and what more it might have said, and why it didn't. Why the sense of national coherence and belonging the 31-year war crystallized may have slipped away without anyone being sure where it went, or why.

But first, where did you start? You looked at files and at church walls with "rolls of honor" on them, read war histories, regimental histories, old newspapers, asked families what they remembered and old men what they knew. If you were lucky, people dug out things they'd had in drawers for years. And bit by bit a picture formed.

When Britain went to war in 1914 Canada went to war, automatically, because she was a colony, a big, awkward and increasingly self-conscious one, but still a colony; in places like the village, a devoted colony. Within days of Britain's declaration of war, the *Tribune* was reporting that young people were parading through New Brunswick streets. Bands were playing. Lieut. Hugh Mariner Teed left to join his regiment, even as "great interest in the war situation prevails" in Dorchester and "a large number in the province announced their willingness to fight for the Mother Country." The feeling was "that England must not sheathe the sword till the haughty spirit of the German autocrat is entirely shattered. God Save The King."

Already the ladies of Westmorland County had collected $1,000 for a hospital ship, the contributions ranging from 25 cents to $50, and when the Sackville band came to town for a night concert, "all the folks within miles were at the courthouse" to hear it. At 90, this was the way Percy Palmer would remember it: "The boys in high school hoped the war wouldn't be over before they got a chance to get into it." Yet the war wasn't everything; it had to share space with news that Silas Tower had four cattle in the pound at Dorchester Cape, the village's Methodists and Presbyterians held a joint Sunday School picnic, two local parties were motoring through the county, and everybody was admiring the five-seat McLaughlin-Buick touring car recently purchased by storekeeper J.H. Hickman. Within a month the Honorable Henry R. Emmerson, M.P., died, and it was a milestone. He'd been premier of New Brunswick, been in the Liberal cabinet of Sir Wilfrid Laurier in Ottawa. He also would turn out to be, as time would coldly confirm, just about the last of the long line of prominent political leaders who called the village home, which is another way of saying that even as its people headed into the greatest challenge they had ever faced, the village itself had reached a milestone in its descent from the very considerable eminence it once had known.

By late August the newspapers said there were 20,000 soldiers at Valcartier, Que., waiting to go overseas. By September there were 32,000, and Lieut. Hugh Teed was one of them. He was attached to the headquarters of a brigade, and somewhere in that sea of tents there were at least five other men with village associations. Two were privates with the 7th Battalion from British Columbia, the Rocky Mountain Rangers, and both were older than privates usually are. Edwin Oulton had been working ever since he'd quit the village school at 14 to support the family after his father, a judge, died early. Over the years he'd made his way west, from job to job, and sent money home to help educate five siblings. When the war started, he was working in the lumber woods near Fernie, B.C., and no teenager could have made for a recruiting station faster. He had a good mind, and he just knew it was the thing to do, even if he was 30 years of age.

The other private was Harry Archibald Tattrie, and he was nearly 37. He said he was single and a Presbyterian, that he'd been a lineman born in Halifax, and his closest relatives were an aunt in Nova Scotia and an uncle in Massachusetts. He also said he'd soldiered with an infantry outfit at Camp Sussex, N.B., for two years, presumably at summer camps, but in years to come people would not be too clear about what his links to the village were. Someone would say he was a drifter who'd been around for some years, then left, and maybe he was because he told a recruiting officer in Kamloops, B.C., that he had no address. By contrast, there were two teenagers who'd been working for the Royal Bank of Canada and were so young they barely qualified to have the army take them. Harvard Linwood McAllister, the son of Barber Jimmy McAllister, a village character, signed up in the infantry two days before he turned 18 that September. Charles Wesley Elsdon was even younger; he was the son of a senior official at the prison, of a stern father, and their relations were such that he didn't go home to say goodbye, didn't take the oath of loyalty with Moncton's 8th artillery battery till he had his 18th birthday in England that December. Finally, Albert Wright Starratt was 21 when he enlisted in the 8th Battery too. He was the son of the accountant at the prison, listed himself as a painter and said that, like Elsdon, he'd gone to militia camps.

The six of them were in that great fleet of ships that bore the 1st Division overseas that fall as what was called

"Canada's Answer." When they got to England, they were sent to Salisbury Plain to train for battle, and Ed Oulton would remember singing "We are the boys from Canada" and "There's a hole in the bottom of the sea," with some very naughty verses, and a lot of other songs, till they saw the mud. They would never forget the mud because they lived in tents with no floor boards, and it was everywhere. Still Lieutenant Teed found time to court and marry a beautiful young Salisbury woman named Violet Stacey, which apparently made him the first Canadian soldier of the war to wed in Britain.

The 1st Division was floundering in the mud of Salisbury Plain when the village's Pierre Amand Landry, chief justice of the Supreme Court of New Brunswick (King's Bench Division), sat down in Saint John's Royal Hotel and wrote a father's letter to a son about going to war. He told son Bill that "I have been reluctant to write you as my writing might seem to urge you to enlist." In fact, he said, the son must act for himself. As far as the father was concerned, "'Staying home' will be a comfort to my feelings — 'going' will give me a certain pride in you, and a feeling that you are yielding to a call of patriotic duty. Act on your own judgment." If his judgment were to go, the father added, he should "see Sumner at Moncton," that is recruiting officer Roy Sumner, a prominent Conservative as Pierre Landry had long been himself. He should go at it "in a business way," and if he could do no better than a private's rank, "I think I'd wait."

Bill Landry didn't wait. He joined up as a private. He was a 28-year-old engineer, a graduate of McGill University who had for some years worked with Canadian General Electric in Peterborough, Ont., a city which had crowned him men's singles tennis champion in 1911. He also was a feisty and popular young man, and a short one; he stood just five feet five, which explains something that happened the day he came face to face for the first time with Sir Sam Hughes, the improbable Minister of Militia and Defence. The minister was coming for an inspection, and Bill Landry liked to bet, so he made bets with his peers that Sir Sam would stop to speak to him. Then he went to the two tallest soldiers he could find and paid them to stand on either side of him. Sure enough, Sir Sam stopped to speak to this very small man between two very unsmall ones.

"Aren't you," he said, "too small to be a soldier?"

"So, sir," said Private Landry, "was Napoleon."

An amused Minister had barely vanished before Bill Landry was collecting. What's more, a family story says, the camp commandant was so impressed that he put him up for an officer's commission. By March 1915, he was training in Kingston, Ont., to qualify as an artillery officer, and three other village young men were there too, one of them Joe Hickman, another apparently Lionel Teed. "I did not think it was so hard to hold your seat on a horse," a Pierre Amand Landry letter kidded about something the training had done to his son. "The horses there must be wild or your mode of riding must be hazardous." Bill Landry's mode of riding may well have been hazardous because he was that sort of young man.

Chapter Two

THE CANADIANS MET THEIR first great test in April 1915, and a legend came out of it. In muddy, devastated Flanders Fields, in a salient of a stalemated front near Ypres, Belgium, they faced the Germans' first poison gas attack and refused to break when other troops were fleeing in anguish, were leaving wide gaps on their flank. They extended their lines and retreated and held, and when the terror and confusion and mass killing were over, they had lost 6,000 men in five days and a British communique said "their gallantry and determination undoubtedly saved the situation."

Ed Oulton, Harvard McAllister and Charles Elsdon came out of all this intact. Albert Starratt, now a corporal, came out of it with a back wound that would keep him away from his battery for three months. Harry Tattrie didn't come out of it at all. He was reported wounded, then missing, then presumed to have died on or after the 24th of April, at the height of the battle. In army documents it would be recorded that no particulars were available as to the circumstances of his death, just as few seemed to be available about the circumstances of his life.

Lieut. Hugh Teed came out of Ypres a shattered man,

his nerves and energies shot. A medical board found him suffering from anemia, a victim of strain and exposure arising from military duty, incapable even of light duties. In August, the army sent him home, hoping that a two-month leave would help him get in shape to do what he wished to do: return to the front. When he reached the village with his bride, he got a hero's welcome. It seemed that the whole community turned out at the railway station, and a band was there, and there were speeches and handshakes and tears, and everybody agreed that young Mrs. Teed was beautiful even if she had laryngitis and could hardly say a word.

One newspaper reported that "Lieutenant Teed, war hero, was greeted with prolonged cheers. The gallant officer told of life in the trenches, of outrages of which he saw results. He told of a boy nine years of age whose hands had been cut off by Huns. He instanced the case of a girl of six whose face had been punctured by a German bayonet." He told, in other words, atrocity stories prevalent at that time, many of them later attributed to wartime propaganda. As to dangers at the front, "Lieutenant Teed pointed out that he had been there and had returned ... But men are needed, he said, needed more than people here seem to understand."

Later kid sister Connie and others came down with typhoid, and the young couple left for Saint John where people said how striking they were, and how very much in love. Eventually the convalescent leave was extended to a third month, and it worked. In January 1916, shortly after Lieutenant Teed got back to England, another medical board found him completely recovered. That same month his brother Daniel Lionel Teed enlisted in Saint John.

That month, too, Lieut. Bill Landry arrived in Belgium to serve with the 17th Battery, Canadian Field Artillery, 2nd Canadian Division. After Ypres, the Canadians had had chaotic fighting at nearby places such as Festubert and Givenchy, and this same general area is where the 17th Battery took up positions on a stalled and writhing front. Did this even as the army at home was raising more infantry battalions with numbers to identify them, a system that had come out of the tumultuous and quite possibly unbalanced mind of Sir Sam Hughes.

Among others, the army was recruiting a New Brunswick battalion to be called the Kent-Westmorland 145th, and at the first local recruiting meeting on December 20, 1915, there was a rousing response. Boys off the farms that lay in all directions enlisted. Village boys enlisted. So did a young man who was let out of prison to do it. Indeed, the village undertook to raise one-sixteenth of the battalion's total of 1,100 or so men, and it did so well that it was soon resisting the imperialistic overtures of neighboring Sackville and getting used to having men training downtown and going on route marches and marching in a body into churches on Sundays.

Dr. David Beatty of Mount Allison University tells a lot about this in a book entitled *Memories of The Forgotten War*, based on the diary of the 145th's Vincent Goodwin of Baie Verte, N.B. He says the town fathers of Sackville were not pleased to have Dorchester keep its soldiers to itself, for they had rented barracks of a size sufficient to further military ambitions of their own. They thought the Dorchester recruits should come there to join in training with others from the Sackville and Port Elgin areas. Nevertheless, by February 9, 1916, the village was doing so well on its own that Lt. Col. William Forbes, the battalion's commanding officer, announced that "in view of the splendid record in recruiting made in the shiretown of

Westmorland County, an all-Dorchester Platoon has formed." It would be billeted there too. Its motto, proclaimed the colonel, was "For King and Country and to Help Paint Dorchester on the Kaiser's Front Door." Moreover, he pledged, the Dorchester Platoon would "carry its name and individuality to Berlin."

That still wasn't good enough for crusty C.C. Avard of the *Tribune*. He was soon arguing editorially that the platoon *should* be transferred to Sackville because its recruits were "not receiving the training they should and all because the people of Dorchester have put up a 'holler' that the soldiers should be allowed to remain there." Yet, he maintained, "retention of the soldiers in Dorchester is fair neither to Sackville which is paying good money for the rental of barracks, nor to the Dorchester boys themselves who should be undergoing training which is impossible in Dorchester." But by then the village had taken its own military formation to its heart, and manifested no sympathy for a larger community just nine miles away and which, people said, was always after everything it could get. So for some six months the soldiers were around town in their peaked hats and puttees and khaki uniforms with buttons right up to the throat. Moreover, it was just as well that Sackville didn't get its way for then the village would have been largely deprived of exposure to Lieutenant Goodwin.

Young Lieut. E. Mansel C. Goodwin of Baie Verte, that is, who came to town shortly after that first recruiting meeting. To be specific, he arrived December 29 to take charge and at once called a platoon parade. He met lawyer C.Lionel Hanington, an uncle of Hugh and Lionel Teed, and they got a building cleaned out for drills, and within 24 hours there was a doctor on hand and he turned down four of the recruits the platoon already had. Lieutenant Goodwin was then named officer in command of the

Dorchester Platoon. He was a tall, slim and dashing figure in his officer's uniform with the Sam Browne belt, a graduate of Stanstead College, a private school in the Eastern Townships of Quebec, and an enthusiastic soldier. He kept a diary which Historian Beatty came across in researching his story on Mansel's cousin Vincent, a diary that was soon bristling with summaries of military activities. Drills, route marches, pay days, church parades. The arrival of army clothing, equipment, rifles. Of more recruits, one at least under unusual circumstances. Twelve German prisoners of war escaped from an internment camp in Amherst, 18 miles away, and someone reported one was seen in the nearby farm country. Lieutenant Goodwin at once sent two soldiers to investigate, and they brought a man in who turned out to be an Irish sailor. So what did the commanding officer of the Dorchester Platoon do? He recruited the sailor for the 145th.

But his diary had a wider context. He threw light on a village that wasn't what it had been in its shipping and political heyday but still was an attractive and even handsome place, surrounded by small farms and with the Maritime Penitentiary as its economic pillar. He stayed at the Windsor Hotel, that proud 20-year-old "city hotel in the country," and he got friendly with the Tait family who ran both it and the 12-year-old local rink. He went to the Presbyterian Church with the manager of the local linen mills, one of several abortive manufacturing enterprises down on the marsh near the railway station. On a Sunday afternoon in January, he went for a car ride with Mrs. Tait, son Billy and daughter Nina: "Snow in roads but motoring fine. Met wagons and sleighs. Went again after supper."

Above all the diary tended to bear out a Goodwin family saying that Mansel was "a great man for the ladies." Indeed, it suggested that in that wartime winter he may well have seen himself as a one-man cure for lonely and patriotic hearts. Within a week he discovered the rink, the nicest one for miles around: "Meet lots of girls and had a good skate. Went home with Miss Foran." Such items went on, week after week, on into spring: "Church with Mary Mitton ... To rink with Nina Tait ... Walk around the flatiron with Mary ... Band at rink. Had splendid skate. Home with Mary ... Route march. Evening at home of Misses Piercey. Colder ... Rink. Home with Mrs. Foran ... Evening at Pierceys ... Rink. Home with Miss Foran ... Social in Baptist Church for soldiers. Home with Miss Buck ... Rink with Mrs. Winchester ... Fine. Driving with Mrs. Winchester. To Pierceys after Methodist Church ... To Mrs. John Dickie's in evening with Miss Ruth Tingley ... To Sackville with Herb Palmer and three young ladies. Saw a play and had an oyster stew ... Rink. Party down from Moncton. To Miss Emma Chapman's after, till 1 a.m. ... To Moncton with Miss Mary Gaudet, and to Sunny Brae rink for carnival ... Went to see Mrs. Winchester and had a big time ... Parade to Methodist Church. Had supper with Misses Buck and Gaudet, then up to see Jean ... Rink. Home with Miss Cochrane ... To Amherst for Red Cross dance with Miss Gaudet. Had a big time ... To Amherst. Evening at Harpers. Ada was there ... Pay day. To Moncton with excursion from Amherst. Skating and dancing. Home at 4.30 a.m. ... Parade to Church of England. To Forans after. Home with Miss Bishop ... Route march in morning. To Moncton with Miss Alice Shaw and Mrs. Gaudet. Big time at Red Cross dance ... Doctor passed nine men, three turned down. To play with Lulu in evening ... Doctor here for inoculations. To Sackville with him and two young ladies ... Baptist Church in evening. Home with Miss Tingley ... Tea at Lou's ... Up to Molly's with Lou and Carm ... Parade to Presbyterian Church. To Andersons Mills for mayflowers. To Molly's in evening ... Nina in Saint John. Very lonesome ... To ball in Amherst. Meet

Miss Black ... For ride with Carm, Lou and Jean in Mr. Landry's car ..."

The distinguished and, unfortunately, ailing Judge Pierre Amand Landry *had* bought a car, and people in town were talking about his son Allain running it into a cow. In fact, the mere mention of the Landry name indicated that Lieutenant Goodwin was right in there socially in more ways than one. Perhaps also at more levels than one. There were, for instance, diary entries with a touch of mystery. They concerned visits to "No. 20." Lieutenant Goodwin reported he was there quite frequently. He never explained why, but he always said he had a fine time.

From February on into summer, Pierre Amand Landry's son Bill sent home a series of letters which told a good deal about the frontline Lieutenant Goodwin and his soldiers would soon see. They also threw light on what was happening to the warm and buoyant Landry family — six sons, one daughter — raised in a patrician, three-storey house by an Irish-Canadian mother, Bridget Annie McCarthy, and her husband, the most prominent French Acadian of his day. The father was also a man of open mind who could eloquently switch from French to English. Even Bill Landry's real name revealed the way he thought. A former Conservative Member of Parliament, Pierre Landry so admired Liberal leader and future prime minister Sir Wilfrid Laurier that the boy was called Wilfrid Andre in his honor.

But Wilfrid Andre Landry's letters from the front made another revelation. Though he'd occasionally start with a few lines in French, it was in English that he told about life in the waterlogged Ypres salient, about fighting in places he couldn't identify but would add to Canadian history names such as St. Eloi and its enormous mud craters, left by exploding mines, names such as Mount Sorrel and Observatory Ridge and Sanctuary Wood, plus casualties which in June soared far beyond those of April 1915. He told about:

Reputation: "The Canadians are sure thought a lot of. As one English general said, they are not much at discipline but, by goodness, they can fight."

Life in the gun lines: He was one of three lieutenants in the battery and they took turns spending 48 hours at a forward observation post out in no-man's land, "directing by phone the firing of the battery and watching the movements of the enemy." For this and other reasons, he said, life could beat a football game by a mile "for real excitement." The light, he wrote one night in March, "is very bad for observing, being very misty and our glasses magnify the mist. The last few nights have been very dark and the Germans keep sending up flares. This lights up the land between the trenches and the guns and machine-guns on both sides open up on anything they see: working parties and patrols or anybody else who might be above the parapet ... We had a great shoot the other day, firing all afternoon along the whole line, and again at night." It was so noisy, "you could hardly pass orders."

Aspirations: Though it could wait till he'd learned what a gunner's life was all about, he yearned to fly. He watched with fascination as one British flying "machine" tackled four German ones and brought one down: "He'll get his V.C. (Victoria Cross) for that." Enemy planes were "flying about here all the time, trying to locate gun batteries or anything else worth knowing. This information is sent back to the Germans and they open fire."

Repercussions: "One (plane) flew over us and dropped smoke bomb signals. Next day the Germans put 50 shells over and how we escaped without losing our guns I don't know." The first shell just missed six soldiers, then made a hole 3 feet by 12 in the soft earth. He and his men escaped, he said, because they were under cover. "You can hear the report of the gun, then the shell coming like an express train. Although you don't know exactly where they are going, you can form a fairly good idea and after the first one keep well to a flank." The encouraging thing was that on average it took about 1,000 shells to kill one soldier. The biggest worry was rifle bullets.

The people: Even with snow on the ground, "the farmers around here are ploughing their ground (late February) and getting ready to till the soil."

Comparisons: Brother Pierre was overseas as an infantry officer (would become a major and win the Order of the British Empire) but if brothers Jack and Allain were going to enlist they should join the artillery. "If anybody deserves credit in this war, it is the infantry," but the gun lines were the place to be. The excellent French guns were taking a "terrific" toll of German mass attacks against Verdun, and he hoped that great battle would soon end the war in victory. What it would end instead was hundreds of thousands of lives, without changing much at all.

Home: His mother had been ill in hospital for a prolonged period, and they too corresponded regularly. He felt it was "my duty to see this thing through to the end," but it would be "the proudest and happiest day of my life if I can jump off that little old I.C.R. (Intercolonial Railway) at Dorchester and see my father there to welcome me."

Command: "I know every man in the battery by name

and they will do anything I tell them. I am hardly strict or severe enough to really make a good soldier but I get along all right."

Religion: "Communion service only comes around once in a great while, and if there is anything doing it is pretty hard to get to. Sunday is the same as any other day here. Half the time you really don't know what day it is."

Moving: On March 17 he reported being busy for 10 days getting settled in a new position: "You would smile to see me in a cellar strengthened in the centre by rails supported on planks. The entrance is filled with sandbags, leaving a small doorway. The sides and top are covered by sandbags. In front there is a big, high chimney. We took out a brick and have a view of the enemy and our own trenches ... There are two men with me. Bullets are flying everywhere but we are protected. This was a brick farm and we are protected even more by a brick wall. One soon gets wise to all the cover he can get."

Learning: (March 20) "The weather is beautiful. The battery is working splendidly and making a great name for itself. When we arrived, the men could fire 3 rounds in 15 seconds, now they fire 3 in 8 seconds." They, and he, were learning things every day, and one was that socks were the best gift to get. When he got two parcels of them from "the society," he sent some to Joe Hickman "and a few other village boys, including young Burns who used to live in the (Guard) Row." But he found it so complicated that he suggested they be sent direct.

The Canadian soldier: "When he comes into a new place and knows he has to live there, he digs right in and makes himself comfortable. We took over from an English battery and in two days you would hardly know the place. The men built a big cooking stove which is working fine. Fixed up their dugouts, cleaned them, put in good strong beds, fixed up their gun pits, planted grass seed."

As spring came to the village and people began talking about getting ready for gardening, an ailing and lonely Pierre Amand Landry yearned for the maples to bud outside his window, and when the leaves came he wrote an uncle how beautiful this was to see. Up the road in Middleton, 10-year-old Graydon Milton sometimes took time out from doing the chores on the family farm to watch the Dorchester Platoon training on the family's sheep pasture hill. It was one of the few dry spots in the area that spring, so Lieutenant Goodwin would march his men the two miles or so from the village square to make use of it, and the boy liked to see if he could talk one of the soldiers into parting with a military badge.

Then he'd see them march back down the dirt highway where he used to see the Hickman boys come roaring along in their father's car, making a hell of a racket. "Those Hickman boys!", old ladies would say. But Joe and Jack were gone now, gone overseas, as was Frank A. Dobson who'd nearly been killed the winter before the war when a tree fell while he and farmer Ed Turner were working in those woods back up the hill. So were two of the Landry boys whose father, the judge, was sick and in pain. Yes, and a lot of others. More and more others all the time.

As spring came to the Western Front, Lieut. Bill Landry

was around St. Eloi where the enormous, man-made craters were like the cesspools of hell. From his letters:

Action: (April 14) "We have had 16 days of the hardest scrapping any battery has yet had. We have fired more rounds than any four batteries had in eight months. We were at it day and night, getting two or three hours sleep in 24. The trenches rocked at times from the enemy fire ... We were relieved by another battery and, strange to say, Joe Hickman was in it." (April 25) "This is one terror of a war. This morning we buried one of our men killed by a shell. A great favorite in the prime of life. All over the country are graveyards filled with our men. Everybody would go wild if the war was finished and we'd mastered the Germans. Yet none of us want to kill them ... We started a week ago Monday to dig in four gun positions. It rained all week, the men were wet through, and a river flooded us out. Easter Sunday night I fell in five shellholes and was wet to the neck. I was mad clean through after the first two, but the next time I sat down and laughed." (April 28) "Night before last, about 10 p.m., the Boche tried to rush a crater our men were in, but got the surprise of their life when they were bombed back to their frontline, then bombed out of that into their support trenches. Our men came back to their own line, and believe me the artillery on both sides opened up. I was about 700 yards from the crater and about 150 yards from the German fire. It was a wonderful sight, flares going up in a steady stream, lighting the whole country, shells hissing through the air from all directions, the flash of guns, the reports, the explosion of the shells, rifles firing, machine-guns firing, trench mortars ... It was the finest and hardest short scrap I have witnessed. I sure was proud of our artillery and our infantry. Everyone is pleased. A little success goes a long way."

Hero: (May 8) A two-hour trip by horseback and he got a good bath and sleep in the "waggon lines," and fell to thinking about the war: "Germany can't beat us. We may suffer a few defeats but we will always come back stronger than ever." One reason: "the Canadians, when well officered, are good to a man." Another: a young man named [Weldon] Belyea from Moncton. "He's a linesman with the 8th Battery and a better or more devil-may-care boy can't be found. He's done things to win Victoria Crosses time after time but because he's up for office so often for misbehavior he doesn't get the credit. Once his place was shelled out and he got into the frontline and an infantry officer told him to act as a stretcher bearer. He lost six helpers, killed and wounded, getting the wounded out, but got through himself. The infantry major took his name down for a V.C., but was killed soon after. Another time, at Ypres, Belyea was driving with two men; a shell killed them but not him. Another time he crawled over the parapet in the dark and into no-man's land. To see the country, he said. He came to a log, saw a German on the other side, and said, 'What the deuce are you doing here?' Neither dared raise a fight because the machine-guns would open up on both sides. So they both crawled back to their own lines. Major Anderson once told Belyea he wanted some souvenirs. It wasn't long before Belyea came back with a German officer's outfit. He'd crawled out into no man's land and stripped one who'd been killed there. He fixes and mends broken communications wires no matter how bad the shelling is. They tell a good many stories about Belyea."

They may also have told stories about Bill Landry. He was recommended for the Military Cross but doubted (May 23) he'd get it because "the circumstances occurred during a scrap in which we were not awfully successful."

In the village that June of 1916 they were telling stories about Bill Landry's father. He'd become the first Acadian to be knighted, and his son wrote that he was "tickled to death" about it and about word that Sir Pierre had been out for a car drive with no ill effects. He was, in fact, a dying man just when dying was on the village mind. That month, soon after the Dorchester Platoon had suffered its first death, that of 20-year-old Pte. Ernest Gordon McFadden through illness, and just as it was getting ready to start its movement overseas, things kept happening which drove home to its men what it could be like when they got there. By coincidence, they were reported at the very time Sir Sam Hughes descended from a special railway train to find the platoon waiting. He inspected it, then joined in scenes of military and social splendor: the men in their khaki uniforms, Lieutenant Goodwin crisp and spruce in his officer's serge, his eyes studying the crowd for purposes of his own, people milling around a great tent on the lawn of the great stone house at the top of the hill, eating, drinking tea, chatting, and Sir Sam bustling about.

The visit was, by chance, reported in an issue of the *Tribune* which brought home forcibly what lay beyond the seductions of military panoply. The Canadians now had a three-division corps at the front, and in three June days it lost 8,000 men. L/Cpl. Harvard McAllister suffered shrapnel wounds that would take two months to heal. Pte. Joseph Arnold Chambers, a 26-year-old former telegraph operator and son of a former deputy warden at the prison, was reported missing in action with a signals unit, but it wouldn't be long before it was confirmed that he'd been killed after nine months in France. Killed heroically, it was said, with a sacrificial gun defending a withdrawal from no man's land. Robert McKelvie of the Mounted Rifles was reported wounded. My mother's brother, Pte. Frank A.

Dobson, was reported seriously wounded, though there was some doubt that the report was authentic. Lieut. Carleton Hanington of Vancouver and formerly of Dorchester was reported seriously wounded. Cpl. Albert Starratt had suffered his third wound, and the local correspondent had barely written that "Allie's friends wish him a speedy recovery" when word came that he'd died. Died on the 5th of June, three days after Arnold Chambers and two days after he himself was hit by shrapnel.

There still exists a photograph of him. He is just over six feet tall and he looks every inch the soldier. When the word of his death came, the whole village went into mourning. Union Jacks flew at half mast and the Methodist Church was packed for a memorial service.

One week later Bill Landry wrote, "We have been having a pretty strenuous time lately, take it from me." Two days later, just back from no-man's land, he reported that the fighting was "getting pretty fierce" amid terrible weather: "Nothing but rain."

The last thing Sir Sam Hughes said to the soldiers of what the *Tribune* now sometimes called "the famous Dorchester Platoon" was that he'd see them soon, and on June 25 , after leaves to help get the farm crops in and after being feted by the community at a farewell reception, they left for Valcartier. In Sackville there was a big farewell for B Company of the 145th, and when the train came through Dorchester it stopped to pick up the local boys, including a lieutenant of the village's own, Herbert Gladstone Palmer, handsome son of F.C. Palmer who ran a big general store. In all, they numbered 50, according to a photograph, and maybe more because Lieutenant Palmer wasn't in the picture and Sgt. Edgar Cole didn't appear to be and there may have been others. But away they went, singing a regimental song entitled "We've got a number, 1-4-5" and cheering through the open windows and the sounds coming back across the marshes to those cheering them on their way. Not to mention heavens knows how many young ladies lamenting the departure of Lieutenant Goodwin.

What is significant about the men he led away is what their numbers said about the village itself. It easily stood out in the 145th's recruiting area. According to David Beatty, "with the exception of Dorchester, recruiting was extremely slow." Week after week, the *Tribune* complained about the lack of response. By April Moncton clergymen were being asked to preach recruiting sermons. By the time of departure, the total numbers were up to 800 but only because of heavy stress on sermons, band music and exhortations by leading citizens at one recruiting meeting after another, and only after reaching out to other parts of New Brunswick and even into Nova Scotia. By the end, that June, the village and area had raised more men than the entire county of Kent. But it is also true that, in its insatiable hunger for men, the army had also been recruiting an Acadian battalion.

On the day the 145th left for Valcartier, Private Frank Ashley Dobson sat down in a base camp in France and wrote his sister Maude Turner about being wounded and homesick. He'd been shot in an arm while with the 5th Canadian Mounted Rifles, an outfit that had left its horses behind to fight as infantry. He'd been discharged from hospital, he said, spent a few days in a convalescent camp and then made his way to where he now was by two versions of train travel, first-class part of the way, in a boxcar after that. His wound had "healed up nicely and I am feeling fit for active service again." But there was longing in him: "Saw some very pretty country on the way here and it looked enough like dear old Canada to make a fellow feel a bit lonesome." Then: "How I would like to be home today and have Laura with me."

Laura Cunningham was a Nova Scotia farm girl he'd met in Truro when she was in teacher-training and he was a student at the Nova Scotia Agricultural College, and they had become a serious item. On June 21 she had written Frank's sister Maude that she'd been "living in dread as there have been so many casualties" and what a relief it had been to get a letter from him saying he was feeling fine and thankful to get off so lucky. They were writing regularly and if spared, he told his sister, he would "do my best to make a happy home" for Laura Cunningham.

But for the moment, Teacher Cunningham wrote from Brookfield, N.S., it seemed "so useless to just sit here and wait." So there was frustration and anxiety in her life, and in Frank A. Dobson's there was a tumult of satisfactions and apprehensions and hopes. In hospital he'd met New Zealanders and Australians and liked them, and on that recent trip he'd found that "there is plenty of fun even in travelling in a boxcar with the right bunch of fellows." The fact was, he said, that "a fellow sure does have some experiences out here and I wouldn't miss them for anything and am not a bit sorry I enlisted." Then the other side: "Nevertheless I am pretty lonely at times and will be glad when it's all over and I can turn to farming instead ... Hope the (Turner) farm is going along in the best of shape. Wish I could be with you to have some strawberries and cream, the thoughts of such things are enough to drive a fellow mad."

He was a tall, likeable and gentle man, my mother's brother. Frank A., the village called him to distinguish him from his first cousin, Frank L. (for Lawrence) Dobson, who would also go overseas. In the family it was said that when his mother had died young, of cancer, he vanished after the funeral and apparently spent the night alone at her grave, a teenager weeping heartache into the mystery of death, but he would never talk about it. After that he'd gone to live with Maude and Ed Turner on their farm just out of town, and he liked it there and still felt, as he said in his letter, that he wanted to be a farmer himself, a married one.

Once the 145th soldiers left town, the village's two outstanding military scholars had more reason than ever to keep a close eye on events. Bank manager A.V. Smith and the Rev. Byron Thomas, a retired Baptist clergyman, both had maps of the Western Front and both followed and posted the sway of battle as closely and swiftly as possible; certain pins for the Allies, certain pins for the foe. In a world without radio or television, they badgered the local telephone office for any news available. If it was important enough, drastic enough, they said, it should be passed along at any hour.

In keeping with this mandate, Mr. Smith was gratified to get an urgent call well after one midnight. Operator Jean Drillio was on the line and she said she felt she should report that the Germans had taken Cascara but couldn't hold it. He asked her to call the Reverend Thomas at once, grabbed some pins and headed for his map. In short order, he had a call from the Reverend saying he'd be darned if he could find Cascara. It's strange, said Banker Smith, because he couldn't either. Indeed, it was only after some time that they realized this was the trade name of a laxative, and that Miss Drillio had been pulling their legs. They were so furious that her days as a telephone operator came to an end, both night and day.

By the end of June it was confirmed that Frank A. Dobson had been wounded, although not as seriously as first thought, that Pte. Charles Herbert had been severely wounded with the same unit, and Pte. Harvard McAllister seriously wounded with the 16th (Canadian Scottish) Battalion. Just at this time, too, two trains went through town with the soldiers of one more New Brunswick battalion, the l04th, and with their banners and slogans proclaiming loyalties to component parts such as "Gregg's Grizzlies" and "O'Leary's Wrecking Crew," and on July 28 Bill Landry wrote his most poignant story yet about what was happening where they were going. He'd met another artillery officer who asked if he knew a village girl named Carm, and he'd said she was Carmelita Richard, daughter of a prominent lawyer and a friend of his sister Mary. "Well," he wrote, "it seems this officer nearly got hit by a shell which wounded an infantry officer. The artillery officer took charge of getting the wounded man to the dressing station, and all the way back the wounded man kept saying, 'tell Carm I'm all right and not to worry.' He was just about unconscious, having been hit in the mouth, back and legs, but kept repeating 'you won't forget to let Carm know.' After his wounds were dressed, the artillery officer got his name, then cabled his father "to tell Carm."

The wounded officer was George Keefe, and Bill Landry asked his sister to tell Carm he might be minus a couple of teeth but otherwise "will be O.K.." Besides, he said, she should be satisfied that "he must be pretty true to her because she was the only person he could think of." Satisfied she must have been, because eventually they'd get married.

On August l, Lieutenant Landry wrote his father that the battery had just had a letter from a general highly praising it because, "under cover of our fire, two men rescued an officer ten yards from the Hun line in broad daylight." He said he was fine and dandy and brother Pete was too. Ironically, he didn't ask about the father's health as he had been doing for months.

Sir Pierre never saw the letter anyway. He was buried that very day, before his son even knew he'd died. He'd been a shining light in the awakening of the Acadian people after a century of exile and return. He'd been Premier "Roaring Dan" Hanington's right-hand man in politics and in office in Fredericton, an M.P., a judge and, said one newspaper, Dorchester's most distinguished citizen. A second paper, the arch-Liberal Moncton *Transcript* , stressed that the Tory Sir Pierre was "loyal to the Empire and active in promoting its cause." He was, said the paper, "as British in his instincts as if he'd been born on the banks of the Thames."

In late September there was a huge bonfire in the village square because yet another battalion was after yet more men even as the 145th left Valcartier and headed for Halifax. This one was called the 236th New Brunswick Highlanders and all the officers and most of the non-commissioned officers were what were becoming known as returned men; they were back from where the killing and the wounding were.

As it passed through its recruiting area, the 145th got a royal sendoff. When it stopped at Moncton, the crowd at the railway station was so dense that people missed one another simply because it was so easy to do. Cpl. Alexander Fraser was there that night, a rugged Scot who'd been wounded in the Boer War and arrived in the village as an emigrant in the spring of 1914. When he couldn't find the members of his family who couldn't find him, he headed for the Brunswick Hotel bar for a drink. When his train stopped shortly after starting, he got off and had another, and his family never did find him, even after sitting up in restaurants and the station for two nights because no one could be sure just when the train would arrive.

Hours late, the battalion reached Sackville about 3 a.m. with rain pouring down and people packed around the station to say goodbye and a band playing "God be with you till we meet again." But five soldiers from the shiretown weren't there. Privates William Bowser, Dick Whalen and Roy Marshman and two others had taken advantage of a noted physical offshoot of political clout. Nearly half a century back, Edward Barron Chandler had had enough influence to ensure that the Intercolonial Railway would pass just below the village even if this meant that its tracks crossed the marshes in one long, straight line, then swung sharp left to climb a hill. With rain pelting down, the five soldiers knew it would be a laboring train that climbed that hill. So this was a good place to get off for one last visit with their families. Charges of being A.W.O.L. (absent without leave) were threatening by morning. But the village quickly took up a collection to pay their fare and off they went on a morning train, and when they got to Halifax all they got were one-day detentions. One reason may have been that the 145th needed all the hale-and-hearty young men it could get because tough medical examinations at Valcartier had weeded out so many as unfit or overage. When it boarded the S.S. *Tuscania* on September 26, the battalion was down to half strength.

The 145th arrived in England about the time the *Tribune* reported that a village officer was in the Royal Flying Corps after army service, and had written home that he and his pilot had "had some great trips." Especially, he said, one in which their plane was "shot full of holes in an attack on a balloon and a village five miles behind the German trenches." It was a breathless tale of swooping through the air at 136 miles per hour, of the plane being hit and hit again, the engine stopping, of him, as observer, firing 50 machine-gun shots, of the pilot desperately looking for a place to land. Then, when they were within 150 feet of the ground, the engine coughed into life and they headed home with "about 500 Germans firing at us," many of them in the trenches in the terrible valley of the Somme. And what did he do in reply? "I waved at them." Then, 300 feet short of their own landing place, their engine gave out once more. But they made it by gliding in.

The *Tribune* didn't say so but the officer was none other than Wilfrid Landry. He'd never gotten over the urge to fly. "I spent an hour," he'd recorded on May 28, "watching one of our planes flying over the German trenches while the Hun went after him with machine-guns and big guns and he kept twisting and dodging. It was beautiful to see." He'd pulled strings to get into the R.F.C. so he, too, could do such beautiful things. After training as a pilot, he had become an observer or navigator in a two-seater plane spotting for the guns he'd left below.

The letters his family preserved ended with his father's death, but the *Tribune* article showed he'd continued to write them. Even so, it missed one aspect of that hazardous flight, one which indicated he may have been saved by his height. Perhaps because he was so short, he'd stood up to get a good look at the enemy. When the plane landed, he found two bullet holes in the seat he'd left. He came through another crash later; the plane plunged into a barn and men who rushed to help were sure he and his pilot had perished because the first thing they saw was flesh and blood. The two men survived. The cow they'd hit didn't. After that, Lieutenant Landry went back to Canada to become an instructor and a captain.

The Canadians had moved 50 miles south from the Ypres salient and were locked in the ghastly battle of the Somme. It had killed nearly 20,000 Britons on its opening day in July, and by September the valley was a cratered desert and the Canadian Corps was into a campaign that would add names such as the sugar factory or refinery, Courcelette, Mouquet Farm, Regina Trench, Desire Trench to its record and those of Privates George Malcolm Bishop and Clove Armand Saulnier to its dead. Bishop was a blacksmith, a native of Cape Breton who had enlisted in New Brunswick in August 1915 and was reported missing on September 15, 1916, two months after joining Nova Scotia's 25th Battalion at the front. He was killed by a sniper's bullet when he was nearly 39 years of age. Clove Saulnier wasn't much younger. A native of Memramcook, he said he'd been a carpenter, a driver and a gas engineer when he enlisted in Edmonton in January 1915. He was 35 when he was reported wounded and missing on September 26, a few months after joining the 15th Battalion. His next-of-kin, his father, lived in College Bridge, part of Dorchester Parish.

By October 17, when both Bishop and Saulnier were still considered missing, three decimated Canadian divisions were moving north to the Arras-Lens sector of France, and a month later the 4th Division followed after its own brutal introduction to battle. In two months the Canadians had advanced roughly two miles and suffered 24,000 casualties, even as the 145th infantry battalion had ceased to exist. Almost immediately after its arrival in England, the Dorchester Platoon had discovered it would not "carry its name and individuality to Berlin." Instead, as often happened, the entire battalion was broken up to provide reinforcements. Its soldiers scattered, some to train as machine-gunners, some to try to stay together, some to go where military service took them.

Scattered even as Lieut. Hugh Teed was with the 2nd Battalion at the front. Two weeks after his September arrival, the unit sent him off to take a course in the use of grenades. When he got back he became so busy that it was weeks before he wrote a November 23 letter saying how pleased he'd been to get back for some of the fighting on the Somme. Though its very name had become a synonym for annihilation, he said it was a wonderful place to be. He was the bombing or grenade officer, and he talked of the war as of an adventure:

> Dear Father: I received your letter October seventeen just as we were coming into the trenches, and have not had a chance to write since ... When I wrote you before, we were on the Somme for the big push, and I am so glad I got over in time for it. Everything was wonderful and I was sorry to leave as it was more or less open fighting and we junior officers had all kinds of jobs absolutely on our own.
> I was up at the front line, or in front of it nearly every night and several days where we could see everything going on for two or three miles, and it was a wonderful sight. You or anyone else not actually there can have no idea what it was like. Everything pounded to bits. Towns absolutely wiped out in some cases, and no towns with a house standing.
> When the Germans held that country they built large deep dugouts, some of them being thirty or forty feet deep and everything fortified just as strong as it is possible to make it; but our artillery would start to pound and then our men would go over, and some

more of France would be in our hands. Nothing could stop them, and the Germans seemed glad to give up in several cases I know of, as they were nearly crazy with the noise and danger. When one is down in the deep dugouts the noise of a shell bursting is nearly one hundred times as great as above. Men have ear drums burst and the candles put out by concussion. Courcelette and the Sugar Refinery are rather famous that way, as they are both undermined by large dugouts, and were exceptionally strongly fortified. The dugouts are still there, of course, but the buildings are practically no more.

I rather expect if you were here you would drive past or through most of the villages and never know it unless someone pointed them out to you. I know when I first went up we passed through a village and I never knew it till later. I can't give you much of a description of the place, as it is beyond words. Hardly an inch of ground not blown up by shells, mud a foot deep, at least on rainy days, a constant stream of wounded going out during an attack, and practically no shelter.

I spent several days in a hole about three feet deep and with a waterproof sheet over it to keep me dry, but we usually dug a trench and scooped a small hole in one of the walls to take our head and shoulders, and lay in the bottom of the trench, and people moving along had to be very careful not to step on anybody. Of course, the artillery being reasonably well back have to get up wood, sheet iron, etc., to make gun pits and to hide the guns; and the officers and men always have shelter. We did not have the same chance, as it takes, or rather took us all our time to dig trenches and "funk holes" to live in and to get up supplies, which all had to be carried at least a mile; and, I forgot, we had the wounded to carry out the same distance in most cases.

I will never forget the night I took a party up to the front line to carry out the wounded, going through mud up to and above our knees, and then carrying the poor devils out, one being from Plaster Rock, up near Woodstock — I forget his name. I took four men to carry a stretcher, with a relief of four men, but they were played out before we got down to the ambulance, and the chaplain, who was our guide, and myself took turns with the others. It was the hardest work I had ever done, and the wounded were wonderful, the way they bore the shaking, shells lighting everywhere and men falling into shell holes all the time but managing to keep the stretcher level.

The night was dark as coal. We had to pass the Sugar Refinery, and it was the only night I was there that the enemy never shelled the place; and we got through without a casualty. I think we made a record there as we carried out all our dead and buried them either in a cemetery we made there or in the big one five miles back. As far as possible, they were all buried with military honors, which says a lot for the commanding officer and men, who were all dead tired.

I saw Carleton (a cousin) several times but never saw Lionel. I located him the day we moved out but did not get over to see him, as I could not leave the men alone—one never knows when one would be called upon to do something.

When I got here I was appointed Battalion Bombing Officer, and am on my own now more or less. I like the work very much. My predecessor is in England getting patched up.

We are in a very nice quiet part of the line now, and leave is getting along very nicely, so I hope to be back in England about Christmas time. Needless to say, I am looking forward to it very much.

I am living in a very nice dugout with a bed, stove, table and chair that I built myself, and am very comfortable, in fact I hate to leave as there will probably be no such things where we go next. However, we hope for the best, and can usually get some boxes to build things with. When we do go out everything here will be in first class condition for the next bunch anyway.

Your loving son, Hugh.

There was at least one other enthusiastic soldier on the Somme. Adolf Hitler served there, in the frontline, as a headquarters runner, a messenger in a Bavarian regiment. He was 27, Austrian-born, a former derelict in the slums of Vienna, a failed painter who would be twice wounded and twice decorated for courage. He was, in short, a frustrated drifter who became a good soldier and liked the comradeship, the discipline. It confirmed in him a belief in authoritative ways and the heroic virtues of war, though his mates considered him a bit of an oddball and his officers felt that when he got to be a corporal, an *obergefreiter*, that was as high as he should go.

The Somme stirred in Private Dobson, F.A., no enthusiasm whatsoever. Indeed, by the time Hugh Teed wrote his November letter, he thought of the war as a "confounded thing" and hoped it would soon be over. He'd been wounded a second time and was wondering how long his luck would last. He'd gone back to his unit in August, the same month Laura Cunningham had helped get in the hay on the family farm near Tatamagouche; 70 loads, she said, and she knew because she was driving the horses and keeping count and thinking how much he would enjoy it himself. By October he was on his way to hospital from the Somme, and in rural Pictou County she was trying to teach school and, in her own words, going "nearly crazy" with worry. She'd seen a casualty list that simply said he'd been wounded and, she told Maude Turner, she didn't know where to turn or what to do. Then on October 17 she got a card from a military hospital in Greenock, Scotland. This time, he said, the wound was in the left thigh, but "it was not bad and he was doing nicely." It was, she said, "such a relief to think he is away from the front," and near an aunt.

The aunt was Emma (Chapman) O'Neal who'd grown up watching ships being built in a hamlet called Rockland, across the river from the village, and was now the wife of sea captain and shipping executive Edmund O'Neal and, yes, they lived near Glasgow and were as kind as could be to this son of Emma's late sister Annie. In October they had come to Greenock by train, even though it wasn't too easy to make connections, but he wasn't sure how long it would be before he could visit them. His wound was doing fine but it would "be some time before I see France again."

By October 29 he was up and about, had attended a football match, was looking forward to a Hallowe'en party, had had a car drive along the River Clyde, seen more of the O'Neals. The weather was nasty, he said, and it made him thankful he wasn't back in the trenches. Two months later, he was in Hastings, England, after leaving "good old Glasgow." Four days after Christmas, he wrote, "I am feeling a bit blue but of course this is only to be expected as I had such a good time with Aunt Em and Uncle Ned." He hadn't yet had a medical examination and was still having problems with his wound. The weather was rotten and "it doesn't help when a fellow is feeling blue." When he got word of a series of village funerals, he said, "A fellow gets so accustomed to death over here that he doesn't think about such things unless it happens to someone very dear to you." He hoped the war, "the whole confounded thing will soon be over." So did Laura Cunningham. She hoped, she wrote, that he'd be home for the haying in 1917.

Such sentiments were increasingly shared by Ed Oulton. His zeal and enthusiasm were going. He was tired of the licensed murder of battle and the legitimized stupidity of generals you never saw. Months of standing in trench water and mud were doing things to his legs. He was tired of keeping his clothes on for weeks, of yearning for sleep, of eating cold bully beef out of his helmet, of walking through mud up to his knees and feeling bodies below, of seeing too many men die, die mowed down in swaths like grain, die screaming on barbed wire, of seeing too much filth, rats, lice, poison gas and blood. There were occasional leaves in Paris where the lights were bright and the parties went on forever, but you always knew you had to go back to the hell you'd left behind. So, at 32, he was getting closer and closer to asking for a transfer to less hazardous duties, and eventually he would and eventually he'd get it and become a sergeant.

Yet his feelings were a stark contrast to what the Saint John *Standard* of January 11, 1917, said in publishing Hugh Teed's letter of November 23. Its sub-heading said, "New Brunswick Officer Has Thrilling Experience in Front Lines." The opening paragraphs said Lieutenant Teed was both extremely popular and well and favorably known and that his letter "illustrates the optimistic spirit of that gallant young officer, and his unfailing willingness to do his share, while engaged in the cause of Empire." That was, however, Lieutenant Teed's last letter home. One day before it was published, his family was informed that he'd been killed on the 7th. Killed accidentally while showing soldiers how to throw a hand grenade.

One day before his letter was published, too, the *London Gazette* reported that his village friend Lieut. Joe Hickman had been awarded the Military Cross "for conspicious gallantry in action." As an artillery officer, it said, "he carried out a daring reconnaissance and obtained most valuable information. Later, he several times proceeded to and from the front line under very heavy fire and rendered very valuable reports."

By haying time in 1917, Frank A. Dobson was stationed at a machine-gun training base, and the Canadians had been in the battle the country would remember above all others. Vimy Ridge was the one Canadian mythology would single out as a crystallization of the Canadian identity and spirit. Yes, and as a meticulously planned, magnificently executed attack on an escarpment that was a key to German defences and had defied everything the British and French could do to take it. In giving British arms their first major victory of the war, all four divisions of the Canadian Corps attacked together for the first time on April 9, Easter Sunday, attacked in sleet and climbed that ridge and took it. It took three days to tidy everything up, and two of the lives it took would be commemorated on the village memorial.

Private James Allen "Allie" Milligan died there, and it did something deep to the village because of who he was and what had happened before he enlisted. His father was black and his mother white and they were good, respected people living on the Back Road when he, their popular son who did farm work, got into trouble. Some sort of trouble which years later people would say wasn't much, arose in fact from something he did after he'd been turned down to go to summer militia camp; he interfered with the train that took the soldiers there. Whatever it was, it was enough to send him to prison, and prison is where he was when he was offered the alternative of enlisting. He enlisted one day after Lieut. Mansel Goodwin arrived in town. When he died on Vimy Ridge, he was with the battalion Ed Oulton and Harry Tattrie had been in. He'd been with it less than three weeks, and he died sometime between the 8th and 10th of April. That's as definite as his records could be.

Private Lloyd Everett Crossman died at Vimy too, a farmboy from Woodhurst where, in all probability, my mother had had him as a student in the one-room school where she taught for a year before heading for the West. He died that Easter Sunday one year and not quite one month after enlisting in the 145th at the age of 17. Died bravely, so bravely that not one but two of those who led him into action wrote his parents to say so. Lieut. T. Dick, O.C., 2 Section, 14th Canadian Machine Gun Company: "Your son died almost instantly after being struck by shrapnel. I feel his death very much as he was one of the best boys in my section and although this was his first real battle he showed great coolness. We buried him at dawn the following morning, near where he fell." Dick's right-hand man, Sgt. E. Llewelyn, wrote almost apologetically that he was only Private Crossman's section sergeant but was so impressed with him that he wanted to write anyway. "He was," Llewelyn said, "a very courageous young fellow and in the final test one could not have wished for a braver, cooler man."

It would be said that men came down from Vimy not as Albertans or Nova Scotians but as Canadians, and it would be said that this may well have been the hour when Canadian nationalism flowered. Allie Milligan and Lloyd Crossman were among the 3,598 who didn't make it.

Vimy did have a big impact on Canada, but the killing simply went on, and within a few weeks it claimed Pte. Frederick Laurier Emmerson. He had joined New Brunswick's 26th Battalion as a reinforcement four months before Vimy and he died not far away three weeks after it was over. He was killed on May 1, 1917, amid heavy fighting around Arleux and Fresnoy. He was 21, a former bank clerk, unmarried, a native of Petitcodiac, N.B., who went by the name of Laurier as a testament to the abiding Liberal loyalties of the Emmerson clan. He'd been living in Moncton before enlisting in October 1915, but he was a nephew of the Hon. H.R. Emmerson and he liked to visit his home, did it frequently enough that he became a sort of adopted son of the community.

He was the fourth to die in a year that would put more names on the village memorial than 1915 and 1916 combined. There would be nine all told, and three of them were those of men killed in six August days in the fighting around Lens and on Hill 70, six or so miles north of Vimy, as part of an attack designed to help one more major British offensive in disastrous Flanders. Lens was a shattered coal mining town. Hill 70 was a nearby limestone hill dotted with the ruins of miners' cottages, and the Canadians attacked it so they could let the Germans waste themselves trying to drive them off.

Ten battalions started the attack at dawn of August 15, and within 20 minutes they were at the top of the hill, and Pte. William Bowser was dead. He was 27 years of age, a singing man from a singing village, a baritone with a great voice and a great personality, a former carpenter and bookkeeper in his father's mill and woodworking plant. He'd gone to Alberta's celebrated 10th Battalion as a reinforcement after Vimy. He died in a hell of exploding shells and whining bullets, simply vanished as he had that night when five soldiers of the Dorchester Platoon fled a troop train to spend one last night at home. Was seen advancing, taking shelter, reportedly in one of those ruined miners' huts, then not seen. Was buried in what shellfire made of where he was. His body was never found.

In the next three days the Canadians beat off 21 German counter-attacks, and 20-year-old Robert Samuel Sutherland died. Died one day after Bill Bowser and only two days after joining the 26th Battalion as a reinforcement and 16 months after being enlisted by Lieutenant Goodwin. He came from Rockland, described himself as a laborer, and stood just five feet four. Shortly after he died, two village men in the same artillery battery were gassed. Sgt. Bill Hutchinson would be in a British hospital for months; Lieut. Lionel Teed would spend eight weeks in a French hospital and a convalescent camp in Dieppe.

On August 21, Frank Morris LeBlanc was killed in the fighting to clear more of the mining villages on Hill 70. He was a carpenter from Upper Dorchester and just 18 years of age when he enlisted in the 145th. He'd gone to the 50th Battalion as a reinforcement in November 1916, and they'd made him an acting lance corporal without pay in the very month he died.

Hill 70 was where Pte. William Saunders' war ended too. He had enlisted in the 145th and, like Bob Sutherland, he'd grown up in tiny Rockland, was born in 1898, which he liked to say was the year its last wooden sailing ship was built. He grew up in that doomed community, grew up eating its apples and its berries and romping in its forests and fields and river, yes, and looking across the marshes to the village on its two-tiered hill, with the church steeples poking up through the trees and the prison a mile or so on, alone, castled on a hill, and things happened to him which Hill 70 made manifest.

In the rage of battle, he was struck down. Bled profusely. Was carried off, one arm shattered, left hanging, and the blasphemies of combat were still close when they got him to a medical officer, a doctor, who said the arm had to be cut off, and it was going to hurt a great deal because he didn't have the things he needed to make it otherwise. So he gave the 19-year-old boy a stick to bite on and told him to concentrate his thoughts on something that meant more to him than any other. And William Saunders lay there while that shattered arm was cut away, and what he thought about was the Rockland of his childhood, and years later he'd buy the land he'd pictured in his mind.

By the time the Canadians left the Lens-Hill 70 area that October they had lost some 11,000 men, dead, wounded and missing, and British Columbia's Lt. Gen. Sir Arthur Currie, their corps commander since Vimy, was appalled by what they were ordered to do next. But Britain's Sir Douglas Haig said it must be done, the Passchendaele ridge must be taken, said it, as Currie would later learn, because French Army mutinies, terrible losses at sea to German submarines, and a growing urge for peace in London and Paris made a decisive victory vital.

Passchendaele was a ghastly measurement of how far the war had come since the spring of 1915, a tiny community on a minor ridge only seven miles or so from Ypres. When Currie inspected the area in advance, he beheld a wallow of mud that had already consumed thousands of Allied soldiers. He said his four divisions would suffer 16,000 casualties for very inadequate reasons, and he was right: they took that village and they lost almost that many men in less than three weeks.

Lieut. Lionel Teed got back to his artillery outfit just in time for the battle. Capt. Joe Hickman, M.C., was wounded there, and what they both would remember were the things Joe's brother Jack and other village soldiers would remember: that sea of mud with soldiers wading up to their knees in it, or falling off board walks into it, falling off wounded or exhausted and sometimes drowning in it, and the guns firing from wooden platforms to keep them from sinking , and the Germans mowing men down with machine-guns in newfangled pillboxes, and wounded coming back day and night.

All the soldiers knew was that taking that ridge did no more than Vimy Ridge to change what the war had become, a static, paralyzed insanity. But if Vimy's name found its place in the mythology of Canadian nationhood, Passchendaele found its own in the mythology of horror. George Smith fought there, and he would end up with one wry consolation. He was a 17-year-old private, a recent graduate of the Amherst, N.S., High School, when he went into this first battle he'd ever known. He would later live in the village for half a century, and he would say that the one good thing about Passchendaele was that nothing that followed could possibly be worse.

Yet it added only one name to the village memorial. Gunner Edward Hugh Landry, 23, a native of the village and a former railway employee, was fatally wounded on November 7, three weeks after joining an artillery battery on the eve of battle. Sapper John Lemuel Waddell McDowell, another native of the village, died later that same month. He'd enlisted in North Vancouver, spent months at the front with the engineers, come down with lice-caused trench fever and finally gone to hospital with heart disease in January 1917. He died in hospital on November 22. In his 40th year.

In late March of 1918, with the Russians out of the war and the Americans in it, the Germans flung themselves at the Allied lines in a gigantic fury designed to seize victory before it was too late. They riddled divisions and corps and even armies, regained what they'd lost on the Somme, swept over Passchendaele's ridge, and at fearful cost almost succeeded in what they'd set out to do. But didn't.

The Canadians were not in the frontline when this began, but thousands of them were eventually thrown in to help stem the tide, among them Dick Whalen and Roy Marshman and other village soldiers from the 145th; they'd found their way into a Motor Machine Gun Brigade which markedly helped to save a crumbling front. By April 5 the Germans knew they'd failed, and the question was whether the Allies could do what they had failed to do. On August 8 they set out to do it east of Amiens, a city on the Somme. In great secrecy, they had brought the Canadians 30 miles south from the Lens-Vimy front where they'd returned after Passchendaele, made them and the Australians the cutting edge in an attack that turned out to be so successful that the German General Erich Ludendorff would call this "the black day" of the war.

Harvard McAllister was at Amiens, more than three years after Ypres, more than two years after being wounded. Barber Jimmy's son had had his military ups and downs, in action, in hospitals and out, had been re-elevated to lance corporal with his infantry battalion only days before this battle began. He was there at 4.30 a.m. when the ground began to shudder from the firing of guns, and he walked into the thick mist of morning when the attack began. Walked not far. Lieut. G.H. McCreery wrote the family that, "It is with great sorrow that I write concerning the death of your son, number 23556. No doubt you have been officially notified but as his platoon commander I would like to extend my sincerest sympathy." It had been his privilege, McCreery said, to command the platoon since December "during which time I found a very happy acquaintance" with their son, and he thought the family might like to know some of the particulars of his death.

"At the time," McCreery said, "he was in command of a Lewis (machine) gun section and in line for promotion. On the morning of August 8th in the big push in which the Canadians had the honor of taking part, he fell. It was shortly after leaving our jumping-off position that we encountered an enemy machine-gun. He was hit by a bullet from close range and his end was immediate. Needless to say those of us who were left made short work of the enemy crew. His company commander, his pals and myself all feel his loss very keenly, the more because he was always an excellent soldier and best of all a real man and a splendid example for other men."

Lieut. Herbert Gladstone Palmer was at Amiens too, and he'd remember it in the vivid way he remembered things. After he got to England with the 145th, the army had kept him training men there for more than a year, and it was Christmas Eve, 1917, before he got to France, mid-February before he got to the 26th Battalion as a reinforcement, and years later he'd say he felt he could remember every minute, every sight, every thing that happened while he was there. Remember going on a musketry course. Remember the 26th's secret move south. Remember Amiens. Remember the shuddering of the earth, the mist with men in it, advancing, falling, going on. Remember running, shouting, leading his men into a nest of German machine-guns. The killing. The majestic sight of British cavalry galloping past the objectives the 26th had attained. Remember, marveling, that the battalion had so many hundreds of men at dawn and so many hundreds fewer in the dusk that found the Canadians eight miles beyond where they'd started out. The attack was called off after three more days and four more miles of an increasingly costly advance. But by then Lieutenant Palmer was in hospital. He'd been wounded on the second day, and he would fight no more.

Amiens was the beginning of the ending of the war and of what came to be called "Canada's Hundred Days," a different kind of war. When the Canadians took up the attack again on August 26, they found the paralysis of trench warfare was largely gone, that the enemy they faced in hilly, wooded country fought like a wounded, trapped and desperate animal, took a dreadful toll but kept falling back under relentless pressure, much of it from the Canadians themselves. In driving them back across 75 miles of France, Sir Arthur Currie would estimate, his four divisions and a couple of British divisions took on one-quarter of the German Army, 47 divisions, and didn't stop till the exhausted Germans quit and the war came to an end. Which is to say that in the very months when the Americans would say they won the war, the Canadians were winning some of its most important and decisive battles. In doing so, they suffered losses that made August and September their bloodiest of the war and October as bad as Passchendaele; losses that would add another seven names to the village memorial, three of them from one day of battle, a fourth from the day that followed. Four of them from a volunteer army, three from what had happened when volunteers were not enough.

Pte. Raymond Cormier, the first to go, was killed three years after enlisting, two days after the attack began, killed with Quebec's 22nd Regiment. A 23-year-old former bookkeeper, he'd gone to the Van Doos as a reinforcement after the Somme, had been with them through Vimy and Hill 70, and might well have been killed on September 24, 1917; he was with the signals section at battalion headquarters when a shell struck its dugout and killed six men during a heavy bombardment. He escaped with a concussion, but got back to his unit 18 days later and in time for Passchendaele. He survived that too, only to be killed somewhere east of Arras.

Lieut. Lionel Teed was the next to go. He was killed with his artillery battery on September 1 amid the fighting on the very tough Drocourt-Queant Line between Arras and Cambrai. He'd been in France more than two years, and just two months back, on June 3, 1918, he'd been awarded the Military Cross for gallantry in action. He fell dead, the family was told, after one last noble thought. Mortally wounded, he looked up and asked, "Everyone all right?"

One day after his death, Pascal Leo LeBlanc was killed with the 38th Battalion less than three weeks after joining it at the front. He was the son of Napoleon LeBlanc of Memramcook and in his 23 years he'd been a commercial traveller and, since 1915, a rollercoaster number of army things, had qualified as a lieutenant after service in the ranks, later been an acting sergeant, an acting corporal, twice reverted to private, the rank he held when he was mortally wounded. He died just at the time Sapper John Booth Burnett, son of the village station agent, was surviving the deeds that won him the Distinguished Conduct Medal. His citation said it was for "conspicious gallantry and devotion to duty during the attack on the Drocourt-Queant Line. He was a linesman on forward communication and, although badly shaken up by a shell, carried on repairing and laying lines under heavy fire for 72 hours. His work was the best of any man in the section, and his contempt for danger was a splendid example to his comrades."

Those 72 hours ended with the withdrawal of the Germans from what the soldiers called the DQ Line. They retreated behind the unfinished Canal du Nord, and set the stage for one of the most spectacular and risky feats of the war. Beginning at dawn on September 28, after careful preparation and another secret move, Currie sent tens of thousands of men storming across a 1,000-yard wide dry, unfinished stretch of the canal to fan out on the other side, up a hill into a forest, to the fringe of one more defence line two miles or so west of Cambrai. By nightfall, the Germans were falling back again, and three more names were ready for the village memorial.

Charles Elsdon was killed that day, killed at 22, and 3 1/2 years after Ypres had begun his education in battle. Died with the good conduct badge he'd been awarded after Passchendaele, died as an artillery bombardier in the last chapter of a moving story of friendship. He'd only recently found his old school pal Bill Hutchinson joining him in the 8th Battery, indeed becoming his own officer. This son of the man Elsdon's father had succeeded as chief keeper at the prison had been commissioned as a lieutenant after being gassed and spending months in hospital. Once fit, he was posted not to his old battery but to the 8th from near his hometown. Thus he and his lifelong friend came happily together in the last days of the war, only to have Charles Elsdon die doing something he didn't have to do. Lieutenant Hutchinson signed the papers for him to go on a long leave to England, but Bombardier Elsdon didn't go. He'd come through years of battle without a scratch, and he said he'd never missed going into the line with his battery yet and he didn't want to start now. He asked for a delay so he could keep his record intact. He was killed by a direct hit on his gun, and his old school pal was close by when it happened. Bill

Hutchinson would become a newspaperman and write many things, but he'd always say the hardest thing he ever wrote was the letter to Charles Elsdon's parents.

Charles Elsdon and Bill Hutchinson, Lionel Teed and Raymond Cormier and John Burnett were seasoned veterans when they fought through the Scarpe valley, south of Vimy, south of Hill 70, between Arras and Cambrai. Three others who died on the 28th were not. They were green, and they lasted very briefly.

Lester Joseph Buck, a 21-year-old farmer, was one. He'd come overseas in April as a reinforcement for an infantry endlessly in need of men. Which is why Parliament had finally passed the Military Service Act, had imposed conscription of manpower for overseas service. Lester Buck's military career is evidence of what that could mean. He arrived overseas three months after a medical examination, was posted to a reserve unit for the New Brunswick Regiment, joined its frontline battalion just after the fall of the DQ Line, and became a sniper because he was a crack shot. He was killed 24 days later, in his first attack.

It was much the same with Eloi Bliss LeBlanc who described himself as a laborer and gave his birthpace as Malakoff and his address as Scoudouc when he took his own medical examination under the M.S.A. in November 1917. He was enlisted on January 15, 1918, and within less than two months, at 20, he was in a reinforcement unit in England. On September 11, he was posted to the 44th infantry battalion, itself a testimonial to what four years of war had meant; it had become a New Brunswick unit because Manitoba could no longer maintain its strength. When LeBlanc arrived, it was once again rebuilding that strength after the DQ battles. Seventeen days later, on his own first day of attack, he was killed.

One day after that, Pte. Ira Leon King died of wounds

he'd suffered on the 27th, and what had happened to him reveals even more about what the war was doing to the country. He too had taken his medical examination under the M.S.A. A native of the village, he was in North Bay, Ont. at the time, and three months later, in January 1918, he was enrolled in Saint John. He arrived overseas less than two months later, and on the same day as Eloi LeBlanc. He joined the 44th Battalion with LeBlanc too, just after one harsh battle ended, and was mortally wounded by shellfire just before another was to begin. He was three months short of his 34th birthday.

Gunner William Robert Burns was exactly 21 when he died after nearly three years in France. Died on his birthday while heading for Ireland on leave and in an incident that disrupted negotiations for an armistice. On October 10, a German submarine sank the *SS. Leinster* in the Irish Sea, and Burns went down with the ship. He'd said he was a salesman when he enlisted in Winnipeg in March 1915; in fact, he was just 17. He was the "young Burns" Bill Landry had shared socks with, partly because they were both natives of the village, partly because they were in the same artillery battery, partly perhaps because they both had to contend with the vicissitudes of height. At five feet six, Burns was by one inch the taller of the two.

On November 11, one month and one day after his death, the Canadians entered Mons, Belgium, and Sir Arthur Currie rode through joyous crowds. The war at last was over. Had ended in the very city from which the British had retreated under the first German onslaught of August 1914. Which a British officer noted in telling Currie he'd been in Mons then and how pleased he was to be in Mons now. "Well," Currie said wryly "it's taken a damned long time to get you back."

Chapter Two

In the village that evening, there was a great celebration in the square. The weather was cold and raw but hundreds turned out and there was a band and speeches and everything. At 85, Anne (Palmer) Steeves would remember being nearly 13 years old and one of the very few in town who didn't get there though she had every reason to want to, having a brother, Herb, who'd been wounded only recently and a sister, Jen, in France as a nurse with an American Army hospital. What's more, she and brother Charles and sister Julia (Doole) had run errands and done other things to help out because the war got to a stage where their father, F.C., had only a boy named Ernie Card and a married man named Ern Tower to help him run the store. But on the big day she and her sister Margaret were in bed with the flu and they could hoot and holler all they wanted but the doctor wouldn't let them go. So they lay there, indignant, as the sound of music and excited voices passing by told them what they were missing. Anne did, however, have the consolation of thinking how romantic it was that now she'd find out what was going to happen between her sister Mabel (Tooke) and Jack Hickman. They'd been "that way" a bit before he left and Tooke went to Brockton, Mass., to train as a nurse, and they'd been corresponding, so who knew what might happen?

What Jack Hickman's father knew was that both his sons, Jack and Joe, had come through, and how good it would be to have them home, even if they'd have to share the grief of their mother's recent death from the same influenza epidemic that kept Anne and Margaret Palmer in bed on the night of the armistice. In Saint John, Madge and Mariner Teed watched the celebrations from the window of their home on Hazen Street, quietly weeping for the sons who'd cheered on the day the war began. In England, Frank A. Dobson celebrated as an officer cadet. In Belgium,

Brig. Gen. Andrew Latta McNaughton felt regret that the Allies were stopping when Germany had escaped almost totally the devastation she'd wreaked on her neighbors. He was a brilliant young officer who'd made Canadian artillery much more versatile than it had ever been before, and he predicted that Germany would have to be fought again in 25 years.

Socially, no Canadian crowned the hour of victory more splendidly than Lieut. Mansel Goodwin, for he celebrated where celebration reached its imperial apex. Like Herb Palmer and others who'd been with the 145th battalion, he'd been kept in training camps in England for months, had finally reached France in late March 1918, one week after the Germans launched their last desperate pitch for victory. After helping the 2nd Canadian Motor Machine Gun Brigade stem the tide, he and and some of his village recruits were with it at Amiens. For the first time, he saw men die under shellfire, was later at the Canal du Nord and beyond, and his diary recorded the sort of life his battery led. He described an artillery and machine-gun barrage so powerful it made the earth rock, then a direct hit by a German shell that killed one man, wounded two in the crew of one of his section's machine-guns. As the days went by, he recorded being under heavy shellfire, taking shelter in a tank trap, watching aerial dogfights, making a reconnaisance to find positions for his guns, identifying one by the body of a white horse, sleeping on a stretcher in a shellhole near bodies of the dead, his guns firing for an hour and more at a stretch, his wound.

He was wounded around Cambrai on October 7. He'd been in a dugout all day, he recorded, and he decided to visit cousin Vincent in another machine-gun battery nearby. As he walked back, he was struck by a shell. Picked himself up bleeding freely from the face. Got someone to "tie me up," then made his way to a dressing station —

and out of the war. He was soon on his way to London, to a military hospital where he had one operation, then another. Both were unsuccessful, and there would be others. In fact, there would be shrapnel in one of his legs for the rest of his days. But within less than two weeks he was making the rounds at the very heart of Empire:

"Took Nurse Cleland to a play ... To tea and dinner with Mrs. Siddall ... Out with Nurse Tait ... Mrs. Russell came to see me and we had tea and a dinner party ... Met Miss Whitlock and had tea and dinner in Soho Square ... met Mrs. Russell and had lunch in Trafalgar Square and dinner in Soho Square ... Took (Nursing) Sister Cook to a matinee and tea at the Trocadero ... Paid calls on Miss Brennan and Miss Whitlock ... To concert at Albert Hall and was in Earl Grey's box, second from the one the Queen and Princess Mary occupied. Had tea at Miss Sneyd's home." On the evening of November 10, it was "dinner at Miss Wood's." The following morning, he was in a taxi in Trafalgar Square when he heard guns announcing the armistice. He did not join crowds surging through the streets. Instead, he returned to the hospital and, with fellow wounded, was soon on his way to Buckingham Palace: "Lady Sybil had received permission for us to enter the inner court. We saw Princess Mary in a window. An immense crowd gathered in the square and we sang and shouted, 'We want the King.' The King came out dressed in the uniform of an admiral and the Queen followed in a fur coat and carrying a Union Jack." From there he went to a restaurant for a "very nice dinner" with two nursing sisters, then for a stroll with them down Oxford and Regent streets: "The streets were crowded with happy people and the lights were on, making a gay scene. People crowded into and on top of taxis. There was dancing on the road and nearly all the women wore flags on their heads.

Piccadilly was crowded, both the circus and the street."

He returned to Canada in January 1919. Five days after disembarking at Saint John, he returned to the village for a carnival and dance. And, he recorded without elaboration, to "renew old acquaintances."

Of the 25 soldiers whose names the war itself would put on the village memorial, William Robert Burns was the 24th and last to qualify. The 25th was different. The fighting had been over nearly four months when John Frederick (Jack) Hickman was killed on March 5, 1919. Killed in Wales, in a transit camp called Kinmel Park near the great port of Liverpool. Killed during riots by Canadian soldiers infuriated mainly by what an official inquiry called "delays, postponements and cancellations of sailings of ships to take them home."

Five soldiers died there in two days. Historian Desmond Morton says one of the five was "killed by a stray bullet as he waited in a hut." This was 21-year-old Jack Hickman. He was in that transit camp with another village man, Allen Drillio, and was not involved in the riots themselves. His brother Joe had been decorated for gallantry and wounded. So had Lieut. Fred Foster, M.C., the village friend he'd gone camping with the month the war broke out. Jack Hickman himself had repeatedly seen action, only to die by chance, though rumor would tell another story. Many wild and unfounded rumors swept Britain, and Hickman was involved in one of them. It was said in print that he "was so horribly tortured that his body was removed from its burial place for fear of public exposure." It is true that the four other victims remained buried in Wales. It is also true that Jack Hickman's body was disinterred. But the reason it was, a brother would say years later, was the wish of the Hickman family that it be brought home. It was on its way within two months of his death.

Thus Jack Hickman became the only one of the village and area war dead to be buried in the village itself. Fellow soldiers Henry Emmerson and Bill Hutchinson were among the pall-bearers at the military funeral service, and Bill's kid brother Larry was there too. A big, strapping kid, he was, a teenager who'd worked at one part-time job after another to help the war effort: gardening, sawing wood, in a sawmill, on a threshing machine, in a fish store, as waterboy on a railway gang, with men drilling for oil. He'd also picked potatoes for J.H. Hickman, Jack Hickman's father, who ran not only the big hardware and general store in the square but a lumber operation as well. He had a teenager's hero worship for Mr. Hickman, had seen him standing there, dignified, white-haired, stricken, at Mrs. Hickman's recent funeral. He came with hundreds of others when their son was buried in the village Protestant cemetery, and he would never forget the way the father stood, ramrod straight in grief's stark silence, as the earth took the body in.

Took it in and buried with it something that was doubly doomed not to be. For both Jack Hickman and Mabel (Tooke) Palmer died at roughly the same time, he in Wales of that stray bullet, she in Boston in the great influenza epidemic that had killed Jack Hickman's mother and would take even more lives than the war itself.

Even at the time of their dying Adolf Hitler was

discovering, with ecstacy, that he could make men listen to what he had to say, that there was something captivating about his passion and his voice. He was an army political agent assigned to keep an eye on a tiny Workers' Party, one of many organizations springing up in a chaotic, disillusioned Germany. He got into its discussions and when, that same year, the Allies imposed a harsh Treaty of Versailles, the captivating voice found the perfect vehicle for its bitterness and its hate. It was a combination that would, in time, be intimately associated with the deaths of more people than the Great War and the great 1918-19 flu epidemic combined.

Chapter Three

THE YEARS OF PAUSE and remembering began about the time I was born, and there already existed that lyric poem that pledged that "at the going down of the sun and in the morning, we will remember them." It had been written "for the fallen" by an erudite Englishman named Laurence Binyon long before anyone knew the horrifying number of fallen there would be. Binyon was 45, a renowned authority on Oriental art, when the idea came to him on a cliff in Cornwall shortly after the British retreat in August 1914 from that Mons, Belgium, where Canadian soldiers would march in triumph four years later. "The stanza beginning 'They shall grow not old' was written first," he would say, "and dictated the rhythmical movement of the whole poem." It was first published by *The Times* of London, and it has become a radiant element in annual tributes to the fallen. Yet I have come to hear it with a sense of irony because my quest soon taught me that hardly a soul in the village knew anything about the 25 men whose names the Great War had put on the memorial.

They were not remembered men, they were forgotten men, certainly as individuals but also in a broader sense. Nor, as I'd discover, was this unusual. When I taught a university summer course in 1972, we fell to talking about a sense of history and I asked the 20 students if they could identify a large body of men who'd had a deep effect on Canada's own history. None could. I said those who were left were old now and could be found from coast to coast. No one could imagine who they were. I said nearly every person in the room, some beyond the usual college age, must have some relationship with at least one of them. No one knew. In my opinion, the Canadian soldiers of 1914-18 rank somewhere near the Fathers of Confederation in the Canadian story. The Fathers created the framework of a nation. Half a century later those soldiers sanctified it with sacrifice and crystallized it with spirit. Yet none of those 20 students knew who I was talking about.

The second thing my quest taught me was something about remembering itself. I asked Herb Palmer to go to the memorial with me because he was one of the very few people left who knew much about the 25 fallen. He was, moreover, a romantic. The war mattered to him. So I asked him to go and he went — after he first got me to go to the Protestant cemetery with him because, he said, someone should know something about some of the people buried there, and I was a logical one because I wrote things.

It's a serene and beautiful place, that cemetery, and Uncle Herb — as my family called him — told me interesting things, including the fact that there were at least a dozen sea captains lying there. But what I recall most distinctly is how much it mattered to him that this be done, that certain things and certain people be remembered. On a planet that is much less than a dwarf in an unfathomable universe and peopled by a species that slays its own in multitudes, it mattered to him that these few names and these scant facts be offered up to an immortality enormously indifferent to the crusades of the human soul. Yet it was for the same reason that I asked him to go to the war memorial, and we weren't there long before I sensed a funny thing about human beings: they think remembering is important, but they don't seem to come with many pegs for hanging detailed memories on. Herb Palmer stood in front of that memorial and he talked about those 25 names but, in the end, what he cast upon them was a thin, pale illumination. It took less than 10 minutes, which is pretty thin gruel for immortality or even for a book.

So the third thing my quest taught me was that if I was going to tell much about those 25 names or even the 16 from my own generation, I was going largely to have to find it for myself. Then when I did find things I tried to link them up with my own version of that highly imperfect apparatus, the human memory. And that's when it struck me that my own first name was an artifact.

I was born February 5, 1919, one month before Jack Hickman died. It's obvious now that this was at the beginning of the pause, but my parents didn't know that. My father had had a brother killed and my mother had had a brother and first cousin wounded and, as far as they were concerned, I was born into the euphoria over victory. So they named me Douglas in honor of Field Marshal Sir Douglas Haig, the British commander on the Western Front, the man who sent Currie's Canadians into Passchendaele.

Euphoria makes people do these things. One of my friends was even called Douglas Haig Cochrane. Our parents had no idea that Haig's own name would eventually become stained by a hideous remembering. Nor was that what village people were thinking about when they buried Jack Hickman. What they *were* thinking about fell within the parameters of pride and regret and gratitude and relief and, above all, shock that what had happened had happened. They knew it was momentous and historic and they felt the 25 deaths must be honored.

The ones who'd gone to war felt this and the ones who hadn't felt it, and that's why war memorials began to emerge. Cities, towns and villages erected them and there had never been anything like this in the country's history because there had never been anything like what caused it.

The village soon was raising money for a monument. People pitched in over a period of years and there were plays and raffles and other events, and on January 16, 1925, there was an announcement by a firm in Amherst, N.S., that made gravestones. The J.A. Tingley granite works said they'd been awarded a contract to erect a village memorial that would consist of "three bases, die or pedestal and statue," would be 13 feet high and seven feet square at the base. The statue itself would be a Canadian soldier with a rifle resting at his feet and it would be made of blue/white Westerly granite from Westerly, Rhode Island, whereas the base would be made of New Brunswick gray granite. J.A. Tingley himself had cut the statue in Oxford, N.S., two years back as the first of its kind in the Maritime Provinces, and he'd do this one too.

The memorial was unveiled that summer with its helmetted soldier at attention, with a rifle in his hand above a four-sided base with the names of the 25 village and area dead chiselled into stone. It was unveiled on July 1, Dominion Day, and the day is important because it linked the ceremony with the birth of modern Canada, and the year is important because the ceremony came within months of the Balfour Declaration which expressed a great irony: that her soldiers had fought a war of independence from the Britain they supported, had made it illogical for Canadians to remain something they no longer felt themselves to be. It recognized that all the Dominions were no longer colonies, were Britain's equals under a common Crown. The Americans had won independence by revolting against British rule. The Canadians had won theirs by fighting at Britain's side. It was a strange way to do it, and it would be hard for Americans to understand and it would take a long time for Canadians to make it mean what it came to mean.

There is a photograph of the village ceremony showing the leaves of summer, the floral tributes, the big crowd and the frame which held whatever it was that hid the granite soldier until the proper moment. There are funny looking cars in the background, and some people seem to be bowing, and there are men in uniform, and all in all it's obvious that the photograph concerns an important event, which indeed it was. There is every bit as much significance in where the memorial is because that says a great deal about what people felt, and why it became an instant and integral part of the village mind and the village soul. They put it at the very heart of things, in front of the courthouse, near the town pump, in the square, in the old devil's half acre which in the distant and prosperous days of the Golden Age of Wooden Ships and Iron Men was where sailors and farmhands and lumberjacks and Liberals and Conservatives and Catholics and Protestants drank and talked and fought and a considerable clump of taverns existed to help do it. On the day of the unveiling, a number of young boys were either posted at the core of the ceremony or appropriated it for themselves. There they are in the photograph, in a perfect spot to see what's going on, which is one way one generation seeks to imbue another with what it considers important. I was six years of age then, and I may have been one of them, if for no other reason than that my mother always tried to see that her four kids got to things that mattered, like church and Sunday School and school-on-time. But if I was there, I don't remember.

More about memory — collective memory — came to me when I tried to hitch my mind to what my research found. The village in my day had a proud sense of identification with an era of sailing ships and economic securities and political clout. At a seminal time, it had been the home of both Edward Barron Chandler, a Father of Confederation, and Albert James Smith, the leader of New Brunswick's fight against it. Chandler built the Teeds' great stone house and he had been Smith's legal mentor. They lived within 150 yards of each other, and one snapshot will cover both their graves. Yet the collective village mind remembers nothing of the days when they fought over union.

With the 145th Battalion, it's even worse. I never heard of the 145th till Dave Beatty wrote his book. It was only then, in the 1980s, that I realized that at least six of the names under the granite soldier were those of men who'd enlisted in the 145th and that others were men I'd known in growing up without knowing they'd been in the war at all. When research revealed that the *Tribune* used to speak of "the famous Dorchester Platoon," it also revealed how easy it is for men to be forgotten, even when their names are chiselled into stone so they won't be.

Even so, if you knew the local family structure, you could draw certain conclusions about the 25 names. For one thing, they made it clear that their war had called forth an effort that cut right across the boundaries of society, religion, politics and blood, had tapped the energies of an entire community as could no other force or phenomenon known to man—an extraordinarily revealing and very tragic thing. But in the end it was the 25 individual files in Ottawa which made it possible to create a statistical profile. There was with two exceptions a curious gap between men in their early 20s and men in their 30s, which may say something about the character of response. What's more, only Hugh Teed married. No less than five were in their 30s, and one nearly 40. The average age of the others was between 22 and 23. The only six-footer was Albert Starratt and if you didn't count him the average height was 5-8. Six, almost 25%, were French Acadians. Eight were Roman Catholics, eight were Baptists and the nine others were Methodists, Presbyterians and Anglicans, which proportionately was pretty well the way things were in the village itself. Almost invariably their wills made their mothers their beneficiaries, which may say something about the position of women in society. A few came down with venereal diseases overseas. The enlistment forms didn't bother with education, which says something in itself. Only the two Teeds were officers. The only ones who wrote their names with flourish were the bank clerks Elsdon and McAllister. Surprisingly, despite the paramount image of the horrors of the trenches, nine of the 25 died in the fluid last hundred days. And a number came off farms that have long since ceased to be.

It was when you fed in information like this that your memory began putting together things about what it was like to grow up in the years of the pause, amid the soldiers who came back, and how your generation was shaped for the response it would give when the pause was over. How it was imbued. For it was. In subtle and complex and even mysterious ways, it was.

I began to wonder why I wouldn't remember the unveiling of the village memorial when I did remember quite clearly a kindred occasion just two years later, wonder if this was because they gave us something to make us imbuees? So again I am remembering: It is July 1, 1927, and on the courthouse lawn, with all the ceremony a village can command, we do honor to the 60th anniversary of the founding of Canada. On this first day of the summer holidays, we school kids stand there in our best clothes while maple trees rustle and sombre parents shush dogs that want to celebrate for purposes of their own. In addition, there are things that are not said because they don't need to be. Even the kids know that a lot of the men in the audience are called returned men. For another, in every child's hand there flutters a Union Jack. A year has passed since the Balfour Declaration and it will take another four years to enact the Statute of Westminster to confirm what the Declaration says, and even then Canadians will fly the Union Jack.

Just two years after the memorial went up, it seems to have been there forever, and already it is part of the way the young are shaped, are imbued. For what began as a testament of pride and grief would become an instrument of indoctrination. Indeed, the war that put the memorial where it is even dictated when this ceremony should be. It might have been enacted 10 years earlier, on the 50th anniversary of Confederation, but the year of Vimy Ridge and Hill 70 and Passchendaele was not a year to celebrate. But now, belatedly, we do honor to the founding of the country without any mention of the Sir Albert J. Smith who led New Brunswick's fight against it, or of the pressures of the Motherland which broke his hold on the power he won in 1865; indeed, if those present think of anything in this regard it is that Lady Smith died only last year as, regrettably, the last really honest-to-God wealthy person in town.

Yes, and the speeches speak of the village youth as the sinews and hopes of the country's future and there are those names on the monument that are sinews and hopes of youth destroyed, yes, and somewhere in the audience there are boys whose names will, in time, be there too. Yes, and to each child is presented a medal, a small burnished coin bronzed brave with the image of the face of the distant King George V, and with a motto, a legend, on it which commemorates this great occasion. Then we march off and that's where this memory ends, except that at times in my research I would find myself wondering what ever happened to the millions of medals handed out on that historic day. For I've never seen one since, and I wonder if there is some attic where humanity leaves and ultimately forgets the trinkets it creates to try to convince time it matters. But they *were* imbuing things.

It was years later that I first noticed Jack Hickman's gravestone in the cemetery and wondered why it was different. Yet it was out of the yard where he grew up that something more would come to me about remembering, and about heroism, and about the fallen. It would take me 60 years and more to grasp it, but all these factors were there and they all eventually came together because the American Charles Lindbergh flew the Atlantic. In 1927 he became the first man to do it alone, and was lionized as an instant, electrifying and universal hero. I was eight at the time and he most certainly electrified me, and this in turn helps explain what happened between Mr. Cormier and myself, and what this may signify.

What did happen took place in our backyard. There was the stump of a giant elm tree there. It was at least six feet high, and decay had made a hole in it where you could sit as in a cockpit and travel wherever your imagination took you. This is how I became involved in the life of Charles Lindbergh, and how Mr. Cormier became involved in my own. Mr. Cormier, Mr. Anthony or Antoine Cormier, an Acadian, worked around the Hickman property across the street from our house. They had a big place and a huge barn, and he did odd jobs. Milked the cow. Did the garden.

Kept things cleaned up. Came and went so quietly that it would be easy to be only vaguely aware that he came and went at all, even though this took him right through our yard on a narrow dirt road to the racetrack and his own home. He came that way to get to his work and he came back the same way. Came right past the tall elm stump with the cockpit in it. Not always, but quite often.

None of which mattered until Lindbergh flew the Atlantic, and two ladies who roomed with us gave me a book about it. That was probably in 1928, and that's when I started climbing into the elm stump and becoming Lindbergh. Totally, of course, in private because it would be embarrassing to be caught talking to myself, both broadcasting the event and making it happen, making engine sounds, crowd sounds, wearing a winter cap that looked like the one Lindy himself wore. Or close enough.

That's exactly what was happening when Mr. Cormier suddenly popped out of nowhere, heading home late one afternoon. Was suddenly and unexpectedly and, yes, shatteringly seen immediately adjacent to a seething Paris airfield where at least a million Frenchmen were roaring a tumultuous welcome as, tired, hungry, triumphant, I piloted "The Spirit of St. Louis," my trusty single-engine plane, in for a landing that would make me part of forever. Yes, Mr. Cormier was suddenly seen. In his work clothes. Walking with the bit of a limp he had. Humming. Humming a little tune: tum, tum, tum, tum, tiddely, tiddely tum. Apparently not yet aware of what was happening only feet away, what he was doing to it, of the amazement of a million tumultuous Frenchmen as "The Spirit of St. Louis" simply vanished, as the broadcaster vanished with it, into a downheaval of modesty and embarrassment and silence. In which the pilot stared straight ahead, yet observed, spied out of a corner of an eye, beheld Mr. Cormier's reaction to what he could hardly fail to see. Saw him limp on. Heard the tum, tum, tum, tum, tiddely, tiddely tum. On and on. Saw his back. Saw him moving on, without one sign of recognition, without saying a word. Just went on. Limping, humming on. Yet indicated, somehow, that he was engaged in the protocols of privacy, and would respect my own.

Which was the way I remembered him — with gratitude — till now. Then, writing this, was struck by the ironies of heroism. That one man could become, for a less compelling cause, the hero that the village war dead didn't. That 25 names had been on the memorial for three years and they meant nothing to me, and wouldn't for years. That I can't remember ever hearing them mentioned as the names of individuals. That Jack Hickman had grown up in that big house across the street and I had no idea who he was or how he died. That already his and the other names were vanishing from the village mind even as Lindbergh's became one that wouldn't. That Mr. Cormier may even have been thinking of his own son Raymond who'd also died in the service of his country. And whom I'd never heard of either. But then the names on the war memorial were a looking back to horror, and Lindbergh's a looking ahead to hope. As one enthralled Parisian put it, he had "given us the continent of the sky."

It was only during my research that I began to see Jack Hickman's gravestone as a sort of link between those who came back from the war and those who didn't. It struck me that if it was an anomaly it was peculiarly fitting because so, in some ways, was the way the returned men fitted back into the village and the country. For there was something awkward and uneasy about what the fit became. Even now, in a non-military country, it's a complex subject, seldom ushered out of the closets of the public mind. On the one hand, the returned men brought home songs people would sing for years: "Pack Up Your Troubles" and "Mademoiselle From Armentieres" and "Keep the Homefires Burning" and "It's a Long, Long Way to Tipperary" and a lot more. They brought with them also words the language had already embraced: shock troops, trench raids, dugout, Flanders Fields, poppies, Western Front, no-man's land, Blighty, shellshock, and a lot more. They had made place names like Ypres and Vimy part of the geography of the Canadian mind, the Canadian Corps a legend in which the Canadian people took great pride. They had crystallized a Canadian sense of being, a Canadian reality. Yes, and in the village, as elsewhere, both civilians and returned men joined wholeheartedly in erecting the war memorial, and every Remembrance Day they would do honor to the dead.

Yet a yet was there. It says something, I suspect, that my parents and Douglas Haig Cochrane's parents named us for a British general. The Canadians produced a very good general in Sir Arthur Currie, but I have never met anyone who was named for him. The fact is that he died relatively young and some people thought he died with a broken heart because of brutal things Canadians said about him. Again, the very term returned men was rooted in the Canadian mentality. It signified the importance of something that had happened somewhere else. It was a code-term for a difference for which Canadian life was ill prepared. Britain, France, Germany, Europe had had centuries of experience in reabsorbing into society the men they'd sent forth to fight; Canada had virtually none. With its memories of revolution and civil war and a frontier ruled by guns, the United States would continue to choose presidents who had done their time in battle. Canada would not only avoid them, she would twice choose as prime ministers men who could have served but didn't, men many ex-soldiers loathed. She would, moreover, keep them in power for close to 40 years. The United States would glorify its war heroes in movies, books and song. Canada would largely confine her own to the margins of the public mind, never quite sure how to make a music of their memories, or whether it was even proper to try.

The United States nicknamed its World War I soldiers "doughboys" and would call its World War II soldiers "GIs." Britain called her own "Tommies." France called hers "poilus." There was a tang of affection, of pride and spontaneous theatre, in all four. Canada's soldiers had no equivalents. No one sang songs about them being Yankee Doodle Dandies. Sometimes they were called "Canucks" but there was something awkward about the word. Indeed, it's a curious comment on the whims of semantics, and on the country, that the overseas survivors of 1914-18 generally were identified — identified, not romanticized — as returned men while the survivors of 1939-45 would be identified — identified, not romanticized — as veterans. The difference says something but nobody seems to know what it is.

At any rate, the term returned men stuck for a long time, and in the opinion of one of them who became a noted historian, it came to have pejorative implications. He was Professor A.R.M. Lower who had served in Canada's tiny 1914-18 navy, and he wrote that the term was used invidiously by Canadian civilians to signify "difficult, maladjusted and barely respectable individuals." In fact, any such feeling was taking shape that February 1919 when I was born. Within a month soldiers would lend substance to public apprehensions through the riots that took Jack Hickman's life, and nowhere more so than in my birthplace, for it was fermenting with divisive anger about what the returning would do to Canadian life.

I was born in Winnipeg when the city feared that the soldiers were returning with the seeds and poisons of the godless communism that had taken root in Russia. The Winnipeg general strike that came a few months later has been called a nasty milestone in Canadian labor and social history. My parents were Maritimers who had headed west in the pre-war days when the prairies were filling up. George How was a banker and bookkeeper and the son of a Nova Scotia clergyman. Althea Dobson was a secretary and the daughter of a Dorchester storekeeper. They met in Winnipeg and got married there in 1911, and 10 years later my father died and my mother became a 31-year-old widow with four children and not much money. At a time when thousands of Maritimers were heading for Boston and Montréal and the West itself, she decided to go back home because relatives there would stand behind her, and that's why I got to know a disproportionate number of returned men in a small and intimate context.

Well into my 70s, I increasingly think of what my mother did as a very fortunate thing, though many outsiders tend to think of Dorchester as a prison town, as a place where bad news comes from. But for the purposes of this book a number of things about the penitentiary are important. Above all, it was in the village but not of the village as I came to know it, because somehow it contained within its great stone walls the anger, menace and despair of those it held captive. Again, its presence was more than balanced by an opiate, if vague, sense of a local history/mythology with its own golden age. Nor did this massive, frowning edifice prevent the community from being a wonderful place to grow up, the sort of place where a Tom Sawyer or Huckleberry Finn or Anne of Green Gables would have felt at home. In fact, it was the pillar of the village economy, the one major employer in town. Finally, in hiring staff it gave a preference to returned men, so there were an unusual number of them around.

Nor do I remember them as A.R.M. Lower's "difficult, maladjusted and barely respectable individuals," perhaps because they had become custodians of the difficult, maladjusted and barely respectable individuals who kept ending up behind bars. In my mind, they became ordinary men returned from doing extraordinary things, and made larger by the fact. I know now, yes, that I saw them in that monolithic way that turns individuals into generalities, so that what one had done they all had done. But it would take me years to realize this, and the fact remains that, to me as a boy, what the returned men had returned from came to be packaged in names like Ypres and the Somme, Vimy Ridge and Passchendaele. It would take me years to sort these and other battles out by reading books, but the very names sounded bugles in my mind, and the reading would only make me feel that having the returned men around must have been something like it was to have the men back from Troy and Agincourt and Trafalgar and Waterloo. They had lived with great events that had entered into them, and what the reading said was that their Canadian Corps had lived those great events with a certain tragic splendor of its own.

Lived it, the reading would say, in a war so impossible that old Kitchener of Khartoum — Lord Kitchener, the British war minister — threw up his hands in 1915 and said he didn't know what it was but it wasn't war. And a Canadian general would imply much the same when he said years later that he hadn't studied what happened in the first four years of it because there was nothing for a professional to learn from a conflict that put two sides into miles of rat-ridden trenches and repeatedly threw them at each other to fight for yards of ground. It was, in short, a war fought under the disciplines of the grotesque, fought moreover by an unusual Canadian generation, a generation that had grown up in a country that had found its stride in the opening of the West, in years of prosperity that had supplanted years of economic hesitations and doubts. For I, for one, suspect that in a war that did so much to destroy faith in mankind's progress, Canadian soldiers and airmen kept a rendezvous with fate as men not quite like any other Canadians before or since. That, at a momentously destructive hour in human history, they in paradox bespoke the explosion of an energy, zest and optimism that had been building steadily in a country groping toward a realization of what it was.

In Lower's words, they represented "frontier energy in the trenches." America's *Time* magazine would say, "The world's memory of Canadians in battle is a bright memory. They seemed to shine out of the blood and muck, the dreary panorama of trench warfare. They seemed to kill and to die with a special dash and lavishness. In a war at a time when glory had already lost its meaning, the Canadians in France kept the sheen of glory." Sir Douglas Haig recorded that at Passchendaele two Canadian divisions knocked out seven smaller German divisions, including "four of the very best." They had faced the flower of the German Army, he wrote in his diary, and they were confident they could whip them every time. That is something no German probably ever admitted, but Hindenburg himself, their top soldier, once said that the best troops Britain had were from what he called the colonies, the dominions, and he said there was a reason. One reason undoubtedly was that the best of the British Army was gone by late 1916. But that wasn't what Hindenburg meant. He meant that many of "the colonials" — a lot of them British-born — had come off the land and out of the forests, and when the Briton C.P. Montague saw the Canadians going into the attack beside Australians and Britons in 1918 he saw vividly what that meant. The troops from the Dominions, he wrote in *Disenchantment*, were tall and bronzed and vigorously healthy. The British, children of a brutal industrial age, were short and stunted, brave men but quite different men.

The Canadians were tough, ruthless, and they were proud. When Sir Arthur Currie visited the wounded after one battle, he told a sergeant he hoped he was very proud of his regiment now. The sergeant sat up in bed and said, "Sir, I always was damned well proud of my regiment." These were the qualities that made them celebrated as trench raiders and shock troops, that led Britain's Prime Minister David Lloyd George to say that "whenever the Germans found the Canadians coming into the line they prepared for the worst." They equated the appearance of the Canadians, echoed British correspondent-author Sir Basil Hart, with impending attack.

The returned men brought all this home with them, and more. They came back, yes, to become fathers and grandfathers, mortal, common men with all their frailties, their problems and their grocery bills. Yet when an American visitor told us village kids the Americans had won the war, we were white with fury, for at least part of what had entered into those who fought had become part of us in turn. They deserved the high and peculiar rank of men who shaped a nation with their deeds. Yet they neither claimed nor sought any such status for themselves, and they would never attain it. They had found their innocence and their youth being channeled into the carnages of Europe, and realization of that alone might explain what happened after they got home: that they were numbed by what fate had done to them. But it went beyond that, into the way the country was and the way they were, into something that had to do with how they fitted back into national life, or didn't, something that got lost in the vacuums, the failures, the riddles of human communication.

They say old soldiers are garrulous men but the strange thing, looking back, is what the returned men turned their war into. They talked of it among themselves but rarely among others. The one I identified most with was my Uncle Frank. He walked straight as a ruler, and I thought it was what the army did to him, but someone told me that was the way he'd always been. Anyway, I remember him as a tall, straight man who meant a lot to my mother and had humility and, yes, dignity and a quality that reminded you of good leather. I would come to suspect that the war took a lot out of him and also put a lot in, and from what I came to know about his last years I am sure of it. He never got back what he'd lost and he never got out the stuff bottled up inside, and eventually it got to him. But long before that I used to wait for him to say what it was like to be a machine-gunner, to be twice wounded. He never would. As a teenager, I once asked him point-blank but all he did was put some wood in the stove and talk about something else.

This was the way he was, and the returned men approved of the way he was and the way Henry Emmerson, Jr., was more than the way Herb Palmer was. Henry Emmerson might have been expected to talk since he came from a political family and had politics in mind. He had come home once with shell shock, gone back and become a major, a company commander with the 4th British Army. But he was a quiet man who didn't say much publicly even when he did get into politics. On the other hand, some returned men thought Herb Palmer talked too much and there were stories about him like the one Jack Hickman's brother Bill used to tell: that Herb came over one night just after Bill got in some prize rum and they left their wives in the living room because Herb wanted to talk. They went out to the kitchen and he talked about the war until finally his wife came and said to let her know when he got through Amiens because then she'd take him home.

Years would go by before I'd learn more about Herb Palmer's war. For one thing, a prison guard would say a convict told him he fought under Lieutenant Palmer at Amiens and that he was as brave as they came. Later still, Mac Heckbert of Saint John drafted a history of the 26th and provided further details. On the opening day at Amiens, they revealed, Herb Palmer's company encountered stiff resistance from a German machine-gun nest. Its advance was stalled until he led his platoon in a charge, captured the machine-gun nest and opened the way for the company to continue to its objective. He was later cited for a Military Cross which he never got, perhaps because there were so many acts of outstanding bravery. He was wounded the next day as the advance continued. He'd live to be an old man and the older he'd get the more the war would come back to him; he'd call someone and say something had reminded him of it and away he'd go, and the reason other returned men might scoff was because this sort of thing violated an unwritten code.

For them, the war became the badge of a special belonging, of something separate and distinct and even sacrosanct, something they wished to not share, to not corrupt by boasting and not degrade by talk. In their minds there was a hierarchy of measurement peculiar to themselves, and for which Will R. Bird had his own explanation. He'd grown up in rural Nova Scotia only 40 miles or so from the village, and he'd fought overseas with the 85th Battalion. After the war, he became a writer and he once wrote about the returned men. They were, he wrote, prisoners of war, a separate people, "as if branded by a monstrous despotism." Made captive, made different, he meant, by what they'd seen and done, different from what they'd been, different from those who had not known what they had known. So that, in the village, in a sense, the war became a sort of no-man's land which people usually did not enter. The returned men did not talk about it because they'd been there, and others did not talk about it because they hadn't, and kids found that what patrols they sent into no-man's land came back to report the trenches empty and their curiosity unfulfilled.

Among themselves, the returned men ultimately seemed to judge anyone's right to talk about the war by what he'd done and how long he'd done it. Above all, they turned brute, unlovely facts into traumatic possessions, jealous secrets jealously guarded. What they had returned from they left behind except in memories they largely refused to share. Perhaps in memories they found impossible to share for a reason that would come much later to be known as the guilt of survival, of having lived when so many good men died. On a national as well as a local scale, essentially what they turned their war into was silence. A silence which helps explain why, on the very subject of our wars, New Brunswick poet Alden Nowlan once wrote that Canada "has no history, only a past," one way of saying that not much of the returned men's epic, and its historic consequences, became imprinted on the public mind. In the final analysis, they never found their Homer, though they did homeric things. Whatever the reason, in my youth I never saw any evidence that they wanted it any other way. Or knew what to do about it if they did.

Most of them worked at the prison on what was known as the staff and, in my recollection, they were as a group good men with good families. Maybe the depression of 1921 had something to do with this, because it made jobs hard to get and a government job especially good to get. Whatsoever the reason, it did bring men to town from all over the Maritime provinces, and since they were all or nearly all returned men they evolved a camaraderie, a feeling on the staff and even in the village, that otherwise might not have been there to the same degree.

They did share a belonging. They spoke the same language and they formed their own institution which became a club, a voice, a retreat. Like returned men everywhere, they fussed about what sort of an institution it should be, but on March 1, 1927, they formed a branch of the Canadian Legion. The charter members inluded Ed Oulton, Herb Palmer, both Frank A. and Frank L. Dobson, Edgar Cole, George Smith, Walter Amisson, Harry Buck, David Cormier, Ray Read, John MacNichol, John Houlihan, Burnes Cumming and Harry Ison; 15 men in Branch No. 16, one of the first in the country. A number of them had been wounded. Cousins Frank A. Dobson and Herb Palmer had. Edgar Cole had been wounded and gassed. Harry Ison had won a medal, had come out of the frontline unable to see because of a wound to his head, his eyes, but carrying a comrade who had lost a leg and who told him where to go. George Smith had been wounded in the last Hundred Days. There were others. Minutes of Legion meetings eventually got lost, so there is no record of what its returned men did and felt and decided. Chipper at 90, George Smith would say a typical meeting might consist of minutes of business and hours of poker, but Branch No. 16 was soon spreading the gospel in other towns.

They also became part of the town that unfolded for the young. You'd see some of them vanishing into meetings of the Masonic Lodge, going to one of the five churches, or sitting on implacable wooden chairs at school closings or Christmas concerts or plays by the Dorchester Dramatic Society, or shopping in one of the four or five stores or just coming up the hill from work — the ones who lived in town — and wearing the khaki uniforms with the colored ribbons that said what they'd done in the war. They all had to live within three miles of the prison gates then, which meant that the village was full of them, and that people felt secure in the midst of the biggest collection of criminals east of Montreal. Again, their kids went to our school and became a happy part of our lives; every time a new "guard" family came to town it would be appraised for athletic sons and/or pretty daughters, priorities which tended to reverse themselves as you advanced in age. What also happened was that when local society divided along various fault lines, one of the most important separated people who were grown up from those who weren't, and that in important ways the returned men ended up on one side and their kids, all kids, on the other.

Under such circumstances, one question I now ask myself is how the significance of the returned men and their war came to mean what it did to and in our lives, or at least to and in mine. Looking back, it's strange to think of two generations sharing the same village, one with a war buried behind the trenches of its mind, the other heading for a repetition, each generation going its own way. The fact is that, very largely, we lived separate lives. Indeed, if there is any one thing that stands out about the returned men I knew it is this: they could not even remotely be accused of infecting a new generation with concepts of war as glory. Instead, a silenced epic aged inside them, and the bugles never rang as they might have rung in younger minds.

Yet if they were putting the war behind them, letting it find its place in history, Adolf Hitler was creating the conditions for another. He turned the Workers Party into the National Socialist (Nazi) movement, dominated it and saw it as the instrument for a rise to power that would let him fulfill the plans set out in his book *Mein Kampf* (My Struggle). Written in prison after an unsuccessful revolutionary *putsch* in 1923, it attacked the Versailles Treaty, scorned democracy, communism and Jews, preached the superiority of the Aryan race, said France would have to be conquered before Germany moved east in the interests of *Lebensraum*, the space to let Aryan superiority flourish. And he meant every word of it.

The reality is that the returned men themselves were history in a village big on history, but didn't fit into either of the two forms in which it existed: what was taught in school and what the village taught itself. It was the second kind that made the prison less important in young lives than it might have been, and you wouldn't have to look further than Helen Petchey to realize this. Her father Fred, a returned man, began in the early '30s to work on the staff, and years later she'd say that from the first she was instructed by her peers in the glories of the village Past. "All I heard," she said, "was history," and eventually she would put a lot of it down on paper. But at the time there she was in the home of a man who had taken part in events that dwarfed anything the village had ever done or been, and she thought of history in another way.

In fact, it would come to seem strange to realize that there we were heading for a great historical event (war), living through a great historical event (the worst economic depression ever) and living among men who'd been through a great historical event (war), and we thought of history as something else. Certainly the school did. What we were taught was that what had mattered most since history began was who was the king of England, and if that weren't enough there were those big maps of the world with the British Empire, our empire, marked in red, and with the ponderous geography of Canada red-linked with an almost unimaginable aggregation of kingdoms, dominions, colonies, mandates and protectorates, plus whatever India was. Yet the music history made in our minds came from what had happened in and around the village itself. There was no textbook to go by and no final authority for facts and statistics, but that didn't prevent the Past from flourishing, the gist of which was that maybe things were no longer what they used to be but what they used to be was, yes, glorious.

The broad outlines were always big on how many lawyers there were. They assembled there because shiretowns had courthouses and registry offices and a small bureaucracy; that's where a trough was with government money in it. The largest lawyer figure I ever heard was 17. I suspect that was on the high side, but what matters was that if you've got lawyers you've got politics, and in the Past you couldn't beat the village for the way it turned lawyers into politicians, and political leaders. For half a century or so people talked about the political power of Dorchester Corner, a little place that had less than 1,000 people, and if the figures went beyond that it was because they took in the parish or counted the inhabitants of that federal institution on the hill who would have been quite happy to be counted elsewhere. It may even be some sort of record that so small a place produced four provincial premiers or, before Confederation, their colonial equivalents, not to mention Sir Pierre Landry who was very big in politics too. Albert J. Smith was one of the four and he later was knighted for negotiating a fisheries treaty as a cabinet minister in the capital of a federal system he had resisted. He was a lawyer and Edward Barron Chandler was a lawyer, and in the first 30 years or so of Confederation two provincial lawyer/premiers came from the village, too, one being the Tory "Roaring Dan" Hanington who, people said, could be heard all the way from Fredericton, and the other being the Liberal Henry R.

Emmerson, Sr., the son of a Baptist divine, who eventually ran into trouble as a Laurier cabinet minister in Ottawa because he wasn't as divine as he should be.

The village they knew was a well-to-do and gracious place, and it got that way primarily because of shipbuilding and shipping. In decades when Maritimers were launching vessels in astonishing numbers, scores were launched in and near the village. There were also three fleets of ships that were owned by village and area people and traded around the world. It was largely shipping that made the money that attracted lawyers, that let people erect big houses, kept four or five general stores going, made people hope the days of glory would go on forever. Which was something the upper crust tried to ensure, so that when wooden sailing ships began to fade, they raised the money to build a "city hotel in the country" and soon added that rink which was so far ahead of others in the area that people in Moncton and Amherst would organize skating parties and come in by train on band nights. They also put up small factories to make chairs, carriages, toothpicks and linens, none of which lasted very long, and in the long run what mattered most of all was that, as a Liberal cabinet minister in Ottawa, Sir Albert J. had enough pull to get the Maritime Penitentiary built in town. But no one talked about it as part of the Past. It was part of what the Past had become.

In the pause, as differentiated from the Past, village boys had their own measurements of importance. This was how they defined the world that bore them toward what was never supposed to happen again. What war stories they could learn were important, especially those about two of the returned men who'd been given up for dead and rescued just in time. One was David Cochrane, one of the British sailors sent to help train Canada's new navy in

1910; he was blown off the cruiser *Niobe* in the great Halifax Explosion of 1917, was about to be carried out for burial when someone noticed his eye flicker. The other was Marcel Belliveau, a hockey star who was found alive in a pile of the dead in the terrible Somme campaign, came home with wounds his wife had to patch up every day.

Reading was important, as long as you didn't have to do it yourself. Civic pride was important, which is why kids boasted that E.C. Palmer was the oldest court crier in the British Empire and that, in his 90s, said he had yet to discover when you lost interest in the opposite sex. Sex education was important, and freely available from your peers. Girls were important after dark and your 15th birthday. Not stealing was important, except for apples. Stories were important. Wealth was too.

Long after Lady Smith died when I was seven, people would talk about how rich she was, as though it cast a communal glow upon their lives. Cars were important. I grew up listening to the first generation of men who talked of them in the fascinated way they had for centuries talked of horses. Saturday nights were important and, to a lesser extent, Tuesday nights, because that's when the farm families came to town and the stores stayed open till 9 o'clock, and things felt metropolitan. Government was important because there was so little of it to go around. The same with sex. School was important because that's where almost everybody who mattered was. But hockey was most important of all.

Hockey on the marshes, hockey on any ice slick we could find, hockey in the closed-in rink if we could raise $1, all told, to hire it for an hour. Hockey enshrined in the gondola from which, by radio, Foster Hewitt made the Toronto Maple Leafs immortal every Saturday night. Hockey enshrined in the legends of that Marcel Belliveau who'd been left for dead on the Somme, had played earlier for the Montreal Canadiens, came home to play in underwear soaked with the blood of his wounds and to coach the village team to the high school championship of New Brunswick in 1927. Hockey that taught the young to run their own affairs because adults left them alone, and they liked it that way.

This was the way our world was when Adolf Hitler came to power in Germany in 1933, was legitimately made chancellor by conservatives who thought they could control him, and quickly began to convert a floundering democracy into a totalitarian dictatorship united by his oratory and mesmerized by his will. Nor was he alone in imposing shadows on our times. Benito Mussolini was ruling Italy with the right-wing Fascist dictatorship he had established in 1922. Japanese leaders with harsh metallic names were expanding an invasion of China that had started in 1930. In Soviet Russia, the communist dictator Josef Stalin was given to authoritarian barbarities, to international skullduggery, to fearing attack upon the communist edifice erected by revolution in 1917; meanwhile, he was starving millions to death to impose a collective agriculture. They shared, these men, a contempt for democracy, for human freedom, a belief in force. They all wanted more than their nations had. They all would take it.

Britain and France were seen as the crucial democratic nations, but both were weakened by the Depression, haunted by ghastly war losses, sapped by indecision. The United States was locked in a mood of neutralism, of refusal to get involved internationally, was led by a magnetic President Roosevelt who was trying to pump life back into an economy savaged by the Depression, doing it through unprecedented state interventions that infuriated the very capitalists he was trying to save. He made radio broadcasts designed to soothe a distraught public; there was nothing to fear but fear itself, he said, and nowhere was he more popular than in Canada. In Canada with her own multitudes of unemployed, with political leaders trying to solve the Depression by tinkering with the tariff, with a population of 11,000,000 deep into a neutralism of its own, as convinced that war was bad as any hippie of the '60s or peace demonstrator of the '80s, and lost in a largely passive hope that it could be wished away.

Freight trains bore countless jobless men to nowheres across a land of vast resources. In the village, they came up from the station looking for food, and seemed to know which houses would provide it. The typical returned man was in his late 30s and working at the prison, raising a family, bringing bread home for 5 cents a loaf and paying $5 or so a month to rent a house in the Guard Row. My mother raised a family of four on $40 to $60 a month; we had no car, no telephone, no electric appliances but we lived in a gracious old house and never felt poor. When a movie was shown at Palmer's Hall it cost 10 cents to sit on a bench and 15 cents on a chair, and the lights went on between reels. Only feet away from the war memorial, unemployed men in their 20s told lies on the courthouse lawn, bummed cigarette butts, loafed, waited for something they were no longer sure would ever return. There were no lawyers left in town. The outlying farms were locked in a long, slow agony of dying as the sailing ships had died. The village itself was locked in its own long, gradual and continuing descent from the glories of the Past.

Even so, it was cushioned in crucial ways. The Depression itself was a sort of cushion because descent was everywhere, and even when government salaries were reduced, the guards found that the economy had cut prices more than Ottawa had cut their pay. In June 1933, on sale,

Palmer's store offered sneakers for 50 cents, shirts for 50 to 75 cents, ladies "full fashioned" silk hose for 69 cents a pair, ladies "house dresses" for 75, three packages of corn flakes for 25. Indeed, things were said about Marcel Belliveau getting two government cheques, one for his work, one as a 100% war pension. It didn't seem right, people said, and even wrote in bitter letters to the government, and the Belliveau family reacted with a private hurt and bitterness. Harry Ison didn't get a pension for his wounds though he might have if he hadn't been in a hurry to get home from the war. But one woman said things about him anyway, perhaps because he had a job when many didn't. She was in his own church and she made sarcastic remarks about the way his head twitched — because of his war.

Yet for the generation of the pause, it was Hitler who would come to rank at the top of the importances in their lives. The very year he came to power the prison had its only riot in years. The next morning, amid the shambles, my Uncle Frank came upon a shaken young inmate who had arrived 24 hours earlier and asked one timid question. "Is this," he said, "what it's always like?" In the way my memory orders things, 1933 was the year things started to become different from what things had always been. It was a watershed. It was the time when the fact that Germany had been fought once began to yield to the fact that she might have to be fought again. The time when the returned men and what they'd done faded into a new reality dominated by a returned man from the country they had fought. It would take me years to grasp that, for them, the cruellest thing of all about those years must have been the sense of how powerless they were to prevent happening to their children what had happened to themselves; that nothing they said really mattered, nothing they felt changed a thing.

It was almost in symbolic answer to such a reality that a new enterprise appeared across the street from Palmer's store, a small, plain wooden building with a front that came down when the day's business was over. It sold chocolate bars, pop, cigarettes, ice cream and the like. Its affable proprietor was one Ernie Partridge who'd come to Canada under the Barnardo plan which sent out young Britons who needed a home. He'd been wounded on Vimy Ridge with Britain's Cameron Highlanders, had only limited use of his left arm, had recently come down with tuberculosis of the spine which ended his working days as a guard. And the returned men had come to his aid. The Legion branch had helped him get set up in business, and he chose for it a name that bespoke their past and his own. He called it the Vimy canteen.

But from 1933 on, in memory, the names and faces that mattered largely were not those of returned men; they were those ultimately made relevant by what was to come. Post-war remembering gave way to pre-war apprehensions, which in retrospect makes it surprising that what I remember best about the year Hitler came to power is that it had the happiest summer I've ever seen. And that one of those involved would become, to me, a double victim, of both the Depression and what it led to. Would, in the process, teach me something about grace.

Chapter Four

AT 14, I WASN'T quite old enough to participate in that memorable summer because you had to be at the boy-girl stage or even beyond, i.e., married. I might be falling in love with Myrna Loy at the movies but that didn't count. The ones who did might number from 6 to 20 or so at any given time, ranged in age from 15 to the late 20s. My brother Jim, just barely qualified although he thought otherwise and fell madly in love to prove it. Some were pretty and lively girls who came to town to visit. Some of the boys and men did have jobs and others were looking for jobs or trying to get into the forces, but most were unemployed. That was the key: that the Depression made that memorable summer possible. Through no fault of their own, a lot of these young people had time on their hands and the opportunity to have fun, and fun they certainly had. They made it themselves, and they had a ball.

Dan Stack was one of the unemployed. He was 24, a university graduate, quiet-spoken, good looking, a gentleman, a superb athlete. In 1927, he'd been the star centre on the team that beat Fredericton High to win the provincial hockey championship. He had gone on to St.

Francis Xavier University in Antigonish, N.S., then to an engineering degree at Nova Scotia Technical College in Halifax, captained the hockey teams in both cases, starred at rugby football. Somewhere along the line his leg was broken and his physical skills were reduced. Yet he'd also been the tennis champion at St. F.X. and he still played it very well, which is why what happened to him became part of what happened to me.

This was so because the daylight pivot of those 1933 activities was a clay tennis court erected by Hugh Dysart, Sr., head of a Boston accounting firm, who had grown up in New Brunwick and eventually married Muriel Chapman, the daughter of a village lawyer. She had gone to Boston to study nursing amd every summer for years she came home for two months and brought with her an increasingly beautiful daughter Florence and a younger son, Hugh, Jr. Every summer, too, Mr. Dysart would come for a few weeks and become a country gentleman smelling of Dill's pipe tobacco and cellar-cooled beer. He was a highly successful man but he would come to believe his best investment was the $1,000 he spent to build that tennis court behind the house where his wife had grown up.

The matches went on day in, day out, summer in, summer out, and this is how young Hugh's life and mine interlocked in 1933 with the lives of our immediate elders. He and I alone played scores of sets for an imaginary Davis Cup. In addition, we played a lot with those who, in our absence, would on many evenings wind up a victrola, put on records and dance the hours away; who had a male headquarters in a huge tent down at the shore where they would gather at night and sing and laugh and flirt and go swimming and have corn boils and marshmallow roasts. None of them spent much money or drank much liquor. They didn't seem to need to. If they did require transportation, the Dysarts had an old Plymouth and the

Chapman boys, Doug and Don, had an ancient open automobile they had restored to mobility. But they never had far to go anyway.

Then one night they had a scavenger hunt, and for the first time Hugh and I were counted in because, I suspect, Mrs. Dysart insisted. Dan Stack went out with Florence, his girlfriend. Every pair but us Davis Cuppers went out hunting as man-woman teams, and we two chanced upon someone who said there was a sheet of paper on the Hickmans' barn door, so we went straight to a clue that let us eliminate those that preceded it. Put it another way: we cheated . Even worse, once we found the prize, a box of chocolates, we climbed into a tree and in the graveyard's darkness spooked those who arrived too late. As a result we got a stinging rebuke we richly deserved. In the Dysarts' front room, we saw a sobbing Florence inform her mother that we had ruined the entire occasion and demand punishment to fit the crime. Mrs. Dysart condemned us with scalding words, ordered Hugh to bed and me into exile. I can still hear the sounds as I walked into soothing darkness: victrola music and the laughter of the undisgraced. They'd even started dancing without a contemplative pause.

Dan Stack was standing near Florence when she demanded justice. He was five or six years older but they'd looked good and happy together all summer. His engineering degree hadn't helped him get a job but such things had become so common that it didn't seem to matter much. Anyway, the scavenger hunt incident was buried where silence stores embarrassments. The guilty were allowed to go back to tennis as though nothing had happened, except that total silence made perfectly clear it had. So there I was playing every day with a voice inside preaching that cheating is cheap, crime doesn't pay. And just as that lesson was burning into my soul Dan Stack taught me another. There was a tennis tournament, prizes and all, and Hugh and I were counted in, perhaps as a signal of our return to civilization. And when the draw came out, who was I to face? The best tennis player in town.

There was no doubt who'd win our one-set match. My only doubt was how determined Daniel Stack was to avenge what I'd done to his beloved, how badly he'd beat me. So there we were on the hard red clay with him across the net in white pants and shirt and playing with an ineffable ease, not even sweating, which I certainly was, and thinking. Yes, thinking, but also giving it all I had to give, determined not to add the shame of easy surrender to the shame of easy guilt, and glory be to God I won a game.

I lost the match but I won one game and, to me, my one was as big as his six. When Dan Stack and I shook hands, I felt better than I had in days. It was only much later that a revisionist memory would make me realize that I hadn't won that game; that he let me win it. Let me, I like to think, especially because he didn't want to add another humiliation to the one already there. But he had to make it look authentic or it would be worse than if I didn't win a game at all. He had to cheat, but against himself, not someone else, and he did it so well and, yes, with such grace, that I really did think I'd made the score 6-1. He expanded my sense of how things could be done without hurting someone else, and in those shy and quiet places where boys acknowledge heroes, he became a hero to me.

So that was another lesson from the summer Hitler's shadow fell across the laughter of our times, one young men and women enjoyed so much that they pledged themselves to come together in reunion 10 years on. They never would though, 1943 being what it was.

In memories of the pause, the next village person who was significant was Charlie Crandall. In that same 1933 he took his Dorchester Army to Saint John for an historic event. He'd come down from Moncton recently to join the staff and though he was too young to have been in the war — 13 in 1918 — he fitted in nicely with the returned men. He looked military. He looked and thought like a soldier even though he was only a part-time one in the militia and what service he'd known beyond that was as a sort of auxiliary helping police try to catch rumrunners bearing quantities of liquor in what the press called "high-powered motor cars."

He loved soldiering in the best sense of that term. The first time I ever saw him was that spring, and that's what he was doing on behalf of the New Brunswick Rangers. Some of us kids were playing pickup ball on the schoolgrounds that evening — Bud and Perc Brian, Bill Palmer, Hazen Greenberg, Bert Emmerson and others — and he showed up with about 15 young men and started teaching them how to be military. They were, in a sense, lineal descendants of "the famous Dorchester Platoon" and it would be nice to report that their presence arose from the impulses of loyalty and public service, but the fact is that, being unemployed, they were in all probability drawn primarily by the pittance the militia would pay them for turning out. In this sense, if Britain's wars were won on the playing fields of Eton Canada's were won in part on the playing fields of eatin'.

For his part, Charlie was a lineal descendant of a rare Canadian breed, of that tiny fraction of the population that believes that one thing you do about nationhood is prepare to defend it, not because you want war but because war is an all too frequent occurrence at the level of civilization humanity has achieved. He had a lieutenant's commission at a time when the militia was at a very low ebb because the Canada that had in 1914 gone to war unprepared was heading for more war in the same way, only more so. In a country full of returned men who knew what war could be, the forces were starved for money and equipment, a travesty, a joke. This was true of the three tiny regular forces, and it certainly was true of back-up outfits like the Rangers for which, that evening on the schoolgrounds, Lieutenant Crandall was imparting the rudiments of parade-ground drill, that kindergarten of the discipline without which an army is a mob.

The recruits wore everyday clothes, and we kids recognized among them both young men who led rakish lives, and others who might have if they had but dared or even known how. What Lieutenant Crandall wore I don't remember, but I knew at once that for the first time I beheld a soldier. He was wiry, thin, bayonet straight, with an open, honest face and a jaw like rock imbricated, smoothed by the sea. Richard Emmerson, one of his recruits, found him "a sterling character," and that's exactly what he looked like. He taught the recruits how to march, to keep step, to fall in and fall out, and he did it with an immense intent. He was that way even when he first had them number off and one young man shouted his number only after the man next to him whispered what it was. After further drill, it became even more obvious that the young man couldn't add: he shouted out the same number at a different place in the ranks. There was laughter but there was none in Lieutenant Crandall. He stilled the chuckles with a look. He was all business. He was also a gentleman.

It was later that year that he took his Dorchester Army to Saint John, in uniform, to join in the celebrations marking the 150th anniversary of the 1783 landing of the United Empire Loyalists, the seminal event in New Brunswick history. For this reason they were accompanied by Bradford Gilbert, an elderly farmer and member of a family which had erected in the village cemetery an imposing monument to its Loyalist past. But it was not his background which led a soldier to make fun of him. What did was Mr. Gilbert's high-pitched voice, and it was fitting that it was this which delivered to the soldier a stinging rebuke. "In my veins," Mr. Gilbert growled, "there courses the blood of noble men; in yours but heifer dust."

This story added to reports that the soldiers of the Dorchester Army had a tendency, off duty, to revert to drinking booze and chasing girls and raising hell, all pursuits in which they had no need for instruction whatsoever. On the Saint John trip, there turned out to be a considerable clandestine consumption of rum but the men soon learned that Charlie had his own way of maintaining order. When a rough, tough soldier got drunk and sassy, he straightened him out, man to man. From then on, it was part of the folklore of the Dorchester Army that Charlie was very good with his fists. It was also part of the folklore that he had very little else to work with.

That July he led the Dorchester Army to Shediac, N.B., to join in an ostentatious greeting for 24 military seaplanes, Isotta-Marchetti-powered flying boats, which Benito Mussolini's Fascist Italy was sending to a great fair in Chicago under General Italo Balbo, the minister for aviation and a former member of Fascist squads which bullied people in the streets. It was no secret that, with such help, Mussolini had eliminated democracy from his own country and had aspirations beyond its borders, but this did not prevent his airmen from receiving the warmest of welcomes.

Soldier Emmerson thought what a splendid sight it was to see their planes bobbing in orderly ranks on Shediac Bay after the first ocean-crossing massed flight in history, and many a young lady commented on the handsome and elegant officers who came ashore to party. As well they might since Balbo's second-in-command described them as men of flesh with hearts of steel. It was, in short, a gala occasion which only retrospect would tarnish with thoughts that within a couple of years some of these handsome and, in certain cases, irresistible young men would be slaughtering the people of black Abyssinia (Ethiopia) with steel of another kind.

In contrast with such great events, it was a matter only of local moment that 1933 was the year the Rev. Leon Levett Duffy left town after being the minister of its highly active Baptist church for 10 years. What people would remember most was that he was blind, that he had a rich sense of humor though he would go about the village with a solemn, theological face and a cane, that he recognized people by their voices and gave fine sermons. What would be more significant in years to come would be the fact that with him, his wife and daughter Lois went 11-year-old son Warren who had had excellent marks in school, was slim and neat and not above wondering mischieviously what would happen if, somehow, there was too little water in the baptistery when his father tried to immerse someone in the ritual of rebirth. In fact, Lois Duffy would say, he was "full of spirit and the old nick."

Again, only local interest was aroused by the arrival one year later of Johannes "Hans" Klotz, a German immigrant who had a son Warren's age, and who took over a farm just off the dirt road leading downshore to where that big tent had perched the previous summer. To be more specific, it was at that Coles Point where the Teed brothers had gone swimming the day war broke out. Klotz and wife and four children arrived at a time when immigrant families were trying to make a living on farms

Canadians had given up on. Some had fled Britain and were trying to create happier times across the Memramcook River and elsewhere, and it was ass-out-of-your-pants rough, and people wondered whether they had realized what they'd be getting into. Indeed, the place Hans Klotz got had no electricity, a well for water, no water pipes, a wood-using furnace in the basement. It was owned by the federal agency in charge of settling returned men on the land, and no "soldier settler," wanted it. Ed Oulton had lived there with his wife and two daughters, but he'd had to leave because it was said to be more than three miles from the prison even when he took a shortcut by snowshoeing across the marshes to work as a guard.

Until cars came in and people began going farther downshore, Coles Point had been the favorite place for swimming and picnics. By 1934 the white farmhouse on the property was empty when the Klotzes arrived. The difference was that Hans Klotz did know what he'd have to face, and figured it couldn't be worse than what he'd faced already. He'd been farming in the Canadian West, he told Herb Palmer, and he'd been driven out by that combination of drought, blight, grasshoppers and economic depression that was turning much of the prairies into a wasteland. The grasshoppers alone, he said, had eaten just about everything but the horseshoes. So he moved into village life as part of the Depression's dark epic of frustration, poverty and grief, and he became part of its education in the imperatives of our times, just as Charlie Crandall and the returned men did.

It wasn't long before his family stirred speculation, and more than half a century later it would still be alive. Only then, in fact, would the village learn many of the details about who they were and what they'd done. Not that this at any given time inhibited speculation, and not that it would have been easy for speculation to match the reality.

For Hans Klotz had led, would lead a restless, seeking and frequently even astonishingly luckless life. He became a sort of human cork bobbing on the surface of vast events that repeatedly crushed his dreams. He was born in the Kaiser's Germany in 1888, in the last years of Otto von Bismarck, the legendary chancellor who had bundled a number of separate states into a formidable and ultimately predatory nation. His father was a Lutheran clergyman, but farmers clustered in the family tree and the boy decided he wanted to own a farm. He became a good storyteller, a gifted entertainer who made pocket money at social functions even as he studied agriculture. Eventually, he set his heart on leaving for South Africa, but his father said it was a warm country that might turn him to drink. So in 1912 he became part of the great influx transforming the prairies.

He ended up with farmland south of Calgary and near the ranch owned by that glittering playboy and future crowned and then abdicated king, Edward, Prince of Wales. He wrote home that he'd seen the prince working like anybody else. He also wrote that things were going well for himself. Within two years, at 26, he owned his farm outright. The trouble was that by then it was 1914 and his adopted country went to war against his native country, and he was seen as a potential spy. His property was confiscated and sold and he was sent to an internment camp. The family story was that the compensation he got was advice to ask the Germans, not Canada, to repay him: "They have the cash." He broke out of internment once; he and two other internees built a tunnel and escaped. They headed for a still-neutral United States, and Hans Klotz made it all the way to Seattle before he got on a train not going where he thought it was. It took him to Vancouver where he was taken back into custody. When the war ended, he went back to Germany and married a war widow with two sons, Walter and Arndt Trebst, and a farm that had belonged to her husband's family. So there he was with a second farm, a substantial farm, only to grow restless in a restless Germany living through that doomed experiment in democracy, the Weimar Republic. By 1928 he was back in prairie Canada, scouting for land, and by 1929 he was urging other Germans to join him in one more migration. His wife's family thought he was crazy to sell the farm he had, but he did, and back he went to the Canadian West with timing that could hardly have been worse.

He, his wife, his two stepsons and two boys of his own, Gottfried, 7, and Uli, 3 — both named for uncles killed in the war — moved into what they called the Adams farm in the Portage la Prairie area of Manitoba. They were barely there before Mrs. Klotz died, leaving him with four young boys to look after. He met that crisis by marrying a single woman who had emigrated with them, married her too quickly, rural gossips sniffed. But within a very short time not gossip but the Depression was foremost among his worries. By 1933, it had driven him off one Manitoba farm and he was trying to survive on another, nearer Winnipeg. Within a year, he fled that too, fled east to try his luck on the New Brunswick coast. Fled into a tributary of the problems Adolf Hitler was creating in the world. For village people soon thought of him as a projection of nefarious things happening far away.

The most important thing happening anywhere was what Hitler was doing in Germany. With brute methods and astonishing speed, he and his Nazi party had turned it once again into a country to be watched and a country to be feared. He had taken it out of the League of Nations. At the very time the Klotzes were settling into their new farm, he won favor with the country's generals by crushing the leaders of a bully-boy private army called the

Sturmabteilung (SA) which had helped him with violence against socialists and communists. The generals, in turn, helped him become not only chancellor but also president, thus giving him supreme command of the armed forces; officers and men began to take an oath of allegiance to him personally. He was demanding, and in abundant degree getting, support to do as he wished, and the methods he employed to crush all opposition were so flagrant and ruthless that people elsewhere found it hard to believe they were happening. Didn't want to believe. Didn't want to spend money to build up the armed forces to fight Hitler or anyone else. Which is what made people like Charlie Crandall exceptional, made what they could do more and more pathetic in the light of what Hitler did do.

Part of what Hitler did do penetrated in depth into the life and mind of Hans Klotz's son Gottfried, and helped make him as luckless in his timing as his father. He was 11 when Hitler came to power and 12 when his family moved to Coles Point. He would remember Manitoba for a farm life he found wonderful, for picnics on the shores of Lake Manitoba and blinding storms of dust and snow; for a school that would make him extol having all grades in one room because he could listen to what the older grades were taught. He liked Miss Foster, his teacher, and his fellow students even though he did strike out one day at someone who made fun of his accent. He became acquainted with cars hauled by horses to save gas and called Bennett Buggies in mock honor of R.B. Bennett, the Conservative prime minister. He had no idea, then or later, why his father had chosen a farm so far from Manitoba; it was part of his family education that children did not ask questions about certain matters. It was of far more importance that his half-brothers Walter, 17, and Arndt, 16, had gone back to

Germany because of estate responsibilities. He missed them.

After arriving at Easter at Coles Point, Gottfried and Uli spent the next two months in one more one-room school. When his teacher looked at the older boy's report card, she was impressed. His father had promised him a dollar for every perfect mark, and he'd missed just once. So she put him in Grade 7. The following September he had a new teacher: Stanley Bateman, who did all he could to help him complete two school years in one. It wasn't easy because the boy kept asking "what do I do next?" But it worked. In September 1935, when Gottfried Klotz entered Grade 9 in Dorchester Superior School, he was just 13 and said to be the first student from the one-room Dorchester Cape School to pass government-set high school entrance examinations.

This was when our paths crossed. I entered Grade 11 that September, and since all three high school classes were in one room we sat six or so rows apart, with Grade 10 students in between. He was a skinny, slightly awkward kid with an accent, with glasses and a nice smile that showed nice teeth. Neatly dressed, wearing boots and often a cap, he walked the three miles or so from his home each schoolday, and sometimes I'd walk homeward with him as far as I went, which by that time was a house next door to where Charlie Crandall lived and very near to where Warren Duffy had lived. I liked him. But it was not an easy time to be a German in Canada, especially when your father was said to have fought for the Kaiser, to get monthly cheques from Hitler's government. The Germans were still the enemy when kids played war, and Hitler kept doing things which indicated that enemies they would remain.

Not long before the school year began, he introduced military conscription and persuaded the British to negotiate a naval treaty that recognized Germany's right to rearm. That was the summer, too, when Hitler-backed Nazis killed Austria's Chancellor Dolfuss in a failed *coup d'etat* . Then during the school year the Feuhrer made his first overt military move; he defied the Versailles Treaty and terrified his generals by marching troops into the Rhineland the peace settlement had "demilitarized." He got away with it, not because he was militarily strong enough but because it wasn't in other European powers to resist. When he informed the Reichstag, it exploded in ecstacy. But at least one of Gottfried Klotz's new schoolmates reacted quite differently. "Next time," he said, "we'll clean those Germans out." That was the way things would be in the boy's three village high school years, and they would make him a hostage of Hitler's ambitions and a victim of his times. Years later no two memories would agree as to how it worked out, but mine is that he faced taunts about being German, that he was called Hitler, that he got into fights, and that I came to respect him because he refused to apologize for being what he was. Like his father, he became part of the education of the village generation of the pause. Only more so.

Until he fell to hanging around the pool room, and probably even then, school was where he became part of that generation itself. School is where he and my cousin Murray Dobson became and remained friends even when Gottfried ran Pop's bicycle into an old basement and wrecked it. Pop was Murray's nickname; Gottfried pronounced it Bop. Pop spent a lot of time around the Turner farm. He loved farming, and from an early age he was as good at it as a man. But he found time on occasion to take Gottfried home to the Guard Row, even though Pop's Dad, Frank A., would at times get angry at things Gottfried said.

It was at school that Gottfried came to know some of

those who figure in this story. To know Bud Brian and how good he was at sports, see Bud and me return to the schoolroom after getting strapped for failing to write the 500 lines we'd been ordered to do. Bud was one grade ahead of him. Bert Emmerson was one grade behind him though he was older. Bud's father ran the garage at the prison. Bert was the son of Henry R., Jr., who was elected to Parliament in 1935. He might have made something of this, but it wasn't in him to do it. He was a friendly guy and he made a friend of Gottfried Klotz, and would take him to the big Emmerson house. Where he was in the middle of a dozen or more children, and his father was a respected man but very strict. For some years he was also hard pressed to make enough money so that big family could eat. This was one reason Bert got me to go with him one Saturday to dig up vegetables.

He was quiet and unassuming and he would never, say, taunt Gottfried Klotz about being German or Hazen Greenberg about being a Jew. Maybe the biggest thing for him about being an Emmerson was that there were so many Emmersons. You'd go to their three-storey, upper-crust house and there'd be kids all over the place, and their mother a perfect lady and their father, without doubt, the boss. He would say he had his own army and his daughter Marion would say, "We were raised in military style." In addition, after Mr. Emmerson was elected to Parliament, there could be cars parked in the driveway all day long and people asking their M.P. to do things on their behalf. Bert was one of four sons. John was younger still and neither was old enough to remember their father coming home from the war in a Seaforth Highlanders kilt. Richard did remember. He was the one in the New Brunswick Rangers, and that happy summer group of 1933. The oldest was Charlie, who was both likeable and different. He'd had a childhood sickness which made it hard for him to learn so he didn't go very far in school. Mr. Emmerson would punish him in exasperation, and at times Charlie would quit working on the family farm property and take off. Vanish. Over the years he did it to a number of places, including Egypt, but when he got home he would fit back right in again as a village institution.

Gottfried Klotz didn't. He got to know and like people like Bud Brian and Bert Emmerson and Hazen Greenberg and he attended weekly Boy Scout sessions, but essentially both his home and his niche were outside the mainstream of village life. Even so, in the end it was he and two of his classmates in particular who would, to me, become most symbolic of what happened to an entire generation.

All three were born within an eight-month period, Bill Palmer on June 23, 1921, Joe Emery on November 3, 1921, and Gottfried Klotz on February 16, 1922. In the same grade in school, they became friends but not pals, though a schoolmate would remember Bill and Gottfried once going at it with their fists. My memory retains pictures of all three but there is just one of two of them together. Bill Palmer and Joe Emery are in the white, wooden Roman Catholic Church next door to the school. It is Christmas Eve and I am there because my curiosity makes me want to see a midnight mass for the first time even if the terrifying Father Bourgeois might order me into purgatory at the very least. It is for this reason that I am sitting well back in the packed upstairs balcony when I behold Joe and Bill come in as altar boys for the glorious Latin ceremony of the mass. Never have I seen anything closer to angels. They are carrying candles and they are wearing white robes with something black hanging below, and their hair and faces and maybe even their ears are ... Well, they are shining with purity, innocence and goodness.

It was only later that I'd learn that being an altar boy was part of the politics of Bill's family life, that he'd use it to bargain with his devout mother. She and my mother were lifelong friends, and my mother and Bill's father were first cousins, and our families were close. Aunt Mary and Uncle Bill, as we called the Palmers, lived in that imposing three-storey house built by her father, Sir Pierre Amand Landry, and I can still see his handsome library dominating an entire room and saying something about books that's been in me ever since. But, as a matter of fact, the big house was getting shabby because Uncle Bill had trouble with the bottle and money was in what was called short supply. This didn't matter as much as it might have since in short supply was what money was everywhere, but it was the way things were when Bill, Jr., was growing up. So there he was, the grandson of a knight, living in a knight's house that said both what the village had been and what it had become. He had an older sister and a younger brother, and he was one of the boys, easygoing, good at sports, smart at school. He loved to fish; he and Tom Lowerison would go through the square with fishing lines over their shoulders and rubber boots on and their two dogs in an advanced state of joy. They'd spend hours fishing tommycod at the Memramcook River wharf where vessels used to tie up when things were good, and still occasionally did. Bill also had at his disposal the barn where we played hockey on bad-weather days, a building so imposing that it would eventually be turned into a house. Attached to it there was a woodshed that had an upstairs with the sort of nooks and crannies that seem, sadly, to have vanished from the earth. There, on a rainy fall day, a bunch of us in the 10-12 age category established a secret and exclusive society which became extinct in the time it took for a fight over procedures and creation of a new constitution. By the end of the afternoon we were up to Society No.4, and wondering what the weather would be like tomorrow. It was, in fact, good, and the surviving society was never heard of again.

Bill was there the night we stopped playing ball to watch Charlie Crandall drill the Dorchester Army. Joe Emery wasn't. I don't remember him playing either ball or hockey, but that may have been because he lived in the Guard Row which had a civilization of its own. It had a playground, and kids also engaged in fights and secrets and flirtations on the dirt road behind the string of houses unless they were busy helping their mothers get the washing out, or helping their fathers in the gardens almost every guard had to have or he'd be looked down upon by the others. Serious is what Joe was, quiet, contemplative, polite, responsible, rational, even if, as was alleged, he could get carried away enough to have a crush on my red-headed sister Peg at the very time Harry Ison's daughter Florence had a crush on him. His father was the chief trades instructor at the prison and the way Joe was may have had something to do with being the youngest child in a family of six to which religion mattered and in which the others were nearly all good looking and the one who wasn't was comical; almost had to be when he was named Oliver. Anyway, maybe we didn't see too much of Joe in the heart of the community simply because he figured walking the two miles or so between his home and the school four times a day was enough. Besides, he took school seriously and usually led his class, and he always looked neat and scrubbed behind the ears. Nevertheless, there were other things yeasting inside him that would eventually come out.

In fact, the village was a sort of confederation of regions divided by how much you wanted to walk. Joe walked to school from one side of town. Gottfried Klotz walked three miles or so from the farm area past the other side of town. Back Road kids walked a mile and more from another direction. The Micmac Indian kids came in along the road leading past the graveyard. The black kids came in from where they lived well along on the Back Road. So you'd see this traffic of the young flowing toward a common destination, much of it through Bill Palmer's yard as a shortcut. Then at noon the traffic would reverse, then reverse again, and at 3.30 it would flow back for the day. The Guard Row kids would re-establish their civilization and on his own way home Gottfried Klotz might meet Melvin Sollows, second-oldest of 15 kids, and get wrestling and the Back Road kids would re-establish another civilization hinged on their own dirt road.

This also happened to be the highway on which a local resident, enroute to work, would take his cow to pasture nearer town and sometimes come home leaning on her because he'd had too much to drink. Regardless, the kids would re-establish their own distinct existence in which the Mitton and Amisson and Ward and Atkinson boys and others, would play ball or street hockey, then gather at Billy Manship's house. One reason was that Billy's grandfather, old Bill O'Blenis, was a storyteller and made kids welcome. They found it a good place to be, especially when the world series was on the radio, or a big boxing match or hockey game, even if old Bill gave a bit of a preference to his grandson in refereeing wrestling matches. Or even if he got going about what a humdinger Billy was at playing the guitar and singing cowboy songs. He was right up there with the best, old Bill would say, which was quite a thing to say when the Maritimes were producing the likes of Wilf Carter and Hank Snow.

Thus there were these differing civilizations that lived apart but flowed together, especially at school but also in other places. Flowed together for the swimming at Palmer's Pond where fresh water from the hills met salt water from the sea, and where one day Bud Brian and "Mousie" Amisson saved a boy in danger of drowning. Flowed together where there were berries to pick, or at horse races or in the square or in the stores or at the rink. Flowed together particularly for sports, and for a special reason: a community spirit grew up because when there weren't too many athletes to go around you welcomed all the athletes you could find.

Gradually, in high school, what began to get to you was not just who was coming into town but what it was going to be like when you had to leave. Leaving had been for years part of the logic of the community mind, for the whole Maritime region lived a paradox: nourished an affection, yes, and often a love it found impossible to sustain. So mentally you prepared for exile, and it helped make me sad because I felt happy and secure at school, and didn't want it to end. Not that I told anyone. There are some things you tell and some you don't, and now when I say I felt secure I wonder how secure I really felt, because there was something else I didn't talk about either. For a year and more my body had spasmodically sought to do embarrassing, bewildering things, to make me twitch as though in a fit, so that I would pray, say, that I would not be told to go to the blackboard or I would have a sinking feeling when the time came to jump into the water or bat in a ball game. The answer I found was my own: to pause, to let on I had something to do before doing what I was expected to do, to steel or freeze my limbs until I could control them and they not me. I thought of it as "it," and it would plague me for years, and I would later regret that I hid it because I suspect that's what kept it going. But I would also come to suspect it may have saved my life.

These were the things that were going on when the

world was increasingly dropping hints about what exile could turn into. Mussolini's Italy invaded and conquered Abyssinia or Ethiopia. The Japanese rape of China went on. When civil war broke out in Spain, both Mussolini and Hitler turned it into a training ground for thousands to help crush a democratic government. All this while Charlie Crandall had his Dorchester Army doing in its occasional and tragicomic way what Hitler was doing with multitudes, and while there developed one other parallel. Nazi Germany was building the first modern highway or autobahn system that would link the country east and west, north and south. Was doing this at the same time New Brunswick was gradually paving its own main highways, was paying men 25 cents an hour to do it, and seeing others beg to take their places for less. My friend Ev Shea was glad to get the 25 cents. My friend John Sweeney was glad to get it. Young Melvin Sollows was so pleased to get it that he didn't even go back to school. All this while Hitler was building the autobahns which would, he reasoned, be a military asset both for defence and as a springboard for attacks on other countries.

It was another kind of springboard that helped Hitler penetrate the mind of Gottfried Klotz. It was the controlled German press, and the man who controlled it was Goebbels, the masterful minister of propaganda whom Hitler called his "field marshal on the spiritual front." Josef Goebbels swept Gottfried Klotz up in a campaign of brainwashing such as the world had never seen. He told the press what it could say and what it couldn't, used it to cast a veil of respectability and plausibility over totalitarian measures and designs, turned it into a tool for spreading the Nazi gospel both at home and among Germans abroad. As one tiny result, German newspapers came regularly into the Klotz home, and the boy read them with a mind psychologically prepared for their message. As a child living in a conservative atmosphere in Germany, he had learned that war was terrible, that the French were to be feared, that communists and socialists were responsible for what happened in 1918, that no criticism was to be directed at the Kaiser for a war he had not started or at Germany for mistakes she had not made. These were beliefs that had helped propel Hitler into power, these and others: that the Germans weren't defeated on the battlefield, that they were "stabbed in the back" by leftist politicians who delivered them into degradation and poverty, that Germany was lured into peace negotiations by the glowing promises of American president Woodrow Wilson only to be bludgeoned into accepting the harsh, undeserved and vastly costly humiliations which France and Britain insisted be in the Versailles Treaty. Even after years in Canada, that grounding was there, and all through the boy's high school years Hitler would feed it, would go on demanding, threatening, bullying, would shriek defiance into supporting demonstrations of public fealty and military power that seemed to grow in strength. Did this while the nations that might have stopped him yielded before his cunning and his iron will. Tried to appease him, to argue to their own publics that much of what he demanded was a justified adjustment of unfair peace terms and that he would be satisfied when the last unfairnesses were removed.

So the boy came to lead a sort of double life, to march to a drummer different from the faint, erratic and sporadic drummer heard by his schoolmates. If they read newspapers, they were Canadian newspapers. If they listened to broadcasts, they heard them on Canadian and American radio. If they heard returned men and other adults talking about Hitler's Germany, it was about a hostile, menacing and arrogant Germany. If they thought of Hitler, as increasingly they did, they thought of him as bad, as evil. If Gottfried Klotz thought of Hitler, he thought of him as doing good things that needed to be done. The family did not subscribe to a Canadian paper for the same reason that it had no radio or car; they all cost money, and money was scarce. Germany had forced harsh peace terms on Russia in 1917, but the papers the boy read didn't say such things. Instead, they provided encouragements for his natural pride in being German. They told him that the country was rising from the ruin caused by Versailles, that its economy, only recently devastated by a massive Versailles-caused inflation, was growing, that the Feuhrer was dedicated both to peace and to undoing the injustices of 1918, to asserting, bravely and firmly, Germany's rights and Germany's place in the world.

It was a message the boy found consoling and a source of pride. He became a believer, and he could be both stubborn and argumentative about it, even in his own later term a "loudmouth." At times he would bristle at criticisms of Hitler and/or Germany, would lash out in what he'd call "fanatical discussions" because he "wouldn't hear bad about them." Even as his father had been out making final arrangements to take over the Coles Point farm, he had rebuked one critic in a Moncton hotel, and that was by no means the only time. At Ernie Partridge's Vimy canteen, Tom Lowerison heard returned man Dick Whalen's son Lee make a disparaging remark about Hitler and saw Gottfried go at him in a rage until someone got between them. And Lee was bigger and older and tougher too.

Given this background, what happened to Gottfried Klotz in the village school was much less difficult and controversial than it might have been. It would eventually be his memory and that of others that by and large he was accepted, that things went well, that he was happy there. Ralph March, the principal, would say he saw him as just one boy among others. Moreover, he worked at fitting in. He didn't boast about Hitler or Germany, didn't try to start arguments. At times John Robinson would walk part way home with him and ask to see the newspapers Gottfried carried and, he'd say, Gottfried wouldn't let him. Also, Gottfried smiled a lot. Helen Petchey, one grade behind him, would remember that the smile was like a banner of friendly intent. Ling Belliveau, Marcel's girl, would remember him being a bit defensive, and my sister Peg would say she saw neither meanness nor pettiness in him. What his own memory would eventually tell him was that there were no fights at school and that if there were any they were probably about him being new. Yet I can still see him fighting someone, his glasses off, his face pale, his hair distraught, his boots gathering dust, the two of them ringed by the brave, shouting faces of the unengaged. That may have been because he was new, but I've heard others tell of fights with him too.

Yet I doubt that any of his schoolmates had any idea of how his attitude was being shaped by what he read as the world headed for the greatest upheaval in human history. It would surprise me to find that one thing that particularly struck him was seeing my eyes on him when the three grades were asked to vow allegiance to the Union Jack. That was the year of the 1936 abdication of King Edward VIII and the coronation of King George VI which may explain what happened, but it left him confused because he didn't know what to do. In the end, he did what the others did, but that only compounded his embarrassment. He considered lies dishonorable, yet there he was doing something he didn't believe in. For the allegiance he believed in was to the country of his birth, and he was shaken by what he'd done and by seeing me watch him do it.

It *was*, for him, a complicated world, as one thing alone

signified. The grandson of a minister, he had strong religious tendencies, and he did one thing about it which would probably have surprised his schoolmates if they'd known. He habitually carried a New Testament, and it meant one more irony. For he believed both in the Christian gospel and in what was being done in Germany by a Hitler who would say "National Socialist and Christian conceptions are incompatible." If that involved a dichotomy, it wasn't the only one. He read war stories and somehow it didn't bother him that in them the Germans were the bad guys. He was also able to rationalize something else. Wasn't, he asked himself, Charlie Crandall doing what Hitler was doing? He was training soldiers, he and Sgt. Maj. Dave Bernard and Louis Knockwood, two affable Micmacs, and what were soldiers for if they weren't for military purposes?

In my final year in school, four boys in Grade 11 were singled out to be trained to spell out battlefield messages with two flags. A man came once a week to instruct us, and we each got $5, and in Ottawa our names were entered as plus marks in the files on national security. Sometimes, as well, Mr. March would climb with us up a ladder into the musty school attic where there was a miniature rifle range. It dated, I presume, at least back to the Great War, though no returned man came to tell us so and we didn't find it relevant to ask; what they had learned, what they'd been, still seemed detached from who we were and what we did. Two at a time, we would lie down with .22 calibre rifles, get a bit of coaching, then fire at targets only yards away. We didn't do it very often, partly because there was hardly enough ammunition to do it as often as we did.

By the June night when I stood up to deliver the valedictory for the Class of 1936, dreading that I would be humiliated by "it" in that hot, packed room, militia officers like Charlie Crandall were preparing to go to summer camps without pay just to keep their units going. At Camp Sussex, for the first time, nobody brought horses because it had been at last accepted that cavalry was obsolete and that the militia must prepare for tank warfare by training with cars. That was the summer the Olympic Games were held in Berlin and the greatness of black American athlete Jesse Owens cast a shadow upon Hitler's assertions of Aryan superiority. It didn't, however, stop the Feuhrer from hailing Mussolini's aggression in Africa, formally making Italy and Japan his allies, encouraging Austrian Nazis to prepare for a takeover of their country, or having his picture taken at fervent rallies replete with masses of troops.

The effects spread through the world. One soft, warm evening, as news of these things drummed in by radio, newspapers, magazines, a bunch of us were kidding with Guy Amisson in the square. He was on leave from the regular army, and one thing led to another, and suddenly we were marching behind him. I don't know how or why it happened, but there we were behind him in his khaki uniform, and only yards away from the memorial with the 25 soldier names on it, and we were laughing and shouting and trying to march as soldiers march.

My first effort to find employment was directed at a bank that encouraged me, then turned me down because the Depression wasn't lifting after all. This was seen by my mother and myself as a disaster. Then, as an old friend of my mother, William Hickman offered to take me into the office of J.H. Hickman, Co. Ltd. until I could find a permanent job. That's how I got into hardware and an education in the economics of disaster and a village I hardly knew. I had to send out monthly statements and they stunned me with information about the devastations of crippling credit, about who paid their bills and who didn't, But in the long run what would matter most was that I taught myself the two-finger typing I'd use in journalism for years.

While this was going on, there was an essay contest for the school's Grade 10. The subject was peace, and Gottfried Klotz submitted 10 hand-written pages that openly brought together for the first time the two strands of his double life. To his peers in one world he revealed the thoughts he'd accumulated in another. The boy who couldn't lie expounded the lies of Josef Goebbels. Hitler, he said, would never start a war. All he sought to do was restore to Germany what was historically and rightfully hers. Then he'd stop. He didn't win the prize. Henry Emmerson's daughter Barbara won it. Yet he was not alone in his views. It was about this time that Canada's Prime Minister Mackenzie King met Hitler and privately dismissed him as a simple peasant who'd never start a war.

King's views would eventually be seen as part of his strong belief in appeasement, young Klotz's as part of the ramifications of innocence. He apparently felt it was possible to dissociate the good that Adolf Hitler did from the bad that Hitler did—if he was aware of the bad at all. But the day would come when he'd regret that essay more than anything else he did at the village school. Regretted it, he'd say, because he felt it would make his schoolmates think he was "a big Nazi."

In November 1937 the biggest Nazi of them all outlined in secrecy for his generals his plans for taking over both Austria and Czechoslovakia. As a beginning of larger things. By then, after laying siege for months, I had landed a job as one of two reporters with the Moncton *Daily Times* and just as William Hickman surrendered to reality and sold out. Years later it would strike me that I saw the Depression end more than a century of Hickman village enterprise in shipbuilding, shipping, lumbering, law, and the retail trade. The sad thing was that the era died without either the salutes of protest or the comforts of eulogy. Died as though it weren't an event but an inevitable release from long disease.

Years later I would think back to my leaving town and about the ones whose names come into this story: Bud Brian: the only boy in town who can walk on his hands, the teacher's favorite in Grade 8, he comes up the hill with his fists doubled. He is very good with his fists and I'm not, and he says, "Are you the one who told people my first name is Francis?" I wasn't, but I lie anyway just to be sure. I say I didn't even know his first name was Francis, and he walks away, perhaps regretting that he had spread the terrible news himself. Raymond Mitton: At the horse races, we get to wrestling and he gets me down. He doesn't seem to know what to do next except that it may matter in relations between the Back Road (him) and the Town (me). We miss one whole race that way. Bert Emmerson: There is a social evening at the Anglican church hall and in a lottery for lunch he draws the name of a new and pretty girl in town. I offer him 25 cents of paper-route proceeds to swap, and he accepts because he needs the money, which is one way of saying the Depression wasn't all bad. Anyway, that's how I got to walk Hazel Drury home. Hazen Greenberg: On a September night, we come in from stealing apples and he is the only one of the four of us with money. He buys a chocolate bar for each of us. This is the way he is. He is the kindest guy in town. Walter "Mousie" Amisson and Lloyd Atkinson: They are being sworn into the Boy Scouts and it is an almost unbearably solemn occasion until someone lets a resounding fart. There is a hush and then everybody dissolves into laughter, even the very proper scoutmaster, and the two boys stand there, not knowing what to do. Billy Manship: We are on a Scout hike and at lunch time he and I are, by chance, paired up. We start a fire that gets a tree burning, and everybody laughs at us, and it creates something that lasts. Len and Ev Shea: Sometimes we swim and sometimes we play hockey or coast or tell lies and jokes, but this evening we are playing softball with their big barn as a backstop, and it is awesome the way their sister Margaret hits the ball, and her destined to be a nun with as happy a face as I've ever seen. Charlie Emmerson: There is a fair and the lights are bright and you can hear the music of the merry-go-round and voices from the crown and anchor board. A slick young man drives up in a slick car with the roof down. He's from Toronto, and his father is big in road construction, and he's Looking For Action. Charlie climbs into the sporty car and in the lights of carnival his face shines like some painting Breughel might have done, with a pleasure in the focus that is on him and in the roaring away, into the night. Frank Tracy: He comes to town to work at the bank and he boards with us and pitches on the town baseball team. He has mainly one pitch, a high, hard fastball, but he can throw it forever.

I'd ask myself, looking back, how it was with them and others in the last years of the pause, with the grip of depression on the land and the grip of a wider apprehension on its people. In some cases I would not know the answer and would be unable to find anyone who did. Even though I made frequent visits to the village, I simply lost track of a lot of them. Dan Stack? Gone. Charlie Crandall? Working at the prison, training soldiers, raising three kids. Bill Palmer, Joe Emery, Bud Brian, Bert Emmerson? Finishing their schooling. Others who'd dropped out of school scrabbled for work where work was rare or non-existent? Billy Manship? Hoboing at times.

Working wherever he could find work. Sometimes meeting Earl Stiles, the jailer's son, who had his own guitar, and singing with him songs about the sorrows and treacheries of life. Raymond Mitton? Heading west to help get prairie harvests in. Heading out with the thousands who climbed on boxcars and roamed a country that had neither place nor hope to offer. Skinny, quiet Gerald Ward, living with relatives to reduce the burdens on his home, clinging to his own share of a no-hope world, to jobs like the one that kept him shovelling gravel with his head down because he feared he'd lose it if he didn't. Len Shea, a hospital orderly. Lloyd Atkinson and Mousie Amisson? Dropouts, hanging in there, doing things my mind has no memory of. Charlie Emmerson? Coming and going. The ones from the happy summer of 1933? Scattered. Richard Emmerson? A militia lieutenant since 1936, now studying to be an osteopath. Doug MacKean, the United Church minister's son? At university. Two others in the armed forces. My brother Jim? Working in an armaments plant in Montreal. My brother Hank? Collecting rents for a trust company in Moncton; in the slums, hating it. Frank Tracy? Pitching for a Moncton baseball team, boarding with us again after my mother moved to the city. Jack Hickman's kid sister Teresa? A nurse in Montreal. Emily Emmerson? A nurse too. Younger kids like Gerald Adshade, Harry Ison's son Edgar, Gottfried Klotz's brother Uli? In their early teens. After five years in Hillsboro, N.B., Warren Duffy lives in Fairvale, N.B., becomes in autumn 1938 a student at Rothesay Consolidated School for his final year; he's been acting as a chauffeur for his father and he's interested in a number of sports but especially keen about swimming, tennis and hockey; when the Dorchester and Rothesay teams meet for the provincial scholastic championship for smaller towns, he finds himself facing boys he knew in Dorchester — and losing the game. In the village school he had attended are

Betty and Margaret McCabe, Margaret and Marion Emmerson, Frances Miller, Rosie and Nancy Nelson, Dorcas Petchey and others unaware they will be among the first women to wear their country's uniform.

Mrs. Klotz and her two daughters? Seldom seen in town, because she felt uncomfortable there. She had a flower garden but not one shaped like a Nazi swastika, as people said. The father? On the farm, milking five cows, sometimes hitching up the horse to go to town to buy and sell and talk about things at Herb Palmer's store or at the hotel bar. Sometimes talking to a Danish immigrant farmer who came to town to sell meat, and admired Hitler. Was still said to have meetings with groups of Germans at his house, to get people to drive him to cities by car for purposes undefined, to have told Stanley Bateman that the Kaiser was a damned fool but Hitler was doing great things for Germany. Gottfried? Forming his own conclusions about Hitler's Germany, rarely if ever, he'd say, discussing them with a father he suspected was less enthusiastic than himself. Lucky enough to get work with a German-born house builder from Moncton in the summer of 1937. At school, to the end, not quite like the others were. When a German zeppelin, the *Hindenberg*, flew directly over the village to an explosive and fiery end in New Jersey, its route was said to be related in some way to what Hans Klotz was telling Hitler, and his son was asked to consider how dreadful it would have been if it had crashed in the village itself. Yet, more happily, he met in friendship people almost symbolic of larger enmities. Met Hazen Greenberg when he came to Coles Point in a gravel truck to get sand, met him and liked him, as Hazen did him. Met and liked jaunty Marcel Belliveau, the returned man with the holes Germans put in him; Marcel Belliveau who came to fish off the wharf, gave the boy and Uli good things to eat and occasionally went to the house to visit the Klotz family. As did his wife. As did his daughter Ling and her sister Ruth who had lived with her grandmother in England and only recently come to the village, who felt when she sat in the cosy Klotz kitchen that she was welcome and that she knew a bit about how different they must feel because she felt that way herself. The returned men? In or near their 40s. Meeting occasionally in the Legion hall. Playing poker. Talking more about the potential of a new war than about the one they'd known.

Chapter Five

THE VILLAGE YEARS OF pause came, in my mind, to a climactic hour on June 30, 1938, on school closing night when people gathered for graduation ceremonies in a world where economic and diplomatic nightmares crowded one another for space. Only recently, badgered by the Depression, the Liberal government had for the first time deliberately budgetted for a deficit. In Europe, Hitler had taken over Austria as the climax to years of terrorism he had inspired to make it possible. Now he was stimulating a crisis over the terrible things he alleged Czechoslovakia was doing to its Sudeten Germans. This was what newspapers and radio kept talking about. Much as he hated war, this was what made returned man Ed Oulton despair at the efforts to appease Hitler, had recently made him get uncharacteristically angry with a friend and argue — as Winston Churchill kept arguing — that it was Hitler who must be stopped. This, on that June 30, was what was in the thoughts of nearly everyone in attendance at Dorchester Superior School.

The room was hot and mosquitoes kept coming in. The blackboards had been cleaned to a faretheewell; the desks removed. There were wooden chairs right up to the raised platform, and every chair was occupied. On the platform sat the graduates, themselves a sort of symbolic link between what had been and what was to be: five girls in long white gowns, at least three of whom were daughters of returned men, Marcel Belliveau's daughter Evangeline, "Ling", Edgar Cole's daughter Kay and Henry Emmerson's daughter Barbara; three boys about to go out into a world that implied the impending return of what had only recently ended when they were born.

The platform was where younger students came to get prizes or to perform, as Maude Dobson, Frank A.'s daughter, did in playing "Sonatina in D Major" by Kuhlau as a piano solo. When Joseph Arthur Emery rose to pass the torch as valedictorian and class leader, he wore a navy blue suit from Eaton's and he looked less like an angel than a figure infiltrated by agony. William Frederick Palmer sat listening with the composure of one who had no role to perform. Gottfried Klotz wore that habitual smile like some signal that he knew he was not quite like his schoolmates but wanted to be friendly with them all. His father Hans was not present, perhaps because of the world situation and what village gossip made of it. Among the students in the audience, Florence Ison sat watching Gottfried himself, remembering that when, at her request, he had kindly helped her with a math problem someone hissed that she was befriending a spy. Yet when Eileen Spence got up to deliver the class prophecy, she teased him just as she teased the others. The zeppelin which had passed over the village may have gone down in flames but, she predicted, Gottfried Klotz would become the designer of a superior version, and everybody laughed.

Joe Emery's valedictory was the 11th item on a program which ranged from an opening march to the admonitions of a clergyman who urged the graduates to remember that God was the best anchor in such rocky times. On behalf of all students, my sister Peg made a presentation to Principal March who was leaving and who had, she noticed, tears in his eyes. Soon after it was all over Bill Palmer and Gottfried Klotz walked downtown together. They stopped at the Vimy canteen and there was something prophetic in them being there, beside a sign proud with the name of Canada's most memorable battle. They thanked Ernie Partridge for his congratulations and they chose hotdogs from what he had to offer. When he made them he obviously had not too much use of his left arm, due to his war wound, but they didn't say anything about that. They stood in the quiet street and the soft summer night and ate the hotdogs, and they they went home because there was nothing else to do. They had no inkling of the ironies time would find not only in them being at a modest enterprise that harked back to war, talking to a man the war had maimed, but also in the name of the last song on their graduation program, one entitled "Comrades of the Road." Or did they?

This was when teenagers Dan and Peter Hanington, grandsons of Roaring Dan, came to visit Mrs. Teed in Rocklyn, the great stone house. Their widowed father had died in Trinidad and left them with little money, and Mrs. Teed had swept them into the New Brunswick clan because she was a mixture of kindness and certainties, and knew what must be done. Dan already thought of her as "darling, tender-hearted Madgie," but she did *know* things. She drove her Dodge car down the middle of the paved highway because she was sure that's why the stripe was there. She knew what must be done when the pavement went by, and the workers chuckled secretly when their tyrannical boss submitted totally to her will. She knew the Teed family must look after her two nephews, which it handsomely did under the guidance of what was known as "the look." Soon after their 1937 arrival in Saint John, they were cascaded into a Christmas they'd never forget: "Never having had relatives around, it was a revelation — babies, cousins, aunts, friends," Dan would write. "Confusing, but wonderful."

The summer of 1938 was a revelation too, because it swept them up in Mrs. Teed's fluctuating retinue of relatives and guests, filled the great house with laughter and certain hearts with ardor, for the beauty of some of the granddaughters made it difficult for young men to breathe properly. Suffice it to say that I'd been happy in the past to pick as many peas and strawberries as possible for Mrs. Teed and to be accepted in courtship by one of the girls. On holidays and weekends, I was still occasionally courting red-headed Dolly Palmer when Dan and Peter Hanington appeared, Dan, 17 and dour, Peter, 13 and a beam of sunlight. Mrs. Teed was 73 that year, a matriarch among her vegetables and flowers and carrying on a tradition that gave each visitor in residence an identifying, napkin-holding clothespin to be suspended from a long string in the dining room. In the selective apparatus of memory, I see her that way, see Bert Emmerson chumming with her shy, blonde Ottawa grandson Lionel Palmer on the lawn where his namesake uncle got that news in 1914, and in one of those images that live and instantly die see Dan Hanington at a night party at the beach when we walked through wind-wracked trees, on a bluff above the sea, and I see Joe Emery among them, on his face a moonlight that made it pale.

In September Britain and France bullied Czechoslovakia into ceding its Sudetenland to Hitler, and Prime Minister Neville Chamberlain told joyful multitudes at London's airport that this meant "peace in our time." It also meant, Hitler had pledged, that he had made his last territorial demand. In Ottawa, Prime Minister King cabled

Chamberlain, with little exaggeration, that all Canada rejoiced. He was so convinced this was the real end of the Great War that he insisted on a symbolic act. Though the literature of stone stretched across the country by then, the national memorial was still under construction, and even though he was told he was rushing things, King personally wheeled into place the great winged angelic form that crowns it. Present, at his invitation, was the German consul general who may or may not have been embarrassed by the fact that Hitler was already making demands on Poland and furious that he'd been denied a military conquest in Czechoslovakia.

By then, Bill Palmer was enrolled in a two-year commercial course at St. Joseph's University in the Memramcook valley. His hockey-playing pals Bud Brian and Gerry Nugent were there too. Dan and Peter Hanington were at private Rothesay Collegiate School. Joe Emery was taking a business course in nearby Saint John. Gottfried Klotz was working in Moncton for the German-born building contractor who had employed him in the summer of 1937, was in frequent attendance at a pool hall and occasionally embarrassed at night when the three daughters of his boarding house landlord came into his room to tease him. When Murray Dobson's father, Frank A., asked him what he thought of Hitler now, he grinned: "He iss a good pluffer." But even as Hitler provoked a crisis over Poland, confident that bluffing would work again, the boy who had for years defended him entered a crisis of his own. His job ended. As winter settled in, he tramped the streets looking for another just when his father said the family was going back to Germany. He would never tell his son precisely why, but some reasons were obvious. The farm debt he'd owed in 1934 he still owed, and he could see war coming. By now even Mackenzie King could see war coming, was starting to make limited and very belated preparations. If he was still in Canada when it came, Hans Klotz knew, he might well be interned again. On November 28 Nazis looted, smashed and murdered in what would become known as the beginning of Hitler's organized attack on European Jews, as *Kristallnacht*, "the night of broken glass." It didn't change his mind. Neither did a strange letter that couldn't say what a knowledgeable brother-in-law wanted it to say because the Nazis examined mail going overseas. With feigned hostility, he wrote that the family hoped they'd never again see Hans Klotz in Germany. But Hans Klotz didn't get the message; it only made him angry. He, his wife, the two little girls Erika and Margaret and 12-year-old Uli were leaving, he said, but Gottfried would have to make up his own mind. He could go or he could stay. So the boy faced alone a decision that tore at him for days, but in the end two main things made up his mind. If he'd found a job, he would say, it might well have made the decision for him. Because, argue though he might, the pull of German patriotism was not what turned out to be crucial. What did was far more human and simple than that. He was never happier, he'd say, than when he got home. In the end what was decisive was the love of a 16-year-old boy for a home that was going away.

He met Joe Emery and a brother of Joe's on the street in Moncton, and told them what was happening. "If you go back to Germany, you're crazy," they said. "There's going to be a war." They drove him home to Coles Point, and they kept saying he shouldn't go. But he did. That December he was with the family when Hans Klotz left his fifth farm and headed for the Germany he had twice departed. When the word got out, village people were confused, but inevitably there were those who said Hitler's Nazis must have summoned them home.

Never had Gottfried Klotz lived as high as he did on

the German liner *Bremen*. A marvelous experience it was, all the way from New York: the food, the quarters, the fun he and Uli had, the shining faces of the two little girls, the confidence of the Germans aboard. But when he got back to his native land for the first time in 10 years, he saw things which surprised or even shook him. He saw the Nazi swastika flag all over the place, and he preferred the flag it had displaced. He didn't like the red in it because red was the color of communism, and communism was bad. He saw people raising their arms and saying, even shouting, "Heil Hitler", and he thought it looked silly. He was surprised that it took 12 hours to get through Customs. When they left Bremerhaven for Dresden, he found himself swearing in poolroom English because the train was cold, frequently delayed and so packed that Uli had to sit on a toilet. Above all, there seemed to be soldiers everywhere; in the streets, in the train and trying in one station after another to scramble aboard. Soldiers laughing and singing because they were going home for Christmas. Soldiers in infinitely greater numbers than Charlie Crandall's Dorchester Army.

After years of separation, it was wonderful to be back for Christmas, wonderful to see Walter and Arndt, though they were soldiers too. They'd been called up for 30 months, and said they were counting the days till they got out. But when a cousin Gottfried's own age came to visit it was different. He was in the *Hitlerjugend*, the Hitler Youth, and proud to be. When you were in the Hitler Youth, he said, you were at the cutting edge of the almost magical things the Feuhrer was doing and going to do for Germany. You were part of an elite that would lead the way to a glorious future, and if Gottfried was smart there was nowhere else he'd rather be. This was while Hans Klotz was working out arrangements for his sixth farm, and while his two boys stayed with relatives, which is where that cousin came. Came and said a lot of things, and the first thing Gottfried Klotz knew they were arguing.

It went on for hours, and the cousin back from Canada found he was using some of the very arguments he had argued against. His cousin was throwing at him the sort of statements he had thrown at others, and he was throwing back statements which even William Lyon Mackenzie King would have found quite acceptable. Democracy was corrupt and inefficient and stupid, the cousin said. Democracy was far more than that, Gottfried Klotz said. Opposition political parties were unnecessary and potentially dangerous, the cousin said. Political parties might be stupid and occasionally corrupt but they were a necessary ingredient of freedom, Gottfried Klotz said. Freedom, said one cousin, was what came after the security and wellbeing of the collective state. Freedom, said the other, was rooted in the individual. Hitler, said one cousin, was a braver and wiser guide than any combination of political parties could possibly be. Hitler, said the other, might go too far.

The same Hitler, Hans Klotz found, was at least the nominal owner of the farm he wanted. It took weeks to find it and make arrangements, but the entire family was happy with his choice: a nice farm in hill country on the outskirts of a village called Mulda, south and east of Berlin, in Saxony not too far from Dresden and the Sudetenland Czechoslovakia had been forced to cede to Germany. It was one of a good number called Hitler farms which you were supposed to join the Nazi Party to get. Somehow, Hans Klotz got this one without joining, which may have been a sign that Hitler needed all the farmers he could find, including Hans Klotz and a son just turning 17. Indeed, the Klotzes moved in just as Hitler marched troops into the rest of Czechoslovakia, bloodlessly took complete control of a heavily armed and fortified country which he said was a menace to Germany but which looked on the map like a big thumb jabbing into the countries to the east, or, if you'd read *Mein Kampf*, like a springboard pointing toward where he intended, one way or another, to go.

In that March 1939, Dorchester High was winning another provincial hockey title, only this time against schools from communities comparable in population; winning against a team from Rothesay, one of whose stars was Warren Duffy. Bill Palmer and Gerry Nugent were up to their ears in hockey playoffs in the Memramcook Valley, Bud Brian was the leading scorer in Moncton junior hockey, and on weekends Bill and Bud would go to Elmer Lewis's garage on the outskirts of the village, and they'd kid young Ruthie, Elmer and Vinnie's girl, and they'd play cards in the kitchen. Around the table, nobody talked about Hitler's latest move the way people had talked about the Sudetenland. The outrage seemed to be gone, not because people accepted what he'd done but because they finally accepted that there was, in all probability, just one way to stop him.

In one sense, the Klotzes' new farm was like Ed Turner's farm where Gottfried's friend Pop Dobson spent so much time. It too was snugged up near a village, in this case one of some 3,000 population. But Mulda itself was far enough out in the country to insulate it from towering events. The boy Gottfried passed that year without seeing Hitler or other high Nazis, or any of those tumultuous and imbuing party rallies designed to inspire zeal at home and awe abroad. In the family, it was accepted that Uli, Erika and Margaret would go to school, but that he would work with his father. This would mean, among other things, that he would never possess a classroom knowledge of the German language, but it wasn't long before he was educating himself in the language of the streets. Like the rest of the family, he soon felt at home and soon began registering the subtleties of daily life. There was a synagogue in Mulda, and there were people who didn't like what they heard about the persecution of the Jews. There were people who didn't like the public burning of books Hitler found distasteful, who didn't like it that a prominent local man had gone to jail because he'd made a joke about Josef Goebbels. But there was broad agreement that it was wise to keep your thoughts to yourself because there were informers everywhere. At the same time, the boy sensed an undercurrent of foreboding. Hitler's generals had repeatedly been appalled at the risks he'd taken against their advice — and repeatedly cowed by his successes. They knew that Germany's enemies could have crushed her if they'd had the will. They feared they might crush her yet, and they were not alone. Ordinary people kept wondering why other countries had let Hitler get away with so much, and whether he'd finally go too far. Sometimes they even wondered why Germany's enemies didn't kill him.

When I think of that summer of 1939 I think of Wordsworth's lines about the still, sad music of humanity, of a drifting toward a reef that would inevitably be reached, of a dancing to a music that would inevitably die. Late in August a weekly newspaper in New Brunswick's Miramichi Valley printed an unusually tall headline which someone in the *Daily Times* newsroom clipped and stuck on a wall as an example of structural impurity. Garbled it was, but its message was clear. What it said was: PEACEFUL OR TERRIBLE WAR DEPENDS ON HITLER.

Everything seemed to depend on Hitler now. He was bullying the Poles, notably about the port of Danzig (now Gdansk) which, after the Great War, had been given to Poland along with a corridor to it through German territory. He kept throwing Jews and others into concentration camps, kept turning tens of thousands of Germans into screaming advocates. He had Czechoslovakia's factories turning out arms. He knew Britain and France were at last rearming, but felt sure that in the crunch he had next in mind they would posture and pontificate, then again back down.

In the village, Ed Oulton was more certain than ever that backing down was wrong. It hurt him to say this because his troubled legs kept reminding him of the trenches. When he sat hunched beside the radio, his daughter Shirley could almost see rising in him again the bitter disillusion she'd been told he'd come home with before she was born. When he passed the war memorial on his way to work, the 25 names it bore seemed to be mocked by futility. He had become the epitome of the ultimate sadness of his time: of men who had fought one dreadful war only to find it had set the stage for another.

In *Mein Kampf*, Hitler had said Germany could not win a two-front war. On August 24 he closed a deal with Josef Stalin which ensured that he would not have to worry about one involving Russia. On September 1, he invaded Poland. When Britain and France demanded his withdrawal, he scorned their ultimatum. On September 3, they surprised him: they abandoned appeasement and declared war. In Mulda, people had no doubt that he had at last gone too far, and were not surprised that as a result war had come. What did surprise many of them was that the same powers that had declared war on Germany for what she'd done in Poland uttered no protest when Russia took a large chunk of Poland and all three Baltic States, and within two months invaded Finland.

In the village, Harry Ison, his head still taunted by what war had done, sat by the radio listening to the news that war had come again, and what his daughter Florence saw when she looked in would stay with her forever. He was silent and alone, and there were tears running down his face. She'd grown up listening to him play "The Last Post" at Remembrance Day services. For the rest of her life, she'd break up every time she heard it.

On September 10, after waiting a week to emphasize the country's independence, the Canadian Parliament declared war, and Gottfried Klotz's homeland became formally an enemy of the country where he'd spent more than half his life. He and his classmates had ceased to be "Comrades of the Road." In the village he'd left behind, there was no cheering on Rocklyn's lawn, no cheering anywhere. For war seemed to come not with the tang and thrust of spring but in the way the Canadian winter comes, inexorably, like a gray November becoming a December with ice and snow.

What happened in the country after that was to a crucial extent what hundreds of thousands of people decided it should be. Primarily for one reason, Canada placed upon individuals a burden borne in most modern nations by the state. Parliament overwhelmingly ruled out conscription mainly to soothe and placate French Quebec. After bitter experiences in the Great War, a national decision of great pith and moment was forged the way the history of Canadian fragility and compromise suggested it should be: no one would be forced to fight. Each individual would face the responsibility, even the agony, of deciding what to do. With one political move, Parliament turned the nation into a laboratory of choice.

Teresa Hickman was one who knew at once what her choice would be. She could remember the fuss over brother Joe's return in 1919, the family dog suddenly exploding into affection. Her mother had died when she was three and her father not long after Jack's body was brought home, so she'd been raised in the homes of siblings. By 1939 she was 25 and a nurse in Montreal, and when war returned she promptly enlisted as a nursing sister. In one generation, her family had linked what ended in 1918 with what started in 1939, and not through her alone. Brothers Harry and Bob would both serve in Canada as army officers.

Like her, Charlie Crandall responded at once to the first of what would become two starts to the war. The New Brunswick Rangers started mobilizing shortly before it began, and he was soon on duty as adjutant in Saint John. Then anti-climax: the unit patrolled vulnerable points and coastal beaches, trained and waited. In Europe: more anti-climax. Hitler quickly crushed Poland, then the Germans and the British and French looked at one another in what became known as the phoney war. Since it was that way for eight months, it is hardly surprising that there were many like the aging and slightly disoriented widow who went about the village inquiring whether the services of her irascible son would be required on the fields of battle. She met a local sage who informed her that British airpower would soon bring Hitler to heel. She went to church and expressed gratitude to the Lord. Then a second sage informed her that the war would be long and hard and would require the services of her son and many others. Whereupon, she went to church and asked the Lord for mercy. In the end, one sage would turn out to be quite correct in saying the war would be long and hard, the other quite correct in saying her son would not be required on the fields of battle. For he would spend the years of conflict in a home-front recruiting depot, then devote the ensuing years of peace to importuning the government for a pension for flat feet.

Yet even as she was seeking advice, the village's John Sweeney and Russ Bowes, veterans of highway construction, were hitchhiking in search of an outlet for patriotic fervor. So were two others who hailed me on Moncton's Main Street: "Mousie" Amisson and Harold Forsythe, rough, open, likeable, and well into the sauce. They'd been trying to enlist only to be spurned, had sought liquid solace and now the whole patriotic exercise had come down to one thing: how were they going to get home? We headed for the bridge from which I'd often hitchhiked and I told them that, in their condition, they had one hope of making it. Hide in the grass beside the road, I said, and that's where they were when a half-ton truck stopped at my raised thumb. I had available, I told the driver, two young men brokenhearted over the indifference of their country. He was taken aback when they presented themselves, but already the war was making a difference. Put them in the back, he said, and they climbed in with overflowing expressions of gratitude. We were waving goodbye when it occurred to me that Harold was the one I'd seen fighting Gottfried Klotz in the village schoolyard, and I wondered where Gottfried was.

Against such a background, it is striking that within weeks an infantry division was getting ready to head for Britain under the same Andy McNaughton who had erred by four years in his 1918 prediction that Germany would have to be fought again within 25. Starved for funds, encouragement and equipment though they'd been for years, regular and militia units still managed to provide the minor miracle he would take overseas. That's why one evening late that fall there was a time for soldiers in Moncton's Brunswick Hotel. For two generations of soldiers. Dozens of returned men came to say goodbye and good luck to Major Russell Dickie and his gunners of the 8th Battery. They came together in a room just off the lobby and there was drinking and laughter and singing, and memory would make of it something else. Because there was symbolism in it.

The way you could sense this best was in the songs. Someone was playing a piano and they belted out "Pack up your troubles" and "Mademoiselle from Armentieres" and "Tipperary" and "Quartermaster's Stores," and they sang many others that had been sung in one war and would be a bridge into another, and they partied and they drank hails and farewells. Then they shook hands and the two groups went their respective ways. As the returned men left, some looked back just briefly with things in their eyes that could have been pain or sadness or nostalgia or an almost indefinable regret. Then they took their memories and the responsibilities of middle-age and went home, and Russell Dickie's gunners took their youth and their incipient hangovers and left to do the soldiering the returned men could no longer be expected to do. The whole thing was fleeting and informal and emotional, and it's moving to remember because I'd never see its like again. There were no prayers or exhortations, but a torch was handed on and I suspect that's when the 3l-year war began to take shape in my mind.

The trains that bore the ill equipped, ill trained lst Division to Halifax that December picked up units across the country, and when one of them got to Moncton the 8th Battery marched up Main Street to join them. Russell Dickie had spent years in the militia preparing for exactly this. He'd been raised on a farm just outside the village and for years his family had been running an electrical business in the city. Now he was taking his battery off to war, and all his men seemed finally to have uniforms and packs on their backs. When people called out farewells, they'd grin. There was no band to help them keep step, and probably they most felt like heroes when they heard the shouted welcomes from hundreds of soldiers with their heads out the windows of the train. The newspapers had not been able to report that this was to happen, but there were hundreds waiting to say goodbye, and when the train pulled out you could hear hundreds of men singing "Roll out the barrel," and it put a lump in your throat.

One of them was Ellsworth Taylor. He came from Taylor Village, just across the Memramcook River from where Major Dickie grew up, and the family figured he'd enlisted mainly to get away from agricultural drudgery. In Halifax, devil-may-care Lee Whalen, son of returned man Dick, was among those who went aboard a troopship with the regular army's Royal Canadian Regiment. Medical officers went too, to prepare the way for the 1st Canadian General Hospital. Teresa Hickman and other nursing sisters waited in Saint John, and she'd always say she got seasick even before they left the dock in a small ship that had never been intended to brave the Atlantic's winter. But when a storm did strike, there was at least one consolation: an insufferable British colonel was catapulted through a glass door to the detriment of his flesh, his dignity and the chair he was in. There was blood on the floor but no one hurried to clean it up. There also were two British officers who kept calling the Canadians "you colonials" until one nursing sister told them off. Thus began the renewal of mass Canadian links with the Mother Country.

Even as the 1st Division sailed, the village faced a situation which confirmed that it's not easy to get a war off the ground. This concerned a teen-ager who enlisted, and simultaneously found himself in love with a girl he'd known for years. They walked around hand in hand and everybody said how nice they looked, he in his khaki uniform and all, gallant, maybe doomed, and she trim and pretty. Even the movies couldn't beat it for romance, except where her father was concerned. He said his daughter shouldn't get married; she was too young. But she did anyway, being 16 and headstrong and thinking time was of the essence when, in fact, it wasn't because the army kept changing what it wanted the groom's unit to be. All in all, it would be another two years before it went overseas, which meant there was no rush. But nobody knew that when it mattered because it was always difficult to know what the army, let alone the war, would do at any given time.

It was even difficult to know what you were going to do yourself, which is one way of saying that in the first few months of the war who did I find at an air force recruiting station in Moncton but me. Here I was living the lifestyle of a man making $14 for a six-night, 60-hour week and ready to throw it all away for king and country. I had discussed it with no one; it seemed to be an intensely personal matter. Yet I arrived on His Majesty's premises with no clear idea why I was there. On one hand I *was* tired of night work but on another I would have been quite happy to continue in a non-lethal capacity for the rest of my days. What it came down to was that I was doing what something instructed me to do while declining to be specific about details.

I told someone I'd like to be a pilot. I couldn't drive a car, wasn't even very accurate in pounding nails, but here I was saying I wanted to fly an airplane. The fact is that pilots were what thousands of young men wanted to be, and if that didn't work out then they wanted to be in a plane anyway. They didn't want to be in trenches. They wanted to be in the air. It had a lot to do with what Canadian fighter aces had done in the Great War, but it was a fact. Once, in 1942, about 20 overseas-bound infantry officers would be in an army mess when someone asked how many had first applied for air crew. Every single one raised a hand.

So the competition was tough, and in the fall of 1939 it was worse than tough because the air force could take its choice and wasn't ready to train in large numbers the choices it made. Which adds comfort to what happened to both Joe Emery and me. At that recruiting depot, I looked up one day and there he was. There he was and patriotism, he'd say later, seemed to have very little to do with it: "I'd say the motivation was mainly that there was a great adventure shaping up and I wanted a chunk of it." That's what quiet, orderly, erstwhile choirboy Joe Emery would say, and what he said in that fall of 1939 was that he wanted to be a pilot or in air crew too, and we considered the possibility that we might even end up in the same plane. As things turned out, the air force told Joe to get a bit older and heavier. At 20, I was old enough but they assigned me to abeyance too. The humbling part is that it took them very few minutes to make up their minds. They said night work had eroded my eyesight and not to return until I obtained glasses. So I got glasses and went back and this time it took them some 10 minutes to put me back in abeyance. They said I fell short of fighting trim and not to return until I didn't, which, they said, would obviously take some time. I hadn't, of course, mentioned "it," the problem I kept hidden, but I was eliminated so quickly it didn't matter anyway.

For Bert Emmerson, what mattered was that things got complicated. At 18, he'd started trying to get into the air force, in fact right after graduating in June with the Class of 1939. But his application got lost. He put in another that fall and finally he'd be accepted in January 1940, whereupon the air force sent him off to become a ground wireless operator, which he didn't want to be. He got sick and failed the course and when they asked him to repeat it he refused. He said he figured he'd "be of better service to my country as a pilot or a wireless/air gunner." It would take months before he got what he wanted, and that was only the beginning of his problems.

Like Joe Emery, what Dan Stack was up against in trying to make air crew was age. The difference was that Dan was too old, at least to be the pilot he wanted to be. He turned 30 in May 1939, and that alone ruled him out. Florence Dysart had vanished from his life by then, but he had finally found work. He'd worked, I'd find out years later, as an electrician with a Moncton firm, left after a year to set up his own business, only to have to give up for lack of capital. Then he got a job with a car dealer in Amherst and he'd been there for two years, running the parts department, when the war came. Within weeks, he was on the air force's doorstep and making such an impression—"an excellent candidate...above average...an outstanding type...keen, determined, likeable"—that an officer "strongly" recommended him for air crew even though he was four years over the age limit. He was accepted in February 1940, only to be informed in April that his application was "one of many of good standing that have had to be held over because of an excess of offers of service over actual needs." But in May he made it. The giant Commonwealth Air Training Plan had finally reached a stage where it was looking for potential pilots and observers or navigators, and the air force made him a sergeant and posted him for training. He was 31 by then, and they said he should be an observer, not a pilot.

So away he went, and it would be years before I'd learn that he may or may not have given up on civilian life because he never knew something that might have been. His old school pal Jacques Bourque would tell the story. While Dan went off to university, Jacques had applied at the village branch for a job with the Royal Bank. He thought he'd made a favorable impression — until someone told him he'd never get a job because he was French. There was a year at college, a year of hockey with the Saint John Beavers. His small size was against him so he started selling vacuum cleaners door to door and ended up as Quebec manager for the company. Four years later he went on his own, established an electrical appliance business in Quebec City.

One day in the late '30s he got a letter from Dan Stack wondering if they could team up in a broadened electrical business. Jacques wrote back that the fit seemed right, that Dan would have trouble because he didn't speak French, but that, together, they could overcome all problems. He sent the letter to the village, and never got an answer. Eventually, on a visit, he went to see Dan's mother, and she made a sad confession. Dan was working in Amherst when the letter came, and she'd never let him see it. She couldn't stand to think of her one child going so far away. So he went much farther away without knowing what might have been.

The month he finally got started in the air force was when the war really took off. In April Hitler had taken Denmark and Norway. In May his armies overran Western Europe with lightning blitzkreig attacks by tanks, infantry and airpower that quickly conquered Holland, Belgium and France and drove the British Army home. In London, Prime Minister Neville Chamberlain was replaced by

Winston Churchill. In Ottawa, the cabinet that had planned a not-too-expensive war started pulling out all the stops. In Germany, people were enthralled by a Hitler magic that seemed to have no bounds. He had appalled his generals once more, and been right once more, and in Mulda there was surprise and exultation even in those who had feared the penalties his acts could bring. Indeed, so sweeping were his victories that there was speculation in the Klotz farmhouse that the war might soon be over.

The boy Gottfried felt the euphoria. The radio, the press assured him it was justified. Letters from soldiers Walter and Arndt left no doubt that the assurances were true. Indeed Arndt had had an excellent position for watching one of the great military dramas of history — as a driver for General Heinz Guderain, master of blitzkrieg. What Gottfried would remember of that spring was that it was like having your team blessed with an overwhelming victory. It was, he'd remember, easy to be proud and pleased. Still, he was in no hurry to enlist. It was his old classmates Joe Emery and Bill Palmer who were, they and a lot of others from the village he'd left behind.

The air force finally accepted Joe in June, the month Bill, Bud Brian and Gerry Nugent graduated from their commercial courses at St. Joseph's University. On the 12th, all three got diplomas "with distinction," and all three knew what they wanted to do next, though it would have been hard to tell from the graduation ceremonies why they felt that way. His Excellency L.J.A. Melanson, Archbishop of Moncton, the presiding figure and main speaker, stressed at length "the importance of hard work and fidelity to Christian principles as a condition of success in life." Rev. Dr. L. LaPalme, president of the university, expressed pleasure over its continuing growth and wished all the students happy holidays. The valedictorian thanked the Holy Cross Fathers for their devotion and guidance, and said the graduates were determined to succeed.

France was crumbling. Mussolini's Italy was two days into a jackal's entry into the war against her. The Germans were within two days of taking Paris. Britain stood alone with what help the Dominions could give her. Western civilization was in monumental crisis. Yet, according to lengthy newspaper accounts, the speeches ignored it all.

This just at the time a village soldier was lamenting his absence from a frantic military response to the chaos in France, and another former resident was fleeing through the chaos he missed. But for one thing Private Lee Whalen would have been with the Royal Canadian Regiment when it and two other 1st Division battalions were dispatched from England to help form a defence line across France's Brittany peninsula. An evacuation through Dunkirk had ended on the 4th, had saved 340,000 British and French troops, and this was a desperate effort to salvage something from utter defeat. Whalen had been with the R.C.R. for five years, only to find himself posted to a reinforcement depot even as the Dunkirk evacuation went on. He'd lost an eye in a recent hockey accident and that eliminated him when the time came to get the unit ready for action. So he wasn't there when R.C.R. soldiers sailed June 13 with scant ammunition, scant rations and enthusiastic British shouts ringing in their ears. They arrived in France one day before Paris capitulated, and found the country in the final stages of military disintegration, refugees everywhere, people thinking they must be mad. By train, the R.C.R.s got some 200 miles inland before sanity returned, and they fled back to Brest. They got to England's Plymouth on the 17th, and were soon telling Lee Whalen what they'd seen and done. In fact, they had in all probability escaped a bloodbath.

The rampaging Germans were very close to Paris before the former Sarah Ellen "Nellie" Palmer, 64, her husband and three daughters fled with an ultimate destination in mind: the Teeds' great house. She had grown up in a prominent Dorchester family, had become an accomplished pianist and singer. Her husband, 75-year-old Dr. George Ryan, a New Brunswick-born dental surgeon with a fashionable Paris practice, had scoffed at the possibility that the Germans would take the capital of France. They hadn't taken it in the Great War, he said, and they wouldn't take it now. But daughter Alice, 28, argued that the best place to be was the country they came from. When they did act it was just in the nick of time. Son George had already left to join the British Army. Then son Donald got out to join up too. With the Germans overrunning the country, Alice and sister Helen made their way to St. Jean de Luz in farthest southwestern France and got away on a ship that took them to Britain. Kathleen, 19, had been travelling behind them with American friends, and actually saw the ship sail without realizing they were on it. Then in the streets she chanced upon her newly arrived parents, and they got out of a French frontier village just as German troops came in. Got over the Pyrenees into Spain, to Portugal. Once safe in London, Alice and Helen went from one hotel to another for five days hoping to find them, finally sailed for Canada on a liner without knowing what had happened. They were heading for the great stone house on the village's hill, and they hoped the others would be too.

Why? Because their mother was a close friend of Madge Teed, had been taught by her in the Anglican Sunday School, liked to recall gala balls and other social festivities in Dorchester's heyday as shiretown. She had gone to live in Paris when her husband, a graduate of the University of Pennsylvania, decided to do what his older brother had done: set up a dental practice where civilization was at its peak and there was a large colony of well-to-do Americans with teeth to be cared for. One year, after the 1924 death of her husband and when her son Gerald was at Oxford University, Mrs. Teed and daughter Connie spent months in Paris, and for some time Nellie and George Ryan lent them their home near the Bois de Boulogne. So they, in turn, were informed that they would always be welcome in the Teed home, and that summer of 1940 it became a timely invitation. Helen and Alice got there in July. They had called from Halifax and when they arrived Mrs. Teed was at the station waving a cablegram saying their parents were safe in London. They arrived in August, and Dr. Ryan eventually took over the practice of a Saint John dentist who had enlisted. Kathleen went to college, her sisters to jobs in Toronto.

By the time the first Ryans arrived in July, Warren Duffy was trying to get into the air force and not making it because he was one month short of 18. But he'd be back at the Moncton recruiting depot within days of his August 25 birthday, and he'd say his hobby was making model airplanes and that he'd "been interested (intensely) in aviation" for years. When they asked him what he'd like to be he scratched out everything but one word: pilot. Bill Palmer and Gerry Nugent were asking the air force to accept them too, and Bud Brian was doing the same at a recruiting station in Moncton for a frontline medical unit destined for the army's 3rd Division. There were clumps of village soldiers now in the New Brunswick Rangers, the Saint John Fusiliers and the 8th Hussars, but it was this new 14th Field Ambulance which, more than any other, attracted village men. Attracted Bud Brian after he'd taken time out from his studies to lead Moncton's junior hockey league in scoring. Attracted Earl Stiles from the first job he'd ever had, as a medical orderly in the Moncton hospital. Attracted Len Shea with his own orderly expertise. Attracted in all a dozen or so young men. Gerald Ward joined partly because Hitlers's crushing victories made up his mind, partly to get away from the draining and hopeless life he'd known. Alvin Mitton, Raymond's kid brother, left a job on the hotel farm to go. Herman "Newt" Cooke was getting $5 a week and board after four years of showing movies around the province; he was in Fredericton Junction when something in him said, "that's enough," and he quit to join the 14th Field. In the main Moncton branch of the Royal Bank, Frank Tracy and Paul Cogger were working late one night when, at 29, Frank suddenly said, "Let's join up." Next day they did.

Dan Hanington was one of those who didn't need Hitler's victories to make up his mind. There was a saying in Teed family circles that you could always tell when the Hanington strain was pronounced, and this may explain why he would classify himself as follows: "I am not one of your forceful Haningtons. I am one of your stubborn Haningtons." From the minute war broke out, he'd known with stubborn certainty that he would finish his last year at Rothesay Collegiate School and then enlist as his cousins Hugh and Lionel Teed had long ago. As sergeant-major of the R.C.S. cadet battalion, he'd been in the honor guard for the visiting King and Queen in June 1939. As they headed into their last year, virtually the entire Sixth Form planned to enlist the minute it ended. At 18, Dan was one more keen to fight in the air. Then his favorite teacher became an almost instant hero with the Royal Navy, and that did it: "If the Navy was good enough for George Whalley, it was good enough for me." By July 1940 he was a temporary midshipman in the Royal Canadian Navy, that is someone known as a snotty until he became the officer he aspired to be.

As such, he was the envy of Lionel Palmer, his first-cousin-once-removed. As a grandson, Lionel had been for years a member of Mrs. Teed's summer retinue, a tow-headed kid with a slow grin and a quiet voice. His Ottawa parents had named him for the uncle killed in 1918, and somehow he made his way into the army too in that terrible 1940. But not for long. His father spoke to his old friend H.R. Emmerson, M.P., who told the authorities Soldier Palmer was too young to enlist, no matter what he'd said when he did. So they sent him home, disgusted. But he'd be back. Warren Duffy was, in his own opinion, luckier. By November, he was at No.1 Manning Depot in Toronto, burning to become a pilot. By then Bert Emmerson and the rest of the Dorchester team that had beaten his own for a provincial hockey title had enlisted too, or soon would. It was what was happening. The crisis in Europe wasn't scaring people away. It was drawing them in. The streets seemed to be full of uniforms, and in the village young men were streaming away. For a second time, virtually all who could go would, and this time young women were going too.

Picture Section

Corporal Albert Starratt, killed in 1916 with the artillery. The Methodist church was packed for a memorial service, and the whole village grieved.

Left: The "famous Dorchester Platoon," recruited in 1916 to "paint Dorchester's name on the Kaiser's door."

Above: Sergeant Bill Bowser, killed on Hill 70 in 1917.

Members of the Dorchester Platoon: Dick Whalen and Bill Bowser, two in middle of front row; back row, Alexander Fraser, Roy Marshman and Fred Miller. Others unidentified. Whalen, Bowser and Marshman were among the five soldiers who slipped off a troop train to spend one last night at home.

Lieutenant Mansel Goodwin, the Baie Verte officer who gallantly tried to soothe as many village ladies' hearts as possible.

The Teed family of Dorchester, New Brunswick, Christmas 1913. Left to right, back row: Emily, Hugh, Lionel, Jack and Margaret. Front row: Gerald, Madge (Mrs. Teed), Constance, M.G.Teed, and Dorothy.

Joe Hickman, winner of M.C. in WWI.

Jack Hickman. Killed just after Armistice 1918, amid soldier riots to get home.

Royal Flying Corps. Bill Landry, son of Sir Pierre A. Landry, served in the First World War 1914-1918. He is the officer on the right, sixth man in, second row from the front. Photo taken in England near Thetford.

Bill's brother, Pierre Landry, met King George V and Queen Elizabeth when they came to Canada in 1939. He reminded the king that they had met previously in France during WWI. Pierre is third from the left, beside the queen.

Thomas Edwin Oulton — France, WWI.

Frank Ashley Dobson, WWI.

The ceremony at the unveiling of the war memorial, July 1, 1925. Note the vintage cars in the background, the young boys up front, some of whom may now have their own names on that memorial.

Theresa Hickman, R.N. in World War II.

Ina Brien's grades one and two, 1925: at least 10 of the boys served overseas, another in Canada. Raymond Mitton, far right, second row, was killed in Normandy, three others landed on D-Day. Douglas Cochrane, centre, second row, was the son of the man who survived both the Halifax explosion of 1917 and the torpedoing of a ship 25 years later. Far left, front row, the author; Bill Palmer's sister Eileen whose Toronto apartment became a villagers' rendezvous; Hazen Greenberg, the gunner who wrote homesick, homespun letters, Tom Lowerison who served in Normandy.

Seven of the Dorchester dozen in the 14th Field Ambulance in England, 1941: l. to r., front row, Bud Brian, Len Shea, Leo Fabien LeBlanc, Herman "Newt" Cooke; back row, Roy Anderson, Gerald Ward, Percy Atkinson.

Raymond Mitton with his daughter and the bride he didn't know was pregnant when he was killed in Normandy, July 8, 1944.

Flying Officer Dan Stack, victim of both the Depression and war, killed in action, 1941.

Warrant Officer Bill Palmer, killed in Italy, commissioned after his death.

Obergefreiter Gottfried Klotz, twice wounded with Germany's Wehrmacht.

Gottfried Klotz (left) and Joe Emery at 1988 high school reunion.

Flight Lieutenant Warren Duffy, D.F.C., hot-shot pilot with the R.A.F.'s elite Dam Busters, killed doing what he loved to do: fly.

Flight Lieutenant Joe Emery, D.F.C., survivor of some 70 missions with the elite Royal Air Force pathfinders.

Gunner Adrian Howe and the smile that lit the world, killed in Italy, December 1943.

Betty Jane McCabe kept track of those who died in the R.C.A.F.

The Emmerson family's contribution to WW2. Top left, clockwise: Nursing Sister Emily, FO Bert, Trooper Charles, Margaret, ambulance driver; center, Lieutenant Richard. Missing: Marion of the RCAF. Their father, Henry R. Emmerson, MP, went overseas in 1915 and was wounded.

Chapter Six

NATIONALLY, THE SECOND FIGHTING phase of the 31-year war led to a Canadian effort which Winston Churchill, among others, would call magnificent. Yet to this day no one can say precisely why, though its size alone may make the village as good a place as any to seek a focus. As one yardstick, it produced none of the so-called zombies created by a draft instituted for home defence in 1940, i.e., soldiers who refused to volunteer to go overseas. Instead, village people responded to the war as to a phenomenon too powerful to resist and almost too stirring to capture accurately in the language of their kind. In 1939 and especially in 1940 the 25 names on the war memorial ceased to be a warning and became a charge. As a group, the returned men watched happen what had happened to themselves, withdrew into an expanded silence and regret, preached neither the virtues of service nor the wisdom of avoiding it. Harry Ison's boy Edgar, for one, was too young to go when the war started but the time would come when he could, and all his father would say was that it was up to him. "If you want to go," he said, "go," and Edgar didn't even finish school. He went.

No Mansel Goodwin came to town. No equivalent of

the "famous Dorchester Platoon" left it. Young men went in ones and twos, and once women's services began to recruit, so did girls and young women. It didn't seem to matter what church they went to or what their father did or where they lived. They vanished into the air force or the navy or the labyrinthine army, vanished from one village and emerged in others called ships or companies or squadrons or battalions. Some to fight. Some to join what Churchill would bewail as the Tail, the six or seven men or women it would take to keep one man engaged in destruction. Apart from marriage, they took the greatest single step they'd ever take, but they did it quietly and they left little or no record of why, so that years later you came upon varying clues and differing explanations. A number of those nearer 30 than 20 left to vanish into industrial expansion, into jobs the Depression had denied. Curiously, and for one reason or another, the combative ones, the ones who picked or got into fights, weren't the ones who would end up where the fighting was. Some were turned down, some hung back, others went into the Tail, some not because they wanted to but because that's where their age or health or talents consigned them.

Some who got into frontline units were not those you would have expected to. Some got there because it was what you did when your country went to war, which, I suspect, covered Dan Hanington and most of the young men from that happy summer of 1933; they became officers in fighting units. Bill Palmer said the only reason he wouldn't go was if his ailing mother needed his help; in the end, it didn't stop him. A team player, he spurned offers to help him get a job in the civil service, said he couldn't stand to think of friends sticking their necks out when he didn't. A loner from a religious family, quiet, undramatic and outwardly unadventurous, Joe Emery surprised me when he made that statement, years later, that the war loomed as a great adventure he didn't want to miss. Earl Stiles said he joined the 14th Field Ambulance because doctors he admired were joining it; it mattered to go with people he knew. It mattered to others from the village to go with the 14th Field because it was recruiting when they were psychologically ready to go and it was drawing friends they'd be glad to have around them. Besides, said Earl Stiles, "the infantry was something else," it was where the killing was worst. Reg Bowser came back from Boston because of a newspaper photograph of a woman holding twins. She was the widow of Alex Trueman who'd grown up in Sackville and had died as a fighter pilot. Reg Bowser wanted to be a fighter pilot too but got washed out in training, as so many would, went on to do valuable work as an air force draftsman. My Moncton cousin Charlie Cosman was persuaded to join the band of the Saint John Fusiliers because they needed a good trombone player. He said he'd only go if they'd also take his pal, my brother Jim who had eye and heart problems, complications from rheumatic fever, and musically was limited to the mouth organ. He got a clandestinely flawed medical exam and in they both went. As much as anything, I suspect my older brother Hank joined the air force because he hated collecting rents from people who could ill afford to pay them. A number went into the air force to fly, but didn't make it for various reasons. Murray Dobson didn't make it because of color blindness, spent much of the war with air force teams salvaging what was left of crashed planes in a country turned into one vast airdrome. The air force slotted his brother Glenn into ground crew too, made him what was known more colloquially as an erk or, in army pejoratives, a pigeon. It did likewise to Herb Palmer's boy Ted. My cousin Bob Turner was too old to get overseas, served as an army officer in Canada. Three other cousins from

Vancouver, sons of village women, served in fighting units.

The flexibilities of age were stretched to the limit. Young Gerald "Jud" Tower was rejected by the forces so he went to sea in the merchant marine. Ernie Partridge couldn't resist a second war; he'd leave his canteen and become a merchant seaman too. Gerald Adshade was young enough to be Ernie's son, but he'd lie about his age and go. Guitar-playing Billy Manship would try all three forces, only to have all three reject him. Yet in numerous cases the forces took two, three and even more from the same family. All three of Marcel Belliveau's children went, Ferdie into the 8th Hussars, his sisters Ruth and Ling as nursing sisters. No less than seven Emmersons went, plus the husbands of four. Warden George T. Goad left the prison staff to become the highest-ranking officer the village produced: a full-fledged colonel as the army's Provost Marshall, the man in charge of its disciplinary corps and of the country's prisoner-of-war camps. His red tabs of rank also had another advantage. He could get the train to stop at the village station when he came home to visit. Then there was Everett Terris who was on the prison staff and had told so many tales of a varied career that it was eventually estimated that he could be 150 years of age. But off he went anyway, into the Provost Corps.

Thus was the village swept clean of most of its eligible youth and of others who'd be young no more. The war scattered them from Britain to the Middle East, from Italy to Australia, from South Africa to France, pitched a second generation in a row into historical events that dwarfed the history that had shaped their minds. It did there what it did from coast to coast, and it was only years later that I began to suspect it wasn't relatively easy to explain why. Certainly, given the deal on conscription, it was an unusually united Canada that went to war. Went, as Prime Minister Mackenzie King put it, to fight for freedom against a base and menacing Nazi Germany, to fight "at Britain's side." To renowned Quebec journalist Andre Laurendeau, there was a simpler reason. Canada went to war, he'd argue, solely because Britain did, in essence because of a colonial mentality. He could not imagine, he said, Canada fighting Germany if Britain stood aside.

Canadian servicemen would rarely discuss why they were overseas, and it would make them slightly uncomfortable if and when they did. Years later, Ross Munro, our top war correspondent, would say they didn't really know in any profound sense why they *were* there. Nor, in my experience, did they give much thought to a number of factors that might have mattered yet somehow didn't. Hitler's Germany undoubtedly threatened human freedom, yet for more than two years the United States, proclaimed champion of freedom, would see no need to fight, and only did then because she was attacked by Japan. Indeed, it is a salient fact that alone among Western Hemisphere nations created by European emigrees, it was the English-speaking Canadians who went to war without significant question, indeed would have soundly defeated any government that wanted it any other way. Though French-speaking Quebec gave qualified approval, the indications are that it would not have been unhappy to stand aside, even after the fall of France. Latin America stood largely aloof. Certainly Britain stood for things richly worth defending, and certainly there was an historic Canadian sense of kinship with her. Yet she had not for years been for Canada the crucial shield and market she'd been for Australia and New Zealand. The call of the blood could be powerful, yes, but in the village men rallied to the colors with blood that had no historical cause to feel affection for her: Acadian French, Irish Catholics, blacks, Micmac Indians, a Jew, a boy of German stock. Nor did more than a few families retain personal ties with Britain.

In the final analysis, numerous things that might have mattered didn't matter decisively. It didn't seem to matter that the country had become independent. It didn't seem to matter that Canada had been isolationist for years. Or that Mackenzie King was an uninspiring leader. Or that experience had shown that nothing menaced English-French compromise, the core of Canadian existence, as war did. Or that the war was far away, and that the last one in Europe had only bred this one in Europe. Or that the country had no interest in the traditional loot and lure of battle. Or that it was shabby, unmilitary, grotesquely unprepared, dotted with memorials to the cost and futility of what had come again.

All these things were thrust aside, not in a blaze of fervor but by a dogged resolution. In the village, as elsewhere, there were no bands or banners or exhortations. None of the white feathers that implied cowardice in the Great War, little of the passions that wave flags, shout slogans or fret that what has come may soon be gone and take its glories with it. There seemed to be no sense of glory anywhere. Yet something written by Historian A.R.M. Lower would have the tang of truth. Never, he'd write, had English-speaking Canadians seemed more at peace with themselves. Partly, in their collective mind, they found a certain exhilaration in doing something the United States wasn't doing, in having ties the Americans didn't have. Yet somehow they also saw themselves not as an exception in the Western Hemisphere but as a norm in tune with world events. The inarticulate imperatives that had erected war memorials had found another cause.

There is no question that other things, human things, did matter: adventure as in the case of Joe Emery, drudgery as in the case of Ells Taylor, a hard life as in the case of Gerald Ward, a dead-end job as in the case of Newt Cooke. Boredom mattered. Regular meals mattered. So did the poverty that made a private's $1.30 a day look good. Nor is there any doubt that Hitler mattered and that response to the cause fed on its own momentum, that a vast suction developed out of propaganda, news, streets full of uniforms, an overwhelming mood that came to mean that any able-bodied man who wasn't in the forces knew people were wondering why. Beneath all this there lay a level of awareness of what Germany stood for, what Britain stood for, *and* something else. The response at least of English-speaking Canadians didn't make much sense unless there was something else. Some crystallizing force building on some latent and, yes, imbuing force. Some compelling and unifying factor which, I suspect, came out in what servicemen would say when the uncomfortable subject did come up; the subject of what took them, as volunteers, thousands of miles from home. If they answered, they'd be apt to grin and say, "We're doing it for George," the King. It was about as articulate as they'd ever get, but it was probably close to decisive truth. The Rt. Hon.Vincent Massey, Canada's wartime High Commissioner in London, once chanced upon a Canadian soldier in Britain and asked why he'd come overseas. He'd come, the soldier said, because he'd seen the King and Queen on their historic 1939 tour and he'd said to himself that if war came "I'd fight for that little lady." And for the symbol she symbolized.

In the most fateful hour any people can face, the Crown appealed for help and a nation responded. Responded as part of something larger than itself. Responded with an empire or a commonwealth, call it what you will, responded with an astonishing example of what a symbol could mean and what it could do to imbue people. The Crown had survived a complex record of greed and justice, arrogance and decency, conquest and contribution, blood and irony and Henry VIII. Only recently it had stumbled under the burden of a weak and obstinate king. It was mossed with elements of the archaic, the absurd and the imperfect, and it had been callously exploited in the royal tour of '39. But it was also an institution that spoke from coins and stamps and mail boxes, from rhetoric and heritage and family albums. From ceremonies such as that of 1927. It remained for many an object of respect and even reverence, and in crisis it turned out to be a symbol represented by two admirable and beloved people with two storybook daughters and a storybook shine on everything they did. It was something men and women could rally to, did rally to, many — in the opinion of an old man looking back years later — because of something beyond a colonial mentality. Went, as volunteers, with a deep sense of allegiance that made being Canadian more complex than being Canadian alone. Went feeling they were what 1931's Statute of Westminster said they were, what the soldiers of 1914-18 had made them: citizens of a country the equal of Britain under a common Crown that was coming to mean something more than British hegemony. If there is irony in this, it befits a country that must be one of the few in the world that achieved independence and has no folk memory of it happening. A complex and even mysterious country that often can only be analyzed through the interpretation of silences.

Whatever the background, the Crown did become a reason that gathered other reasons in. In the laboratory of choice, it legitimized them all, and did it in a way that could baffle outsiders. I'll never forget the awe in the voice of an American editor recalling years later how Canadians, Australians, New Zealanders and others from the ends of the earth rallied to a common cause, a common symbol. "They did," he said. "By God, they did." Whether the Crown is a symbol today's Canada needs, whether it is or isn't a relic Canada must outgrow if she is to find her own "identity," it is a fact that the men she sent into battle in 1939-45 could hardly have felt their Canadian identity more. By and large, I suspect, they felt they were not fighting someone else's war, they were fighting their own. If this be paradox or irony or the corruption of heritage, so be it. It happened, and there was nobility and magnificence in it. Which is one way of suggesting that the Crown has been one of the most flexible and meaningful political instruments the world has ever known. Name one that meant more in the crunch.

It was the chemistry of the Crown that brought some little girls to the village in deadly 1940. They came from Britain as part of a large scheme to get children out of a country that faced air attack and quite possibly invasion. They came from Middlesex, England, and they already knew about bombings and nightly visits to air raid shelters. They were called evacuees.

Winnifred Hoare was one of them. She was 10 years old when she arrived at the station after crossing the Atlantic by convoyed ship, and she had all her possessions in one small satchel. She went to live in the Guard Row with the family of Mr. and Mrs. John Grant, and she impressed them at once with her maturity, with her warmth and acceptance of a new life in the home of strangers thousands of miles from her own. Her sister Dorothy arrived with her and went to live with Mr. and Mrs. Donald Grant.

Winnifred found a new father in John Grant. She came to adore him, and when she and his young daughter Florence walked up the hill to meet him after work he would often do her a signal honor: let her carry home the bread he had brought from the prison kitchen in a white cotton bag. When she had to have mastoid surgery, only he could change her dressings and dry her tears. When Mrs.

Grant fell ill with cancer and the family had to move, it was a sad Winnifred who went to live with a couple in Moncton. Half a century later Florence (Grant) Peck would write from California that she believed a third sister came to the village from England but she couldn't remember her name or whose home she went to. She would also admit to feeling a touch of jealousy about the carrying of the bread, but she regretted far more losing touch with Winnifred, and not even knowing whether she and Dorothy eventually returned to England. What she did remember was that the little English evacuee "gave new meaning to my definition of bravery."

In Mulda, Gottfried Klotz faced a laboratory of choice in a limited sense. He knew he'd be called up in 1941, at 19, with the so-called Class of 1922. He also knew he could enlist earlier, but he didn't. He hung back as well from joining the Hitler Youth, but under the influences of the hour, he eventually did. When he got past its age limit in 1941, he did something that made his father furious. He joined the *Sturmabteilungen*, the SA, the bully-boy outfit that no longer occupied the prominent niche it once had. The father was angry because he knew what it was. The son was surprised because he hadn't realized what it was, and as it turned out what he joined was a mounted unit and about all he learned in his part-time duties was how to ride a horse properly. When he got into trouble with a saddle he explained to an instructor that he had always ridden horses bareback. Only Red Indians in the Wild West rode bareback, the instructor said, and recruit Klotz said the Wild West was where he'd learned. But mainly he waited. He worked with a father who got into dairy farming and couldn't help contrast agricultural conditions with the disappointments he'd known. Besides, as Hitler consolidated his hold on Western Europe, turned his airpower on Britain and prepared for an invasion of her shores, there was even the consolation that the war could be over by the time Gottfried's draft call came.

In England, Nursing Sister Hickman was with No.1 Canadian General Hospital in what became an increasingly rough place to be. When the nurses arrived, they'd found the doctors looking after an unusual clientele. The hospital was at Marston Green, between Birmingham and Coventry, and German bombing or the anticipation of it had led to the evacuation of sick babies from Birmingham Children's Hospital. Sick babies were the doctors' sole patients, and they took it seriously. "There was," Teresa Hickman would recall, "great competition among the fathers." The spring fighting across the Channel, the Dunkirk evacuation, the growing air war soon changed that. Sick and wounded soldiers began coming in even as the 1st Division was said to be the closest approach to a mobile, armed and fully manned division in a Britain painfully aware it could be conquered for the first time since 1066. Its soldiers were marched from one place to another to try to create the impression among both German agents and the British population that the country had far more armed soldiers than it actually did. It also gave the soldiers a magnificent chance to witness aerial dogfights as Hitler tried to knock out Britain's fighter planes and clear the way for invasion.

In Mulda, even as this aerial Battle of Britain raged, four French prisoners-of-war were assigned to the Klotz farm to help bolster production. They were young and likeable and it wasn't long before Gottfried joked with them as they worked together. Yet one thing gave him pause. Hitler may have crushed their army and their country, might be poised for an invasion of Britain, but they were convinced he'd lose the war. They said so, and they very obviously believed what they said.

The epic Battle of Britain reached its climax in British victory that September as Hitler made a major tactical blunder. Faced by indomitable men, he turned from the destruction of fighters to give priority to the bombing of cities, to what became known as "the blitz." In November, his planes devasted England's Coventry, a fact that made older people in Mulda unhappy. He would kill a lot of people this way, and he would cause many sleepless nights at No.1 Canadian General Hospital, but he'd lose his chance for invasion, and this is what was unfolding as Bill Palmer came to his own moment of truth.

When friends took him out for a farewell dinner in Moncton that fall, they expected and he hoped he'd become a pilot. He had behind him the recommendations of the village priest, the village postmaster, the proprietor of the Windsor Hotel and the vice president of St. Joseph's University. But he wasn't in one of those light initial training planes more than a few hours before he discovered that what he felt was not exhilaration and zest but tension, inadequacy and nothing where confidence should be. In Manitoba, he looked down upon prairie snows and had difficulty gauging his plane's height as it neared the ground, came to feel he could do nothing right. It was an experience that would be widely shared as Canada got deeper and deeper into turning out hundreds of thousands of Commonwealth air crew. But all he knew was that he couldn't be, didn't want to be a pilot. It even went beyond that. War in the air may have entranced his Uncle Bill Landry, but it no longer entranced him. He felt he didn't want to fly, period. He asked to be grounded. It was a shaken young man who spent Christmas in Winnipeg with friends of his parents.

Certainly it was a contrast to what happened to Dan Stack that very day as a climax to exciting weeks. He'd been found to be an "above average navigator," had graduated 18th in a class of 42. On the first of December he was commissioned as a pilot officer. He arrived overseas on Christmas day, the day the army announced the formation of a two-division corps. Four days later London had its worst night under German air attack. Teresa Hickman and others on the staff of No.1 General were wondering what the winter would bring to the industrial area where they were. It would, in fact, bring many bombs, some very close. The patients, servicemen now, not babies, would spend many nights under beds and under mattresses piled on beds, and she'd get pneumonia and become a patient too. "It was," she'd say, "not comfortable."

As for Maj. Charlie Crandall, he could only wonder that December at the vagaries of a war for which he'd prepared so long. He was a company commander now, and at least the New Brunswick Rangers were no longer patrolling the shorelines of New Brunswick. Instead, they were patrolling the shorelines of Cape Breton.

I was in Halifax with The Canadian Press then, a part-time soldier in a reserve force signals unit, and in a ringside seat as a reporter on the waterfront of what a British admiral called the most important seaport in the world. When the national news agency beckoned that spring, I had yielded up thoughts of a third run at the air force and entered one of the most memorable periods of my life. The shabby, taut and overcrowded Halifax-Dartmouth area was ringed by guns, stuffed with men from bases for all three forces, with twice as many people as it was accustomed to handling. Sometimes called Canada's Frontline City, its streets were full of foreign accents. It was the funnel for the dispatch of men, arms and supplies to Britain. It was where convoys formed up and departed, gray files almost ghostlike in movement out to sea, warships filing out as escorts, merchant ships with cargoes and sailors from many lands. In the excellent history he'd write of Halifax, Thomas Raddall was right: it was a sight impossible to watch without being moved.

The harbor itself was a spectacle and a bewitching, if frustrating, news beat. A spectacle particularly on the day five liners came in line astern, under a late afternoon sun, thousands of faces peering down from the rails with relief and gratitude for a successful, convoyed passage through a deadly sea. They and others like them bore a varied humanity: German prisoners, often surly and defiant, children evacuated to escape German bombs, battle-seasoned airmen sent over to train more airmen, people on secret missions, models sent to help earn dollars with British style and British clothes, survivors of torpedoed ships, Jewish fugitives from Hitler's Europe, well dressed, guarded, with one seemingly stock answer to questions I might not have had the temerity to ask if I'd known how cold the Canadian government had been to their terrors and their plight. A repeated question: "Where are you going?" A repeated answer: "Shanghai, China."

Strange, exciting, distorted times. Stories going out under a censor's dateline: an East Coast Canadian Port. Military people exercising a smug authority after years in the mockeries of peace. A tiny, make-do navy growing rapidly in both military and self importance, its officers assuming the airs of the mighty (and often condescending) Royal Navy. For me, the luxury of daylight hours, evenings to court. Saturday nights at the Nova Scotian Hotel supper dances where one could blow half one's weekly $20 on girls and booze. The Inglis Street boarding house where Miss Mae Egan, a bustling, devout and kindly Irish Roman Catholic, jammed some 15 relatives, secretaries, newsmen, railroad men and others into a miniature of the overcrowded city, and into something approaching a family.

And the wee ship that won your heart. An unlikely heroine called the *Nerissa*, a former peacetime link with the West Indies, a skinny little passenger ship with one funnel, pressed into wartime Atlantic service, repeatedly sent out alone in the belief that she had the speed to survive. Which she did, repeatedly, until you'd see her tied up, safe again, and some sort of salute would happen inside you. I think she was the ship that once came in damaged and tilting to one side so that the passengers got off walking funny, including British models and Battle of Britain veterans who looked lopsided and tired and happy all at the same time. Fulfilled. But she did it once too often, *Nerissa* did. The German submarines finally got her off Ireland, and 73 Canadian servicemen with her, and Sammy Robertson, CP's London chief and a war correspondent who got to the rail, went back for something and was never seen again. And how do you match something like the epic death of the *Jervis Bay*? In November 1940, a convoy in mid-Atlantic was attacked by the *Admiral Scheer*, a huge German surface raider, and what sailed forth to face it, to obey orders to sacrifice herself so the convoy could scatter, yes, to pay in blood for years of unpreparedness? What sailed forth was this so-called armed merchant cruiser, a peacetime ship with a few guns and an indomitable Irish captain named Fogarty Fegan. And by the time she went down, guns blazing, Fogarty Fegan on the bridge, one arm blown off, gloriously defiant, most of the convoy was saved and other convoys had sought sanctuary in flight, but that was not all. A merchant ship from neutral Sweden had a captain named Sven Olander who had been so awed by what happened, so moved that he did what convoy orders told him not to do. He went back to pick up *Jervis*

Bay survivors and he got away with it, brought them into Halifax and accolades, fame and reporters' questions which they answered as most merchant seamen survivors did. Question: "What will you do now?" Answer: "Go back to sea."

By spring 1941, the ground war was spreading east and south, the Germans had crushed Yugoslavia's army but not her guerrillas, had chased Allied forces out of Greece where they'd gone to fight an invasion started by the hapless Italians, chased them out of Crete, had a budding legend named Erwin Rommel at work in North Africa where the British, Australians and New Zealanders had with great success been beating up on Italians defending Mussolini's colonial possessions.

Dan Stack was flying bombing missions with a Royal Air Force squadron. At Ottawa's Uplands airport, Leading Aircraftsman (LAC) Bert Emmerson finally and joyfully got word that he was being remustered for air crew training. On May 2, Warren Duffy wrote home about how sweet that could be: "I've got some great news. I got through I.T.S. (initial training school) as a pilot. Got my flying kit today and was posted to the elementary school in London, Ont. ... I've got a flying suit, a coverall suit, flying boots, helmet and goggles. It's sure swell." Just two days later his exhilaration spilled over in a letter from London. "Arrived about two o'clock and by three or so I was in the air with an instructor. I was the first to go up. Not bad, eh?...This is what I have been looking for this long time. Something to settle down and really put my teeth to. Now my chance is here and I'm really going to make the most of it, and that's not just a lot of talk either. I mean it."

He was 18 years of age, and he had seen the disappointments of others: "Some of the boys (in I.T.S.)

were washed out for various reasons. Some for math and some for link (mechanical) trainer and a couple for medicals. A few were made gunners and some observers but about 75% got through as pilots. We don't like to lose the boys but it will be the same all along the course, I feel quite sure I can get through O.K. but it will mean a lot of hard work, but I'm ready for that." Like Bert Emmerson, his former schoolmate and fellow Baptist, he was an LAC now, was making $1.50 a day and would get another 75 cents once he started flying.

Bill Palmer was in Fingal, Ont., and back in the air. With the resilience of a 19-year-old, he'd decided to try training as an air observer, a navigator who'd tell a pilot where to go. He'd like to do it and his "educational qualifications are fairly good," an officer reported. But it was flaws in those very qualifications that pinned him into another ordeal. He needed extra help in his studies. He got it from instructors, from fellow students, from sheer hard work, and he'd pass. But the letdown was still in him. "I suppose," he wrote kid brother John,"you were somewhat disappointed that I didn't make it as a pilot, but I just *couldn't* make it. I'll still be in the air though and may get another crack at pilot later on, after I get used to the air." By then Canada's skies were abloom with training planes. Bill Palmer, Warren Duffy, Bert Emmerson, Joe Emery and Gerry Nugent were among the thousands in them or already trained. Dan Stack had arrived overseas just one month behind the first Canadian graduates of the great Commonwealth training scheme. A flood was gathering momentum.

Britain had survived a year since the devastating spring of 1940. The danger of a German invasion had passed. Hitler was moving in another direction. The war had, in fact, entered the year that would make it global, that would turn Britain from an island under siege to a springboard for attack, make the Battle of the Atlantic crucial to this transformation. Already the German submarines were moving deeper into the Atlantic because the seas around Britain were getting too dangerous. Dan Hanington's ship was on a triangular convoy run, Halifax to mid-ocean to Bermuda and back again. She had fled with others the previous November as the *Jervis Bay* went to her death. She was called the *Rajputana* and she too was an armed merchant cruiser, and one day in April she turned over her convoy in mid-ocean and made for Iceland. She had orders to patrol the Denmark Strait, intercept a German blockade-runner reported to be coming around the north of Iceland to break out into the Atlantic.

At this time, the mind of Mrs. Teed's nephew was occupied jointly by apprehension about surface raiders — a massive one called the *Bismarck* was on the loose — and what was happening to his emotions due to a recent swift capitulation to the matchmaking capacities of the most important seaport in the world. He had fallen in love in Halifax as so many did and would. The capitulation would last a lifetime, the *Bismarck* till May 27, the *Rajputana* not as long. She was a liner of some 17,000 tons, a make-believe menace spruced up with eight depth charges and 10 guns dating back as far as 1893 . She had no notable technical facilities such as asdic (sonar) and radar but she did have a grand piano, a large canvas swimming pool, excellent cabins and a wealth of wine. All these she bore when she set out to to find and molest that German blockade-runner. All these she bore when a torpedo struck her and halted her just before dawn on a Sunday morning, the 13th of the month. All these *Rajputana* took with her some hours later when, having survived her furious gunfire, the submarine which had stalked her for hours decided she was not going to sink and finished her off with a second torpedo. A torpedo which Midshipman Hanington watched with horror as it skipped across half a mile of ocean heading, he was convinced, straight toward him and the magazine filled with 20 tons of gun cotton on which he stood.

Of the 42 lost with their ship, most went down when a lifeboat caught on something in being lowered, dumped them into oil-covered waters, then broke loose and fell on them. Others died from oil in their lungs. One dazed midshipman was last seen climbing a ladder on the dying ship's funnel. Another made it to safety from a cabin where he'd been ill with measles and somehow, in the process, every measle vanished. Dan Hanington was one of 318 survivors who spent some time in lifeboats before he beheld "the most beautiful thing I had ever seen" — an R.A.F. flying boat from Iceland responding to S.O.S. messages. Soon a British destroyer picked them up and took them into Iceland where he discovered he'd lost 29 pounds in 24 hours. From there the survivors came to Halifax where we reporters interviewed them and where Midshipman Hanington renewed his capitulation to the charms of Margot Wallace as soon as he possibly could. In the meantime, from Reykjavik, he had sent Mrs. Teed a telegram which would be talked about in the village all summer long. What it said was, "Sunk, saturated, saved. Love, Dan."

The Royal Canadian Air Force had a glamorous way of graduating fliers. With pomp and panoply, it held what it called wings parades all across the country, and all the stops were pulled out on the day Bill Palmer officially became an observer as a climax to memorable events. Since joining up, he'd managed to get to Maple Leaf Gardens twice for N.H.L. hockey games, had looked up at the celebrated broadcast gondola and imagined people back home listening to Foster Hewitt. But even this couldn't match the day he'd marched into the Gardens with the best recruit squadron at Toronto's sprawling Manning Depot. There were 15,000 people in the stands, mostly kids there for an ice carnival, and when that squad marched in the place went wild.

The graduation ceremony was sheer spectacle too. It took place on June 7, 1941, almost exactly a year since the graduation ceremony at St. Joseph's University, and the contrast was striking. This was the first held in Toronto, the first in which men from two schools were graduated together: the bombing and gunnery schools in Fingal and Jarvis, Ont. It was designed to put the focus on observers as a breed, and there was even a guard of honor made up of men who'd been observers in the Great War and were serving again in various capacities. Among the graduates were natives of Britain, Canada, Newfoundland, New Zealand, Australia, Norway, the United States and South America. In the audience were representatives of a number of air forces, trainees from the Manning Depot, families and friends of the graduates. When an opening general salute was given, Monday's *Globe and Mail* would report, "It was a most impressive sight. The men from Manning Depot were drawn up to form three sides of a square. The long line of graduates stretched across the square, and the R.C.A.F. Central Brass Band from Ottawa played." So at appropriate moments did the Manning Depot Trumpet Band. Then the ultimate touch: the insignia they'd earned, a winged O, was presented to each of 80 graduates by Canada's ace of aces, Air Marshal W.A. "Billy" Bishop. He'd shot down six dozen enemy planes as a pilot in the Great War but on this day he wore the observer's winged O he'd worn first.

He also gave a speech and it was quite unlike the speech of the Archbishop of Moncton. It wasn't about the grace and glory and guidance of God; it was about how proud he'd been to be an observer in battle: "I was among the first, I can proudly state, to wear this insignia, and those glorious days will live forever in my memory." Moreover, he said, observers had come a long way from the days when they were looked upon purely as pilots' helpers. They'd become "key men in our great bombing missions," and those who were about to join their ranks had "every reason to regard this as the proudest day of your young lives." Indeed, he contrasted them and all who served with those who might but didn't. "If," he said, "I were a young man today, and not in uniform, I would be ashamed of myself." There was thunderous applause.

The graduates he addressed had been trained not only as observers and navigators but as bomb-aimers and machine-gunners. Some of the 37 from Fingal became officers and some didn't, and Bill Palmer was one who didn't. Nevertheless, the team player in him had found another team, the members of his class had become far more than a collection of individuals. Through the pride and fear and grief that lay ahead, he'd try his best to keep track of them all.

Two weeks after they graduated, Hitler stunned the world by attacking the Soviet Union with a million men on a front half as long as Canada was wide. He couldn't crush Britain but she couldn't decisively get at him either, so he turned east. He attacked the Russia he'd pledged not to attack. He created the two-front war he'd feared so he could strike for the land, the *Lebensraum* , he'd wanted from the beginning. He was supremely confident that he could crush Russia so fast, get control of her vast resources so easily, that he would run no risk at all. Could do this to the Russia that had exhausted Napoleon's armies and crushed Napoleon's dreams. To the Russia ruled by a dictator as ruthless and brutal as himself. Yet in very short order Winston Churchill promised this Josef Stalin Britain's help. He would, he said, make a pact with the devil if it would help defeat Hitler.

At this time the war confronted Mrs. Teed with a problem of her own. It arose when Dan Hanington took his beloved Margot Wallace to the village to be introduced. It arose because Miss Wallace was a Roman Catholic and Mrs. Teed was anything but enthusiastic in this regard. Nevertheless, two factors were at work by the time the devout young lady announced that she wished to go to Sunday mass. One was that she had already captivated Mrs. Teed. The other was that Mrs. Teed knew, *knew*, what must be done. Regrettable as her religious tendencies might be, that child — Miss Wallace was, yes, in her teens — must do what her conscience bade her do, and she must not do it alone. She must be accompanied, and the proper one to fill this role was her host.

So off they went together, past the Anglican church where parishioners would most certainly wonder, down one street, up another to the Catholic church near the school, where the congregation shared speculations of its own. The thoughts of the strict and zealous Father Bourgeois can only be imagined when he saw this attractive young lady with the white-haired matriarch who spent her summers in the big stone house and had religious certainties as virile as his own, only different. But whatever it was, his reaction was eventually tempered by grace and tact. It would become part of the family folklore that he invited both Miss Wallace and Mrs. Teed to return.

Bud Brian's older brother Percy would remember

being with Bud and Bill Palmer and Gerry Nugent shortly before they went overseas. They were all in the village that summer — Gerry's father was station agent in nearby College Bridge — and they fell to joking that if Bill or Gerry got shot down Bud, the stretcher bearer with the 14th Field, would fix them up. But there is also that story that when two of them said goodbye after one last card game at Elmer Lewis's garage, one said he didn't expect to come back. One did in fact say this, and Ed Turner's daughter Frances heard him, but she couldn't remember later which one it was. That's also when Bill Palmer said goodbye to Ruthie Lewis who shared his birthdate and his love of dogs, and promised she'd hear from him, even though she had very little idea where he was going or why. After that he came to Halifax where we said our own goodbyes in an alcoholic state shared by brother Jim who happened to be in town for a concert with the band in which, he professed to believe, he had matured into "the best damn cymbal player in the Canadian Army," more or less. Bill and I poured him aboard an army bus just in time, and he spent a number of days confined to barracks for missing the concert in its entirety.

Bill had expected to sail from Halifax but he got called to Montreal. Someone had decided he should get the experience involved in navigating a bomber across the Atlantic to Britain.

For Mrs. Teed's sister Molly this was a difficult time because the war was about to take the best worker she'd ever had. That's what she called Leo Fabien LeBlanc who was getting ready to go overseas with the 14th Field Ambulance. Mrs. Kerr was a difficult Hanington. She didn't roar like her father but she looked and acted a bit like people thought Queen Victoria must have looked and acted. She lived with her cat and memories of the fine husband she had kept in his place. The cat was named Laddie, and was widely recognized as the most aristocratic animal in town, though a bit mangy. Mrs. Kerr was devoted to him, lived with him in hotel rooms in the winters, whether the hotels liked it or not, and would eventually have him buried in her backyard, under his favorite tree.

She had no children which she said suited her perfectly. As a species, she found them lacking, and since sister Madge's summer retinue contained children in quantity, this was an area for contention and aggression. At times Molly would even say things that made her sister cry. Nevertheless, she could also be very kind and friendly. Her nephew Dan Hanington, for one, had reached an acceptable age and level of behavior, and the only bad thing she said about Private LeBlanc was how regrettable it was that the war was about to take him away. Leo Fabien, he was called to distinguish him from other Leo LeBlancs, and because his father was the Fabien LeBlanc who'd driven Lady Smith about in a fancy carriage.

Over the years, Mrs. Kerr had tried out a number of boys and men to get things done around the house. It was Roaring Dan's old home and had nice trees and flowers, including multitudes of boisterous forget-me-nots, and a fair amount of space, of grounds, and there was wood to be put in and the lawn to mow and that sort of thing, and Mrs. Kerr would sit watching Leo Fabien pile wood in the basement and telling him how to do it, and she would say he was the only person in town who knew how to work. Hence, it is little wonder that, for her, his impending departure was comparable in impact to Hitler's invasion of the Soviet Union.

Nevertheless, she told him she and Laddie would from time to time send him cigarettes, thus contributing to the war effort.

Leo Fabien and most or all of the Dorchester dozen with the 14th Field Ambulance left the village as the Dorchester Platoon had left it 25 years before: with the plaudits of the community ringing in their ears. There was a farewell reception organized by the spirited and indefatigable Mrs. Colin Campbell, and it was a good one. Indeed, returned man Herb Palmer broke down and wept while handing each soldier a gift. He was that emotional. The event was that emotional.

When, shortly after this, the 14th passed through the village from Moncton by train, enroute to Halifax, there was a stop so brief that there was scant time for further farewells. Sensing that this would happen, Earl Stiles and Bud Brian wrote farewell messages and threw them into the night. Half a century later, one Earl wrote would still be in the family. "Hello folks," he'd scribbled, "I am writing to you and I do not know if you will get it or not. We are moving to Halifax and we expect to go right away as our boat is ready. This is the only way I can get word to you as we are watched very closely now. But Buddie and I are going to throw a few letters out at the station as we go through Dorchester. Hope you receive this O.K. I must say goodbye or rather so long until we meet again. Give my love to all and get word to Mom. I will write as soon as possible. Don't worry about me, and may God bless you all. Love, Earl."

They sailed with the 3rd Division in July, and Bud Brian made some money and won a lot of cigarettes by boxing on the long, slow passage to Britain. When they got there, they saw their first blacked-out and bomb-ravaged city. It was the great port of Liverpool near which Jack Hickman had been shot 22 years earlier, but as far as Percy Atkinson was concerned what really mattered was that he'd been so seasick that he wrote home to say he'd be happy if he never saw another ocean, at least until the war was over. But the time would come when you'd realize that this largest single group of village servicemen got to England very shortly before what happened to Dan Stack.

Dan Stack had been overseas for seven months, and he was with 214 Squadron of the Royal Air Force as the navigator in the six-man crew of a Wellington bomber. The Wimpey, airman called the Wellington, because there was a popular funny-paper cartoon character called J. Wellington Wimpey. The plane itself had two engines and it could, at best, get up to 235 miles per hour at 15,500 feet. It would later be superseded by four-engine heavies, but at the time it was as good as the R.A.F. had at a very difficult time for its Bomber Command. The fact was that the Dan Stack who'd been a victim of the Depression was involved in something that made him a victim of what the Depression had meant for military preparations.

When Bill Palmer's class got their wings, a press report said they'd been trained to drop bombs "with the deadly accuracy which has marked British air raids over German soil." When the 14th Field Ambulance got overseas, the emaciated London papers and manicured BBC voices kept implying that this German city or that was reeling from the blows delivered by the R.A.F. The constant implication that Germany was under crippling siege was designed to soothe public morale and help convince a bleeding Russia that the now-mutual enemy was paying a significant price. Yet the reality was that daylight bombing had had to be abandoned as too costly, and that night bombing was anything but effective. That very year of 1941 Winston Churchill was appalled to learn that navigation aids were so inept that in two cases out of three bomber crews didn't come within five miles of their targets; over the heavily-defended industrial Ruhr Valley, it was nine times out of ten. Most of Bomber Command's less than 400 planes were obsolescent and other arms of the forces were pressing to turn most of those over to anti-submarine warfare and army support.

This was the world Dan Stack lived in. This was the publicly-unacknowledged background when 214 Squadron's Wellington number 9750 took off on the evening of August 6 with a crew consisting of himself as navigator, one other officer, a New Zealander, and four sergeants. He was 32 years of age. His air force number was J3118. He was never seen or heard of again. Nor were any of the crew. It would be recorded that "information on file tends to suggest their aircraft crashed into the sea." There were detachments which tried to find out what did happen in such cases, and in this one the search would eventually lead to a cemetery on an island off the coast of Holland. It would unearth a body which it was thought might be that of a member of Dan Stack's crew, but which turned out to be that of a mariner washed ashore.

Dan's mother, again a widow after the recent death of husband William Foran, would get $464.38 from her son's estate, after the payment to a firm of military outfitters on London's Saville Row of PO. Stack's bill for a tunic, slacks, a pair of shorts and a pair of socks. She would also receive a trunk, a suitcase, a prayer book, and a "whole list of personal effects," plus a letter with her son's operational wings and a certificate. In the letter, a senior officer in the records department of the air force said he hoped the wings "would be a treasured memento of a young life offered on the altar of freedom in defence of his Home and Country." The condolences did not take further monetary form. The mother was refused a pension.

As for Jacques Bourque, it was only after his old pal's death that he learned what she'd done to the letter he'd written. In Quebec City, his electrical business prospering, he thought how sad it was to contemplate what might have been if she had passed it on. But who can tell? In the publication village high school students would put out in 1943, there would be a tantalizing few lines. "Daniel Stack," they'd say, "always wanted to fly and it seemed that a war must come to give him the chance. When a boy in his teens, in New York with his family, he spent all his pocket money (five dollars) for a five-minute ride in a plane." So maybe he found what he was looking for after all. In time, his name would be inscribed on a memorial to honor those airmen who have no known grave. It stands in a very historic place, in Runnymede, England, where King John signed the Magna Carta in 1215. In a more intimate context, he was the village's first fatal casualty in what had started nearly two years before.

The month he died the blind Baptist minister he and Jacques Bourque had often seen in town was read a letter in which son Warren said he'd be getting his wings in September, just after turning 19. "We don't know yet where we'll be posted," he said, "but I hope it's overseas."

There was one convoy Lieut. Dan Hanington would remember above all others. It contained 67 ships, it was called SC42 and it left Sydney, N.S., that same August. Four Canadian warships, the destroyer *Skeena* and three corvettes, joined it as escorts off Newfoundland. Lieutenant Hanington was in the corvette *Kenogami*, and such was the pell-mell expansion of the navy that he was one of only two officers qualified to stand watch on the bridge, a situation which could keep him from seeing daylight for months. He also was the navigator and, like Dan Stack, he had very little to work with: "I had to take sights at dusk and dawn or we never knew where we were. We had no electronic navigational equipment, nor did we have radar, so on dark nights or in fog we kept station on the nearest convoy ship by sonar (asdic, a detection device). If we had to leave station, it would take us hours of creeping about listening to find the convoy again."

In such a state, *Kenogami* met convoy SC42 in a howling gale, "and from there on nothing went right. Finally the whole convoy was forced to heave-to until the storm let up. Yet merchant vessels could not keep together since their seakeeping characteristics varied so much, and the convoy was scattered all over the ocean. After what seemed like, and probably was, days the weather improved and the escorts started to round up anything in sight and head for a prearranged rendezvous point." *Kenogami* was shepherding nine ships when the convoy was ordered to alter course drastically north toward Iceland to avoid a submarine wolf pack. "Well, we knew where we were supposed to be and so did Western Approaches headquarters in Liverpool, England, where the orders came from; what neither knew was where we actually were! So I did an elaborate calculation allowing for a much reduced speed during the storm, and we altered course northeast. It was not until Greenland's icy mountains appeared to starboard that we realized we had drifted westward in the storm and were headed for the North Pole. So we wheeled 90 degrees to starboard and eventually found the convoy, still sorting itself out, near the southern tip of Greenland."

Finally they started for Iceland, but the U-boats had found them. "Next morning *Skeena* had a hairy time chasing one through the columns of the convoy. By nightfall the weather was gorgeous; the moon was up, the stars were twinkling. About 10:20 there was a catastrophic roar as an ammunition ship went up. There was nothing left, no ship, no debris, no survivors. That started it; none of us slept for nearly three days. Between sighting U-boats and hearing explosions and seeing starshell and rescuing survivors and watching ships burn and getting false sonar contacts on small chunks of iceberg, there was no time for anything except the occasional sandwich or a cup of 'kye,' that splendid naval brew of chocolate so thick that a spoon will stand up in it. One exception: I had to go aboard a deserted merchant ship to try to destroy the aircraft she carried to attack submarines. The ship had a broken back and was sagging wildly, and the axe I had was not up to the task. I wrecked the plane's instrument panel, collected a few documents and left in some haste and with great relief.

"At the end of 72 hours I was so tired I was writing absolute garbage in the Log, even recounting the sinking of ships that were not in the convoy. Meanwhile, help had arrived, first Captain 'Chummy' Prentiss with two corvettes which had been working up (training) and which took a U-boat by surprise and sank it, then a strong RN escort. By now we had been at sea nearly two weeks and were running out of fuel, so we rushed into Iceland and out again to rejoin what was left of the convoy. By the time we anchored off Scotland we had been at sea 21 days, lost 15 ships, had masses of survivors on board (*Kenogami* alone had 98) and were reduced to a diet of hardtack and canned tomatoes." But what mattered most was that they had brought 52 ships through everything the U-boats could do to stop them.

In the crisis months of 1940 Winston Churchill put Canadian-born Lord Beaverbrook in charge of British aircraft production and it became a legend that Beaverbrook may have saved the country and even democracy by using ruthless methods to turn out fighter planes for the Battle of Britain. But he'd also had another idea: that the way for Britain to get bombers to attack

Chapter Six

Germany was to fly them over from North America. Streams of bombers from unmolested factories. That was why Bill Palmer spent time in Montreal listening to his Uncle Bill Landry, now a well-to-do industrialist, tell tales about the village and war in the air, and waiting for a call from the new airport out in Dorval that Air Ferry Command had a two-engine Hudson ready to go.

On a September evening the Hudson put down to refuel at the new Gander airport in Newfoundland and then took off again with Sergeant Palmer charting its course and no further stops till they got to where Lord Beaverbrook wanted them to be. On the 13th, he cabled home from Scotland's Prestwick airport: "Arrived this morning. Sorry couldn't see you." A day later he wrote that he'd had "a good trip and it was great experience"; only later would he confess that there was a bit of unspecified trouble. He wrote the letter in Bournemouth, a handsome resort town on the south coast of England where the swimming was great and he found Joe Emery among the flood of Canadians waiting to be posted for operational training. He didn't mention the death of Dan Stack, perhaps because he didn't know, perhaps because of its implications for himself. He and Joe and Dan had all attended the village's Roman Catholic church, but Dan was 12 years older and he seemed like someone from another generation. As for the two graduates of 1938, they went to a movie and planned an evening on the town.

This was the month the third young man in their school class was drafted into the German Army, the Wehrmacht. There is a ceremonial picture of him and other recruits being sworn in. Everybody is in uniform and wearing one of those deep, coal-scuttle German helmets. Soldiers appear to be presenting arms. Some men have swords and there is a big Nazi flag but, out front, one officer is saluting another and he's not doing it with the raised arm of the Nazi salute, the "Heil Hitler" salute, but with a traditional army gesture, hand raised to the helmet. You can't pick Gottfried Klotz out but he's in the picture somewhere and, given his command of English, things might have turned out differently for him but it was settled by what was happening in Russia. The big news was what was happening there three months after the campaign began: one German victory after another, the Ukraine invaded, Leningrad encircled, the Crimea isolated, vast Russian armies obliterated.

Yet even as he had left home recruit Klotz knew some older people still feared Hitler had sealed Germany's doom. Nor had the four likeable French prisoners of war changed their minds that he'd sealed Germany's doom long before this. Even as he was about to leave, Gottfried told them they were wrong, that Russia would be defeated in a matter of weeks. So they made a bet. The German who was about to become a soldier bet that the war on the Russian Front would be over by the end of the year. The four Frenchmen who had been soldiers bet it wouldn't. Then they shook hands and said goodbye, and when this happened Hans Klotz must have thought of something he'd done because he feared he'd never get another chance to do it. Shortly after the war began, he got his children together and had their picture taken with himself, the two young girls in front, Gottfried and Uli and Arndt and Walter behind. He was heard to say he wouldn't worry about Gottfried and Arndt because they would survive. But he would, he said, worry about Walter and Uli because they were "so idealistic."

Walter was with the army in Africa now. Arndt was with it in Russia. Uli was 15 years old and still going to school.

It wasn't long before Bill Palmer was reporting on a visit to the 14th Field Ambulance: "I went looking for Bud. He is about 70 miles north of me, not far from London. Gerry is about 70 more north of Bud on the other side of London. I haven't seen him yet. I not only saw Bud but the whole of Dorchester, I think. Everybody is there, or within a few miles. I only had a few hours so I didn't see them all, but saw all Bud's outfit ... the works. Bud seems very content, in fact he and Newt Cooke seem to be very happy here. The three of us went out together."

The 14th Field's village '"works" included Bud Brian, Roy Anderson, Frank Tracy, Newt Cooke, Len Shea, Earl Stiles, Alvin Mitton, Lloyd and Percy Atkinson, Leo Fabien LeBlanc, Gerald Ward and Walter Biddell. The unit tended, however, to be divided up to work with infantry battalions, so it would be exceptional to find the works all in one place at one time, and, typically, there are pictures of some but not all of them taken in England that year, and typically there are other village soldiers in the pictures. In one there are Lee and Paul Whalen, Lee now a sergeant, Paul a private in a signals unit. In another is Wilder Palmer, a village blacksmith a bit old to be in the forces at all, but there he is. Servicemen like himself and the Whalens and Bill Palmer would use the 14th Field as a way to keep in touch with the village and with one another. They'd come to talk about home and what was happening in Russia and how it was going to be a long war.

Even though no one talked about a German invasion of Britain anymore, it was hard to see how the war could be won without an invasion the other way, and not even what General Andy McNaughton said about his Canadian soldiers made many people think this was going to happen happily or soon. Actually, what General Andy said could be seen as an elaboration of what the colonel of the 145th Battalion had said of the Dorchester Platoon in 1916, that it would "carry its name and individuality to Berlin" and "help paint Dorchester on the Kaiser's Front Door." General Andy's version was that his soldiers constituted a dagger pointed at the heart of Berlin, and this took on an extra glow when he had five divisions plus two tank brigades. But nothing much but the arithmetic was changing; besides training, the new ones like the soldiers of the 14th Field were soon doing what thousands had been doing for nearly two years. What they were a dagger pointing at mostly was London and Scotland and the pubs of southern England.

But years later, when you looked at those pictures you'd be struck by the fact that, in one, two of the 14th Field soldiers in particular were side by side. One was Private Bud Brian. The other was Corporal Len Shea. They'd gone to school together. They were both Roman Catholics from Father Bourgeois' flock. There was no special or unusual pre-war background of relations but what would happen between them would turn out to be hard for people to talk about. Meanwhile, Bill Palmer told his parents that, for the time being, the best way to reach him with letters was care of the Canadians' Beaver Club in London. "But don't send any parcels," he cautioned, "until we see how the letters come." As for Pilot Officer Warren Duffy, now overseas too, his policy was parcels as soon as possible. From Bournemouth that October he wrote home that he missed chocolate bars and chewing gum, and would much appreciate some of each.

Even then Gunner Hazen Greenberg was using letters to try to find Bill Palmer and anyone else from the village who was in Britain. He was there himself and making contact mattered to him. He was one of the kids in that 1925 picture of Ina Brien's students. His mother used to send him to school in fancy clothes and, sure enough, in the picture he has some kind of fancy stuff around his neck. But he was always popular, and when we called him Ikey there was affection in it. He was a good athlete and his mother used to throw big birthday parties for him at which we'd eat very well. Her husband Sam had run a garage in town, and then he got into selling liquor when the law said he shouldn't. Not that this was so unusual. The hotel did it, and a prominent God-fearing Baptist, and a man with a small and largely empty restaurant, and a farmer who flew a kite when he had supplies available. Hazen had driven vehicles for years because his father had a truck, and driving them was what he was heading for in the artillery that had lots of guns to lug around. In 1941 he held the rank of gunner, and one letter he wrote could, decades later, make you feel the way he was and hear the way he talked. It was addressed to Bill Palmer's father, and it comes through as a kind of homespun, homesick soldier's classic:

> Please do not faint when you see who this letter is from. I am writing to everyone I can think of. Say, is Billie in Canada yet or over here? If he is over here please send me his address and I will try to look him up. I heard that their (sic) are some air force boys at Aldershot and that is 20 miles from me. It would be great if Billie came over and landed at that camp.
> Well, Bill, this is sure a different country from Canada. Every thing is so backwards that when I walk down the street I don't know if I am going or coming. We can't buy hardly any thing. Cigarettes cost so dam much, and boy they are rotten, and we have a hard time trying to get candy or pop. Hardly any of the Canadian boys will drink the beer but the Scotch whisky is good, that is if you have enough money. They are making us learn the drills all over again, and

they are different here. I am not driving yet but expect to take a test any day now. I have to learn how to fire one of the big guns first ... The country over here is very pretty but we have no use for the English people. They don't like us at all. But the people in Scotland will do everything for a Canadian. I was in Glasgow for a leave, and I am going again next month. I put my name in for a trip to Windsor Castle for Sunday. They let 3 truck loads go every Sunday. The King and Queen are their so I hope I get a good look at them.

Things are as quiet here as they was in (Camp) Petawawa no excitement at all. We hear planes going over nearly every night. But that is all their is to it. We don't even get out of bed. I seen Paul Whalen today but could not stop to talk. I was on parade. I haven't much time to write this letter. I have to play softball but will write you a longer letter next time. I suppose the old town is some dead now. How is John doing? I suppose he will be through school soon. Has he grown any or still as small as ever. I got some cigarettes from him, and I would rather see more Canadian cigarettes than I would pay-day. So tell Billie to bring all the cigarettes and razor blades he can with him. You sure pay plenty for them over here, that is when you can get them. Is Eileen home or is she away working some place or maybe she is married by now. (Ha Ha). I would be some glad if I could meet some of the boys from home. This is all for now. Write soon. Love to the family.

A Friend, Hazen

No. G7352, No. 1 Canadian Artillery Holding Unit, Canadian Army Overseas.

V for Victory

V for Victory was something Churchill got going. He'd hold up two fingers like a V, and BBC broadcasts would spell it out in Morse code, da, da, da, dah, to encourage people, especially behind the German lines. It spread all over the place, including where that former village entrepreneur Ernest Partridge had taken up a new position and become a sort of symbol in himself. He had left his Vimy canteen, gone to sea with the merchant marine, spent hours in the Atlantic after his ship was torpedoed. This plus a dire seasickness and his maimed left arm had led him, in his mid-40s, to conclude that one war would be enough after all and to obtain a position as a doorman at Canadian military headquarters in London's Trafalgar Square. The position had the double advantage of entailing an attractive if subdued uniform and being very near the Beaver Club which made it an ideal place to meet boys from home and to inform the village, through them, that he was making what was called "good money," in this case some $20 a week.

Thus, like the 14th Field, he became a way to keep in touch and to know who was overseas and even in London at a given moment There were more of them all the time and by fall they included Bert Emmerson, a sergeant wearing a pilot's wings. He'd made it. He'd become what so many others wanted to be. His older sister Emily might have been in Britain too but she'd grown tired of waiting for the army to accept her and had become one of some 300 Canadian nurses recruited to serve in South Africa.

The Wehrmacht put Gottfried Klotz in the signals corps, and he liked it. He was, moreover, surprised to find that a lot of soldiers were proud that they had never joined the Hitler Youth. He also found that, as in Mulda, he was faced with a contrast: that in Canada he'd been thought of as someone from Germany and in Germany he was thought of as someone from Canada. Yes, and in Canada he'd dreamt of Germany and in Germany he dreamt of Canada. He seemed to have sprung from some halfway world, and he became used to being called upon for strange bits of information. He was surprised that to fellow soldiers the German language seemed to be inadequately endowed with cusswords. They'd ask him to teach them some in English, and since he had spent some time around pool rooms he was able to oblige in a way which added to his reputation. All in all, he found that he liked not having to worry about getting up early to milk the cows or how the vegetables were doing. What's more, though slated to go to the Russian Front, he still doubted that there would be much more fighting there. Indeed, the Feuhrer still had Germany's war machine running below an all-out effort. Which may have been why Soldier Klotz's training would go on for months.

Nevertheless, by December there were definite signs that both he and Hitler had erred in their strategic thinking, as no one was in a better position to see than his stepbrother Arndt Trebst. Arndt, by then, had seen overwhelming victories in both Western Europe and Russia. He was with tank-expert Heinz Guderain when they got to within sight of a largely abandoned Moscow — and when they started to retreat because they couldn't take it. The Russians had suffered 3,000,000 casualties but were still very much in the war.

At Christmas time, Soldier Klotz was asked to sing songs that evoked the romance of the Wild West and he was able to oblige, especially because he'd fallen into the habit of singing to break the monotony of milking cows. Meanwhile, Arndt spent the holiday season struggling back through what Heinz Guderain would call "the endless expanse of Russian snow during this winter of our misery ... the icy wind that blew across it ... too-thin shelter ... insufficiently clothed, half-starved men."

Chapter Seven

BILL PALMER AND JOE Emery spent Christmas at the very heart of Empire. Now at different stations, they were surprised when they met, though it really wasn't that surprising when they both got leaves and both checked into the London hotel where your typical young, bushy-tailed flying man was apt to go. The Regent Palace had become a cockpit of air-crew saturnalia, and about as close to Piccadilly Circus as a hotel could get. Gerry Nugent was there for four days too, so the three of them teamed up, so many small-town boys at this imperial and hedonistic crossroads, so many former choirboys drifting through Piccadilly blackouts seething with the solicitations of prostitutes, destitutes, pimps, con artists, beggars, crooks, the saviors of souls, the saviors (if possible) of democracy and the accents of half the world. But also going to mass, Bill said in a letter home which said very little at all about what went on elsewhere, other than that he and Gerry "went skating and everything" and that he had two bountiful Christmas dinners and met the Rt. Hon. Vincent Massey, the Canadian High Commissioner, at the Beaver Club. In fact, he said, he went to mass twice with Joe, and they had their pictures taken at one of those places that stuck some in the window, which was how Joe Emery would come to see Bill Palmer's face on later leaves.

On this one, there were several things typical of the world they'd entered. One was that Bill Palmer was embarrassed by a clipping from the Sackville *Tribune* about him guiding that bomber across the Atlantic because, he wrote home, it was being done by dozens, and he'd found it easy despite "a few anxious moments." He'd already discovered there was nothing worse for airmen than being seen by their peers as boasting or even talking about their feats, sins punishable by ridicule and the purchase of drinks. Another thing was rank. Joe, Bill and Gerry were all sergeants, but Joe would soon be an officer — as Warren Duffy was — and rank fitted them into an ancient system with clear distinctions between officers and other ranks, a system designed for war on land and sea when relatively few men with social status led many men without it. In circumstances under which one to seven men flew single warplanes, it took on different meanings. It meant that when Joe Emery became an officer he would eat, drink and sleep in one place and a sergeant in another even if they flew in the same crew. It was a system some Canadians might feel uncomfortable with, but one reason it didn't change was that they became for some time so deeply involved with Britain's R.A.F. So when the three small-town boys left London they all went back to R.A.F. stations knowing they'd serve in R.A.F. squadrons.

Joe and Gerry were in training for bombing operations as air gunners, a role with a tendency to be especially deadly, which is why Bill said he worried about them. He himself went back to Scotland, where he'd spent two months training, then been posted to an operational squadron, No. 228, for an indefinite period. He felt "kind of lucky" but "I don't know whether I can stay as you have to be pretty good to do the work." The work was navigating Coastal Command planes out over the Atlantic where German submarines were moving steadily westward, the work that had provided Dan Hanington with the most beautiful sight he'd ever seen.

Despite the submarines, a fair number of gifts made it to the 14th Field Ambulance for Christmas, but only Leo Fabien LeBlanc got 1,000 cigarettes from Mrs. Kerr and Laddie. I spent the day in Brockville, Ont., in a place where the army trained men to be officers and, if possible, gentlemen. I'd heard a recruiting officer say a Nova Scotia unit needed people overseas and I knew the time had come. Just that: the time had come, though memory also associates it vaguely with a bleak winter's day when I climbed up the gangway to the deck of a freighter. My head was down because it was icy underfoot, and when I raised it a man was waiting for me with a Battle of the Atlantic face. I told him I was a reporter and he said two words: "Fuck off." In a broader sense than he had in mind, that may have been what I did.

After two years and more, the war had become more than a way of life; it seemed to be almost life itself, a sovereign force from which priorities stemmed. It was grimed into everything, a phenomenon with seemingly irreproachable credentials and inalienable rights, not so much something you rallied to as something you were absorbed into. The great suction it had created caught up with me just when two big things happened: I met Ruth Potter and the sparks had barely started flying when I headed for Brockville, and I barely got there before that December 7, 1941, when the Japanese ravaged the Americans' great Pacific naval base at Pearl Harbor and booted the United States into the war.

What puzzled me about Brockville, uncertain and

corrupted civilian that I was, was why they treated like dirt the very people they trained to lead other people into battle. One night I awoke and this was in me. Holy Jesus, I thought, by my own choice the other people they have in mind for me are members of the Cape Breton Highlanders, reputedly the wildest outfit in the entire Canadian Army. At which point, I turned over feeling so absurdly unqualified for what I'd volunteered to do that it was hard to get back to sleep.

When years later I read a letter Bill Palmer wrote just after Pearl Harbor, he was asking questions the whole world was asking. He wondered how long he'd be in Scotland, "especially with things as they are in Japan." With one massive blow, the Japanese had made the war global, and left millions wondering what would happen next.

One thing that happened that Christmas was the fall of Hong Kong and the capture of two Canadian battalions which should never have been there; this and other terrible things as the Japanese swept through the Philippines, toward Indo-China, toward the Dutch East Indies and Singapore, toward New Zealand and Australia, swept onward with barbarities that shocked the world and successes that seemed to have no end. In which a memorable incident befell the David Cochrane who had named his son for Sir Douglas Haig and nearly been buried alive after the Halifax Explosion of 1917.

The bluff, gruff engineer had returned to Britain in the mid-30s and become an officer in the same Royal Navy that had sent him to Canada in 1910. As the Germans and Japanese kept the world on edge, he was sent to the Far East which is where he was for just a bit too long. He was under orders to return to Britain when the Japanese struck, and he and Margaret, his second wife — his first wife had died while they lived in the village — were enroute across the north Pacific when the Japanese torpedoed the ship in which they were passengers. In a 1945 letter to son Doug, he would write: "I got away from Hong Kong but again was caught, torpedoed and had a long, long time in the cold and snow before we were picked up. We lost 68. I had charge of a boat; no compass but I set a course by the sun and got on to the Canadian Steamship Lane which was north, and by luck we were picked up, destitute. Your stepmother was good. She talked Chinese to my crew and greatly helped me, but she has never got over it. She was in hospital for a long time. I am not too bad. I have a touch of neuritis now and again."

It wasn't, his son would learn, the whole story. The fact that David Cochrane was the senior military person in one lifeboat came to mean more and more as days went by and people worried about how much there was to eat and drink and started acting in selfish and funny ways in the cold and occasional snow. The time came when he felt he had to threaten to use his revolver to curb behavior which endangered them all. He threatened several times and finally shot one man who defied his orders. The body was cast overboard while a chaplain said he'd protest the killing if and when they got ashore. Others were dying of hunger, sickness and exposure before a ship rescued them. David Cochrane was haled before a court martial which decided he'd done what had to be done. He would serve in Scotland for the rest of the war and hold the rank of commander when he retired.

Village people knew nothing of their lifeboat ordeal for years. What they did know was that there was a woman in town whose brother was with Quebec's Royal Rifles in Hong Kong and that she worried terribly about what had happened to him. Half a century later they could remember her anguish but not her name, and all they knew about the soldier was that either he died in battle or vanished into ghastly years as a prisoner of war. For that was how it was.

Bill Palmer wondered whether he'd be going to Gibraltar, Northern Ireland, the Middle East or the Far East, though he still expected to be with Coastal Command no matter where it was. He was palling with Canadian Sgt. Bob Long, a pilot he came to consider the best friend he'd made since enlisting. Their duties took him to Wales, Scotland, and various parts of England. Each flying boat carried two crews for long hours over the sea, patrolling, watching for enemy activity. Flying the Atlantic was easy compared to this, he wrote. Twice, he added, he got into action but all he told the family was that his luck was holding.

One way he had of consoling his parents was to assure them that both Joe Emery and Gerry Nugent were heading for greater danger than he was."I got a good break," he said. "I don't know why." His chances of survival were, he guessed, about 10-1 for, and the experience would be "A1 in my job" after the war; the flying he'd detested had become a way of life. By February, he was on a troopship, seasick, had tropical clothes and was heading south. Given his destination, it would have made much more sense for the ship to head east except for one thing: that would have taken it into the Mediterranean, a decidedly hostile place. The Germans and Italians dominated most of it, controlled the shoreline of southern Europe from the Atlantic east to Greece and the shoreline of North Africa from the Atlantic east to Egypt. They were laying violent and regular siege to Malta, that tiny island where British forces held out and launched what defiance they could by air and sea. In brief, as Bill Palmer passed the Equator, watched flying fish, sharks, tortoises, listened to a Roman Catholic chaplain extol the saints, he was heading for Egypt but was, advisedly, going the long way around.

By late March, after weeks at sea, he was in Durban, South Africa, and the longer he was there the more he liked the warm climate, the abundance, the steaks, the lighted streets, the way people treated you. But for one thing — no hockey — he felt it would be a great place to live. On "a native reservation" he had his picture taken with Zulu women. He looked up Nursing Sister Emily Emmerson and they had a happy evening together. She liked South Africa, she said, and the people were nice, often wouldn't let you pay a restaurant bill, enrolled you in golf clubs. She was at a hospital near Durban that was handling casualties from the fighting in North Africa, and from both sides. The ones who stood out, Emily said, were the Italians. When they saw black-skinned natives come in to clean their rooms, they'd often start yelling for help. They feared the blacks might be Ethiopians, and they knew Ethiopians had no love for the people who had conquered them in 1936, and for the brutal way they'd done it.

Though the Germans were very much on the offensive elsewhere, Leningrad — the former and future St. Petersburg — had already resisted months of siege by the time Gottfried Klotz arrived in that area in late March. He was in one company of a nine-company signals regiment and in an area which would live through one of the epics of the war in Russian defiance of the army he was with. He was Obergefreiter Klotz, a corporal, now. He travelled in a light truck, and his company had hens to provide eggs. Its job was to maintain communication lines for the infantry, tanks and artillery doing the beseiging. The lines let one general talk to another and one outfit to another, and thus gave the signals unit an importance which, in the way of soldiers, was seen and exploited as an opportunity. That is to say Obergefreiter Klotz's unit found that the comforts they received and the advantages they reaped could bear a direct relationship to the service they gave or did not give. In this way, life was kept on a higher plane than it might otherwise have achieved.

At the same time, they found the Russian people friendly as individuals but, in Obergefreiter Klotz's words, "very disappointed with the German administration." Hundreds of thousands of Russian civilians had, in fact, greeted the Germans almost as liberators after years of Stalin's tyranny, only to face a new brutality of mass murder and destruction. A brutality conceived by a Hitler who saw them as inferior beings, and carried out very largely by the ardent Nazis of the Gestapo and the *Schutzstaffeln*, the notorious S.S. Hitler didn't, for one thing, simply want Leningrad captured; he wanted it laid waste, its three million people eliminated. In his own small unit, Obergefreiter Klotz encountered resentment and dislike for Hitler's methods, but they did not go beyond where it would be wise to go. If this bothered those who felt that way, they had a way out which he adopted personally. He would say he saw himself as one of millions called to duty by their country and doing what their country asked, as soldiers always had. In war, he'd say, it is your country right or wrong.

For Joe Emery and Warren Duffy, an event on the night of May 30, 1942, was historic, vital and in some respects almost bizarre. It was the first thousand-plane raid on Germany. Four months after taking over Bomber Command, Air Marshal Bert Harris launched it not only to show the Germans what the R.A.F. could do but to save the command itself from its critics. To his chagrin, he had on arrival found it little larger than in 1939, much discredited as a war-winning weapon, beset by navy and army arguments that they could better use what force it had, and so incapable of hitting specific military and industrial targets that it got a new mandate: to attack large built-up areas. Bill Palmer's Coastal Command alone now had 250 and more bombers under Admiralty (navy) control, more than half the number in Bomber Command itself. Dan Stack, if he had lived, would have found a new radar navigational aid, Gee, in use, but it too had limitations in target recognition.

So Harris went for broke. "It is proposed," he told his top people, "at about the full moon to put over the maximum possible force of bombers on a single and extremely important town in Germany with a view to wiping it out in one night." The target finally selected was that large, built-up area on the Rhine River known as the cathedral city of Cologne. The aim: to saturate the defences with 90 minutes of serialized mayhem. If he failed, Harris knew Bomber Command would keep on sinking. If he succeeded, it could prosper and grow.

For Warren Duffy, it was a sixth operational flight after months of training in Britain. In Wellingtons of the R.A.F's 57 Squadron, he'd done mine laying off Denmark and France, raided the docks of Boulogne, France, dropped incendiary bombs on Mannheim, Germany. As for Joe Emery, it was the way Bomber Harris did the raid that got him involved, him and hundreds of others still in training or occupied otherwise than in action against the enemy. To get his force up to the unprecedented and sensation-causing figure of 1,000 planes, Harris scraped the barrel. Borrowed planes from other commands, mustered all his own command could find, many of them obsolescent, used instructors and training crews in training planes, and ended up with 1,046 all told: Wellingtons, Stirlings, Blenheims, Hampdens, Bostons, Manchesters, Whitleys, the new four-engine Lancasters and Halifaxes that would deliver the climactic blows, not to mention the Hurricane fighters that were to curb fighter opposition.

Warren Duffy and Joe Emery, once one grade ahead of him in the village school, were among perhaps 500 Canadians who waited through several postponements, then flew in a gamble within a gamble. For after several days of waiting for the right weather, Harris took a chance on a reasonably favorable forecast because he knew a waning moon would soon make his chances nil. His Canadians went both in R.A.F. squadrons and four squadrons of their own. Young Duffy, the Baptist minister's son, piloted a Wellington. Young Emery, the former Catholic choirboy, flew in an R.A.F. training plane as a wireless operator/air gunner in a crew of strangers. Around them were thousands of men including, in all probability, Gerry Nugent; they flew in ranks and echelons at differing heights in differing planes with differing tasks, passed, disconsolate and wondering, through miles of thick clouds. Saw the city vivid in midnight moonlight when the clouds parted just in time, saw it leap and glow and finally rage with flames. Prime Minister Churchill, enthusiastic from the beginning, had asked how many planes Harris thought he'd lose. Five percent at the most, Harris had said. In the end, the figure was just under four. In all, 41 planes were lost to the long, probing fingers of searchlights, to night fighters and anti-aircraft flak, and to collisions in that packed and moonlit sky.

Warren Duffy got back gratefully and safely and, as he did for all operations, recorded the raid in red ink. "Incendiaries at Cologne," he wrote in his log, "Big DO,1000." Joe Emery got back too but what he'd remember of that night was what a shambles it was, what confusion there was. Yet it was a world sensation, and Churchill warned that it was a herald of what Hitler's Third Reich could expect from now on. It helped Bomber Command survive and grow because it demonstrated both its possibilities and its limitations. For on one hand it devastated some 600 acres but, on the other, this was not enough to knock the city out of the war. On one hand, again, Bomber Command in one night created nearly as much destruction as in all its previous raids. On the other, it had come up against the human resilience that had brought London through the blitz — and would see Germany through ugly nights ahead.

When the R.C.A.F.'s 405 Squadron arrived in the final phase of attack, Wing Commander Johnny Fauquier looked down from one of the new four-engine Halifaxes and saw a city that seemed to be almost totally on fire on both sides of the Rhine. He also saw something else. Cologne's famous cathedral still thrust the majesty and the message of its spire into a sky such as it had never known.

When the news of Cologne got to Egypt, Bill Palmer, that other former choirboy, wrote home that the raid "should shake Gerry (the Germans) up." He'd arrived there via the Suez Canal and been with the R.A.F.'s 230 Squadron since late April, making sorties in Sunderland flying boats: a patrol over the Cyprus coast, another over the Palestine coast, an anti-submarine patrol to screen two disabled destroyers, another to screen a convoy. Then, without leaving Egypt, he was transferred to 267 Squadron at a time when besieged Malta became its key destination.

If in an obscure and distant way, the thousand-plane raid made Joe Emery an associate of the Johnny Fauquier who would be known as "the king of the pathfinders," the epic siege of that Mediterranean island linked Bill Palmer in somewhat the same way with the emergence of George "Buzz" or "Screwball" Beurling as the "hero of Malta." Both Sergeant Beurling and Flight Sergeant Palmer — he'd been promoted — first appeared there in early June, Beurling to remain after piloting a Spitfire fighter on a three-hour flight from a British aircraft carrier, Bill Palmer to come and go as a transport squadron navigator. There were major differences in their roles, but they had a common purpose: to keep Malta in the war, Beurling by feats that would make him Canada's greatest fighter ace, Palmer by flying in people and supplies and taking people out.

Malta needed such help if it was to continue as an invaluable base strategically located between Italy and Africa, as the focus of challenge to enemy control of the Mediterranean, a hotbed of defiance by air and sea, a constant menace to Axis shipping, a threat to the supply line to their forces in North Africa. To keep it in the war had been the aim of Britain from late 1940 on. To knock it out of the war had for as long been the aim of Hitler and Mussolini; for months they had kept up a day-and-night siege which, in that summer of 1942, was sustained by 600 warplanes flying from bases as close as Sicily, just 80 miles away. Hitler wanted Malta "neutralized," and its docks, homes and airfields were attacked with violent regularity. The island's people sheltered and slept in caves, bore up so bravely that they would eventually — and uniquely — be awarded a George Cross for courage. Hunger stalked both them and those who fought around them. Supplies of gasoline and ammunition regularly ran low. Attempts to get convoys through were vehemently resisted. Malta, in summary, was delicately balanced between survival and obliteration, and even as he flew in from that aircraft carrier near Gibraltar, the 20-year-old Beurling saw he'd "come to a war running 24 hours a day."

In joining it, he would be one of those who kept 12 to 18 fighter planes in the air, and it must have crossed Bill Palmer's mind that if he'd made it as a pilot he might be in that desperate fighting too. Instead, he reached Malta in an unarmed plane as a member of a transport squadron with a venerable history. The shift was, he wrote home, "a great surprise." Flying into Malta was another, flying over hundreds of miles of the Mediterranean, picking his way by stars and compass and radio links while the enemy lurked all too close on two sides. Flying in darkness. Landing in darkness, in the pits and holes of airfields regularly attacked, regularly repaired. Leaving in darkness. Heading back toward Cairo before dawn. Benefitting from being at the side of 267's top pilot, Sqdn. Ldr. Alec Noon, a 32-year-old peacetime civilian flier from Africa's Kenya, and one other crewman, a wireless operator.

As they did about numerous things that might interest those they shouldn't, his letters barely mentioned Malta. In one dated June 10 — one day after "Buzz" Beurling reached the island — he said he'd been there "a few days ago" and that the enemy made quite a raid that night. The real measurement came later when Alec Noon was awarded the Air Force Flying Cross and Flt. Sgt. Palmer a mention in despatches. It was later still that Canadian pilot Jack Rice would reveal in an interview one major reason why 267 flew into Malta and one of the problems it faced. It had, he said, an important role in evacuating civilians; in one trip alone Alec Noon's plane came away stuffed with a record 69 women and children. That may have been the time the taciturn Noon himself would talk about years later to his son Chris: "He waited till the machine (a Dakota, a DC3) was full to the brim, then just hoped it would get airborne." And always, Jack Rice said, it was vital to beware of German tricks. One R.A.F. plane was lured to destruction in Sicily by a radio beam set up to trap it. A post-war article published by the Aero Club of East Africa would say Noon's flights to Malta and, later, elsewhere in an unarmed plane "had to be by night, mainly carrying arms, ammunition and torpedoes. The job was enlivened by occasionally being chased by night fighters or stooging around waiting for the current battle to quieten down to enable him to land."

When he heard of his award, Bill Palmer wrote, he was "not quite sure what it's for though I think it is for long and continuous devotion to duty or some such rot." Eventually he learned it was for "work done running the blockade into Malta when it was in such a precarious position." His letters never mentioned Beurling. But then their working hours didn't jibe.

I was a lieutenant heading happily home to Ruth, my lovely bride, when I saw that spring a caricature of the war that had the Mediterranean and much of the world aflame. On the parade square at the Yarmouth, N.S., infantry training centre there were two men. They were alone, one a sergeant, one a recruit, and they were locked in a struggle neither could resolve. The sergeant was trying to teach the soldier how to march properly; the soldier kept marching in a way that was beyond anything teaching could do. Kept slouching. Head too far forward. Shoulders too far down. Arms hanging as though there were a plough handle at the end of them. The sergeant's body demonstrated what proper marching was. His baffled voice ranged from patience into anger. The soldier said nothing. He kept trying to do something he couldn't do.

At times, even now, I find myself wondering whether he slouched to his death on some field of battle, died into the sympathy of the earth that had made him what he was.

He came in my mind to be a classic misfit in a war that made misfits of many by demands they were ill equipped to meet, and I realized, watching, that I identified with him, not the sergeant. Nor did it help that "it," the problem that had started in high school, caught up with me that summer. I'd never mentioned it when I enlisted, partly out of embarrassment, partly because I thought the tricks I'd developed for controlling it might see me through. They did until one day at Camp Aldershot, N.S., a group of us were suddenly, unexpectedly, ordered to run and, in the running, it struck and distorted me, sent me lurching out of control. They sent me to a psychiatrist, and that was the first time I'd ever discussed it with anyone. In the end he said he was going to let me go overseas and they'd see how things worked out. I said that was fine by me.

Aldershot was a place you went overseas from. Ruth and I brided and groomed it in nearby Kentville, in an apartment whose landlord chuckled that the army must be a very tough life to make us go to bed so early. The war was making it happen to thousands, and it was beautiful. But just before going overseas, I went back to my village and saw two revelations about what war had done, was doing, to two generations. A dozen or so people came to the railway station to say goodbye: my mother, my sister Peg, Bill Palmer's mother, aunts, cousins. The only man was my Uncle Frank, and someone was wishing me luck when he suddenly said a totally unexpected thing. "Wait," he said, "till you get wounded a couple of times." Just that. Out of nowhere. Out of the silence that for a quarter-century had masked whatever his war had meant to him. No one said anything about it. Not the women. Not me. Not him. What he'd said was reburied in the emotional no man's land that had made him say it, and into the quiet it had left someone called my name.

I looked around, and there, nearby on the station

Chapter Seven 213

platform, was Billy Manship, skinny, friendly Billy Manship who sang cowboy songs and whom I'd liked ever since we'd set a tree on fire. He asked me to come over, and we shook hands, and he said how sad it made him to see so many friends going overseas when none of the three forces would take him, and as he said it tears streamed down his face. Within a minute or so, war had exposed the twists it had implanted in two men, one with the hidden frustrations of a war he'd fought, one with the raw frustrations of a war he'd been denied.

What the war meant would implant a special memory in Raymond Gallant. He was a village schoolboy in 1942, and he came down with polio. It kept him in bed for weeks, at home in the Guard Row house next to where Joe Emery had lived, and what was special, and memorable, about this was that people kept coming with gifts and food. It touched him so deeply that half a century later he'd call the memory beautiful.

In Bill Palmer's many letters from Egypt, there were other hints and even riddles about what war meant to people. He had arrived there at a crucial time, and he was there because the Suez Canal was on Britain's lifeline of empire, to India, to other imperial possessions and vital pools of oil. He was in the theatre of war Churchill would constantly promote and seek to expand. But the only imperialism his letters talked about was the imperialism of flies, and eventually all that mattered about Englishmen was how they were as individuals. Perhaps he took it all in stride because of maps with red on them and pictures of bulldogs on Union Jacks. But the fact is that he was involved in a campaign fought as a prelude to extermination of the imperialisms that fought it. The entire Mediterranean coast of North Africa was controlled by

European powers, and two of them, Britain and Italy, plus Germany, had been fighting over an area which included Libya, Cyrenaica and, at disturbing moments, British-controlled Egypt, their neighbor to the east. So here was English-French-Irish-Canadian William Frederick Palmer involved in a collision of transplanted European animosities, accepting it as the way the world was, and reorienting himself to new situations. He found that the "British" Eighth Army consisted of British, Australian, New Zealand, South African and Indian divisions and that he was one of four Canadians in a British squadron which also had Australians, South Africans, New Zealanders, Kenyans and men from other places where the British had gone in their long acquisitional past.

As a result of other acquisitions, by the time Italy's Mussolini got into the war he controlled Libya and Cyrenaica not to mention Ethiopia or Abyssinia to the south and east. Along the coast he had erected a great arch to his personal glory, but decided this was a good time to get Egypt which the British had dominated since 1882. Hence they had fought back and forth until finally the Germans had to come in to help the Italians, and Erwin Rommel became the Desert Fox. Before Bill Palmer arrived, the Fox got his crackerjack Afrika Korps and his sadsack Italians well into Egypt, only to be driven far back to French-controlled Tunisia. Then a month or so after Bill did arrive, Rommel struck again, eventually forced his way back over the Egyptian border as the most immediate of three converging menaces. The Japanese were not too far away to the east, the Germans not too far away to the north, in Russia, and there was a real possibility of dire consequences.

Even so, no pessimism was apparent in Flight Sergeant Palmer's letters. On June 10, with Rommel not too far away, he reported that "things look pretty good and should improve shortly." In addition, he found Egypt fascinating even if the heat was terrific and he got Gyppo Tummy or dysentery. Prices were high — you could pay 70 cents for a meal even at a service club, compared to 25 cents back home — but food and cigarettes were in ample supply and he even had a bed with sheets. From 267's headquarters, he could take a tramcar and within 15 minutes be in Cairo, a teeming city with what author Penelope Lively would call its "orchestration of languages ... its smell of dung and paraffin, the felt-shod sound of a donkey's hooves, kites floating in a Wedgewood sky," Cairo with the packed terraces of its Shepheard's Hotel, its multitude of uniforms, with the pyramids "like gray cut-outs on the horizon," with its light-jewelled nights on the Nile. Cairo, where a Canada House hostel was opening. He walked, Bill wrote, to a "very nice" Mediterranean beach, attended church, got months of mail in one batch. He did a lot of flying and found that 267 had its own proud tradition of doing so no matter what the weather was. He was used to living with Britons and others by now, but felt cut off, was still wondering which team had won the Stanley Cup; "it's hard to find out things here." The fact was that he'd become part of a "lost legion" of Canadians in R.A.F. squadrons. Still, on June 23, his 21st birthday, he sent Ruthie Lewis a cable and, in a letter home, repeated something he'd been writing for months: "I'm having a good time; don't worry." But something else crept in, something from gossip, rumors, fears. He wondered what Britain's Churchill was doing in Washington.

What Churchill was doing was coordinating plans with President Roosevelt — and recovering from the only wartime episode that made him break down. In retreating to Egypt, the Eighth Army had taken a calculated risk and left 35,000 soldiers and invaluable supplies behind in Tobruk, a coastal town in Cyrenaica which had faced one siege and was ill-equipped to face another. On June 20, Rommel took the lot, the seaport, troops, supplies. It was, Churchill grieved, a disgrace second only to the fall of Singapore. It made his government totter. Yet on the 26th, Bill Palmer wrote that the Germans were near but "everybody is confident" and he felt the tide was about to turn. In fact, there was a sense of crisis and, according to one account, signs in Cairo shop windows said "German officers welcome here." The Desert Fox, now a field marshal, was pushing the Eighth Army back. Mussolini arrived in Africa and got set to enter Cairo in triumph. But the tide *was* about to turn, at least part way. In the first week of July, the Desert Fox was defeated and stopped so sharply by the Eighth Army that he barely escaped another retreat, this time from an obscure Egyptian place about 70 miles from Cairo. Its name was El Alamein.

If Bill Palmer was out on the far reaches of empire, Warren Duffy, Joe Emery and Gerry Nugent were involved in the one major way Britain could strike directly at Germany. They were deep into what were called tours of operations. Two nights after the first 1,000-plane raid, Duffy recorded "Another big one, 1000" after attacking Essen with flares and high explosives; did it again on June 2 and 5, attacked Emden ("for a change") on the 6th. It went on from there, against Emden, Bremen, Duisburg, Cuxhaven, Hamburg, Mainz, Dusseldorf, Osnabruck, Frankfurt, Kassel. Sometimes he'd go out to lay mines in strategic waters. On July 8, he dropped 500-pound bombs on the dockyard at Wilhelmshaven and in two words recorded what happened: "Shot up." It happened again on July 28, over Hamburg, shortly before Joe Emery's No.7 Squadron, R.A.F., was elevated to an elite.

It became part of the Pathfinder Force which now used navigational techniques well in advance of those Dan Stack had known. Pathfinders had pioneered in target marking. They went first on bombing raids, marked targets and guided other squadrons to them by dropping flares the Germans called Christmas trees. They belonged, says an introduction to Chaz Bouyer's book *Pathfinders at War*, to "a select formation, the spearhead of Bomber Command's part in the awesome destruction of Germany. The air crew members were almost totally volunteers and, despite the terrifying odds against any individual or crew completing the requisite 60-sorties tour of operations, the most feared punishment was to be sacked and posted to another unit. Such was the fierce pride and dedication of the Pathfinder Force."

Its role had taken Joe Emery over one German city after another and even across the Alps into northern Italy. More than once, with searchlights reaching out to catch and blind and intimidate the crew — to him, the worst affliction of all — with night fighters coming after them, more than once he had looked back with wonder on the appetite for adventure that had gotten him into the air force in the first place. But he kept on.

The night before our troopship reached Britain that month, Lieut. Paul "Bones" McCann of New Brunswick's North Shore Regiment got down on his knees and prayed out loud that we'd all do our duty and come through, and not one of the other three in the cabin said a word. We heard, but there was just this silence of our own thoughts. On a bright July day we got on a train that looked small and sounded funny, and we went through a Scottish slum. There were dirty kids in the streets and blowsy women waving, and one pulled a great breast out of her dress and laid it on a window ledge and sang-shouted a welcome to Scotland: "Will ye no come back again." Which was nice since the First Canadian Army we joined was still doing what it had been doing for more than 2 1/2 years.

But things were afoot. This was at the time Winston Churchill went to Cairo with fire in his eye, and Bill Palmer felt honored to be in the plane put at his service. He hinted at it in letters, even as he was swept up in the rumors about why Churchill had come. He'd come on his way to Moscow to tell Josef Stalin no second front could be launched in Europe in 1942 to relieve the terrible pressure on Russia. He'd come to put new generals in charge in North Africa and the Mediterranean: Sir Harold Alexander in overall charge and, under him, Sir Bernard Montgomery in charge of the Eighth Army. Only very recently it and Rommel had taken turns in attacking without changing much, but Egypt was accumulating evidence of change. Guns, trucks, hundreds of American Sherman tanks and vehicles were piling up. Bill Palmer could see them, could hear talk that Montgomery was putting new fire into the Eighth Army and that 267 Squadron would soon be involved in great events.

All he said to the folks back home was that he had seen Churchill two or three times and taken some snapshots of him. In fact, so many political and military big shots flew in Alec Noon's planes that years later he would tell his son Chris he sometimes wondered what might have happened to the war if he'd piloted them into multiple tragedy. And Chris would find confirmation in his father's log that he *had* flown Churchill in August. But all Bill Palmer felt he could do was hint — just as Canadian Douglas Appleton joined 267 and was told that Bill was its top navigator.

August was also the month a raid on the coast of France wove the name of Dieppe into Canadian history. Dieppe was the seaport and resort town in and near which nearly 5,000 Canadians landed on August 19 for what was billed as a reconnaisance in force by nearly 6,100 men, a nine-hour attack designed to help learn what would be involved in an invasion of Hitler's Europe. Two were brothers with the Queen's Own Cameron Highlanders of Winnipeg, one of six infantry battalions sacrificed in that fateful assault. Edward McManus survived. William McManus was one of the 900 Canadians who died, which is why his name came to be on the village war memorial.

The brothers came from Memramcook which was in the Parish of Dorchester and situated four or five miles up the road toward Moncton. It was a small and very French place but their non-French family had lived there since a railway-contractor McManus arrived in the 1830s. They had a big house close to the nearest liquor store. If someone in the village said he was going to Memramcook, it meant he was going to get a bottle, and that he would drive by the McManus house to get it.

By the time war came, William and Edward McManus had gone to university and William was on the staff of the Royal Bank in Saint John and Edward was with the R.C.M.P. in the West. They had an uncle who was a colonel in the Cameron Highlanders, and he told Ed he could get them officers' commissions. If he joined up as a Mountie, Ed knew, he'd go to the Provost Corps, the army police, and he didn't want to. So he got married, and when he told the Mounties they discharged him. Then he called Bill and suggested they both join the Camerons.

On that 19th of August they were both lieutenants when the Highlanders landed at Pourville, a village two miles west of Dieppe, with orders to pass through a bridgehead established by the South Saskatchewan Regiment and operate against an airdrome in conjunction with tanks coming in from Dieppe itself. The battalion went ashore late with its bagpipes sounding amid vicious enemy fire. Its commanding officer was killed immediately, and Bill McManus, the intelligence officer, fell wounded. In leading his platoon across the beach, Ed got tangled in barbed wire and one of his men came back and cut him free and they found temporary shelter in a shell hole. They were still there when they heard a strange sound and realized that a big black goat had joined them.

Bill McManus refused to be evacuated. Ed and his platoon were among those who got two miles inland, farther than any other battalion. They reached a place called Petit Appeville, overlooking heavily-defended bridges across the River Scie which they'd have to cross to reach the airdrome. There were no tanks in sight; they'd never even gotten into Dieppe. Finally, the Camerons were ordered to withdraw. They fought their way back to the beaches, found them raked by fire from high ground on both sides of Pourville. So were Royal Navy craft trying to get in to rescue them, but Ed McManus made it to one of the small boats sent in to take men out to bigger ones. He was climbing in when a soldier was wounded next to him. He pushed him into the boat and they made it to the headquarters ship where the soldier embraced him and said he'd saved his life. Bill made it back to that ship too, but he'd been wounded again in getting away. He died on the way to England.

In all, close to 70 percent of the Canadians were killed, wounded or captured in an assault that would transcend all others in Canadian remembering of the war, be linked with Hong Kong as a symbol of brief, questionable and murderous calamity. At the time, the news spread like wildfire through the army still endlessly training. Officers you knew volunteered to go to the battalions that had lost so many. For weeks, just seeing the 2nd Division's deep blue patch on a soldier's arm made you wonder if he'd been *there*. In time, Ed McManus was awarded the Military

Cross, but all he'd tell his wife was that he got it because his brother was killed.

On August 27 Pilot Officer Warren Duffy completed his 33rd mission, an attack on Kassel. In four and a half months, his first tour of operations had taken him on 26 sorties over Germany, one to France, and six to lay mines. Despite the usual initial Canadian doubts about the British, he had come to admire his British mates greatly: "some of the finest fellows I've ever known." In September, he began what would turn out to be a long spell at an operational training unit, teaching others what battle had taught him. He realized it was important but he didn't like it. He'd already been reprimanded once for flying "at a height other than prescribed" and here he was "severely reprimanded" for flying too low. He missed operational flying. "It does seem funny," one letter said, "to hear that the boys were out on a raid last night and I wasn't there. Oh well, I'll get another crack at 'them' next year."

Joe Emery was still very much involved in these raids because pathfinders seemed to go on forever. So was Flt. Sgt. Charles Gerald "Gerry" Nugent, as a wireless air gunner with No. 44 Rhodesia Squadron of the R.A.F. But Duffy's time *would* come again, in another elite.

I have no idea what the McManus brothers thought when they first joined the Cameron Highlanders, but I do know that when I reported to the Cape Breton Highlanders I had grave doubts about the reception an untough, unsure outsider would receive from the tough, clannish and abrasive coal miners war's absurdities had assigned him to lead. So I was posted to D Company, 17 platoon, and there they were: kids. A likeable bunch of 25 or 30 kids mostly in their teens or early 20s. Rough, yes, tough, yes, but humorous, irreverent, open, friendly, at times delightful.

But I suspect what did most to lead us toward common ground were the shared — and hidden, never stated — afflictions of loneliness and uncertainty.

The battalion was headquartered in a manor house in rural Surrey, and its soldiers had a reputation for being unruly, difficult, truculent. They were still talking of the fact that, soon after their arrival in late 1941, they had seen familiar leaders replaced by a commanding officer, a second-in-command, two company commanders and a regimental sergeant major, the top N.C.O., from a snooty Montreal outfit, the Black Watch of Canada. Bizarre as the mix might be, such a change was not that unusual. Once overseas, one Canadian unit after another saw the departure of top officers adjudged less than "battleworthy." But few if any reacted like the C.B.H. Here were people schooled in historic resentment of outsiders' domination being taken over by officers from a distant world of wealth and sophistication. In the spartan precincts of Aldershot, Hants, that historic heartland of British soldiering, the Highlanders refused to go on parade. They staged a sit-down strike apparently organized by a small group angry over the change in command and over food they found wanting. In fact, the whole thing came as a surprise to many of the soldiers, though one story, apparently apochryphal, is that when the new colonel stalked down their barrack lines brandishing the so-called KR Can, the red volume of army discipline, he was profanely invited to put it where it could be put only with the greatest difficulty. The insurrection was ended by assurances from a general who had served with the 85th Battalion in the Great War. The C.B.H. was not ready for battle, he said. Its soldiers needed, and now had, men who could make it ready, after which the soldiers would again have their own to lead them. Or so the storytellers said.

Time had worn off the rough edges by the time I arrived. No one seriously questioned the right of the Black Watch people to remain. In fact, I suspect I was fairly typical in getting to like and respect four of the five, including my company commander, Major Bill Ogilvie. That is, all but the colonel. He never seemed to look directly at you. He never welcomed me to the unit. He spoke to me once, with a snarl. But at least he no longer went around brandishing KR Can, and he no longer had to. Besides, there was another advantage: the C.B.H. and the Black Watch wore the same kilt.

By September, 267 Squadron had been well outside Cairo for weeks. It was in the desert, up toward obscure El Alamein. Bill Palmer was living in a tent with three English "chaps"; in one letter he even called them blokes. At first he'd found Englishmen "a bit hard to know" but after a year overseas he was "really getting along very well with them." In fact, he'd been palling around with one from the Midlands whose accent even other Britons found hard to understand. He'd been moving a lot, he reported. Been "to a great many places but I can't just say where," swum in the Dead Sea, been to Baghdad, to Jerusalem, to "some of the desert oases where some of our Canadian dates are from; I didn't think they could be so good." What his letters didn't mention was that in late September his plane crashlanded in an oasis called Kuffra. In July, he'd written that "what breeze we get, coming off the desert, is like a hot air furnace blasting at you. I'd give my right arm to have a good old English or Scottish fog for a few days." Sometimes, he said, you even sweated in the air. Two months later he said "the weather is cooler, in fact it gets quite cool in the evenings so the flies are not quite as bad as they were. In time they will disappear. Really they are a menace. You can't rest without a net." Then there were lots of sandstorms, "and they are no fun; they're similar to a blizzard but the dust chokes you and the sand stings."

He was wearing shorts. His arms and knees were dark from the desert sun. He was playing some softball, and "God knows there's lots of space to play in." But he still felt cut off. Letters from home could take a month or more. He never heard from overseas Dorchester boys, and never saw a casualty list so the only way he knew of friends being killed was from the odd letter or the grapevine. Twice he wrote he was sending pictures home in which he didn't look too happy. In one, he said, he looked "very sad and morose." In another, he said, he wasn't "as downhearted as I look." In mid-October 267's Sgt. Walter Plant was killed in a plane crash. His parents knew the name and it would be in the casualty lists, so he confessed that "I'll feel very lost without him as we have been together since last year in England, and the death leaves me the only Canadian sergeant here. But I'm with a good bunch of boys so it will be O.K."

"Don't worry," he kept writing, but he sounded a bit sad and, in his own word, lost, and the nights were getting cold. Still, though, the buildup kept growing along that stretch of sand at the northern end of jungle and enormous Africa even if he couldn't write about it. It was only what Jack Rice said in a later interview that indicated what might have been going on when Bill Palmer's plane crashlanded in the oasis of Kuffra. Rice said his own plane was destroyed about this time by enemy action in that oasis. He was engaged, he said, in "special operations." It would eventually be revealed that these had made 267 part of 216 Group's Mobile Operations Force "which involved Western Desert support and casevac (casualty evacuation)." The post-war article in a publication of the Aero Club of East Africa would say Alec Noon and other 267 airmen established fuel dumps far behind the German lines so Allied fighter planes would be able to pursue the enemy when the time came.

In Toronto, Bill's sister Eileen and her husband Cpl. John Sweeney, R.C.A.F., had an apartment mobile villagers would come to visit or go out for a beer or a hockey game and add to folklore. Did you hear about Percy Mitton, they'd say? Percy who'd come home jobless in the Depression and now held the lowliest rank in the air force. Only recently he'd put up at the fancy Royal York Hotel and someone reported that he'd gone up to the desk and announced that his linen was to be changed at once, and the clerk said "Yes, sir, at once," and it was done. And him with the ass out of his pants only a few years back.

Did you hear, they'd say, about how Melvin Sollows got Doug Johnson to join the navy as soon as he hit 18? Doug who'd been so crazy about hockey that he'd play before breakfast, eat with his skates on, then play a bit more before school. In the shortcut fields at times he'd meet Gottfried Klotz and they'd wrestle for fun or for the hell of it, but Gottfried had gone by the time Doug quit school in Grade 9 and got chumming around with Melvin who'd quit in Grade 7 when he realized he could make 25 cents an hour building highways, and who had also wrestled with Gottfried Klotz, liked and admired him because he was so smart. The navy was a natural for Melvin because he was one of numerous children of Bill Sollows who'd come to the village as a sailor, got married and decided to try farming and do what people called day's work. So now this son had Doug Johnson in the same navy but not in the same ship. Doug was on a corvette making convoy runs to Ireland and Melvin was on a minesweeper and keeping his eye out for Gottfried Klotz in case he'd joined the German navy and was out there on the same cold, hard sea. You never knew, he'd say.

Did you hear, they'd say in the Toronto apartment, that

Gerald Adshade lied about his age and got into the army at 16, and his brother Weldon is in it too, and his father Dave who got a medal in 1914-18, but his brother Doug got turned down? Did you hear about Edgar Ison and Vic Thornton and Ken Campbell? About how they wanted to go into the navy together but it didn't work out, so Vic and Ken joined the army and Edgar joined the air force. He did and he flunked at wireless but not at being an air gunner, the worst place the air force could put you. Did you hear, they'd say, about Betty McCabe? Feisty little Betty who had in 1941 become one of the first 500 21-year-old women to be recruited by the Women's Division (W.D.) of the air force and was working in the records division on Ottawa's Dows Lake and getting a $1 a day allowance to live in an apartment with a W.D. friend. The word was that she was hoping to get overseas when they let the W.D.s go, but wherever she was there would be another village pivot.

There was still another on trains full of uniforms, full of life, the hoboes gone, nobody on the roofs going to one nowhere from another, everybody going somewhere from somewhere with the government paying the bills. Gurney was on the trains, black Gurney Martin, erstwhile farmhand; he'd become a porter and whenever he met a villager they'd talk about home, and Gurney said he'd had a step up, he was "on the linen," but wanted it known that it hadn't gone to his head. And when they passed through Moncton they knew that in an office there was a symbol of what the war had done that the Depression had denied. That at the heart of new electronic equipment that guided trains running endlessly into Halifax was H.L. Smith. The same Harvey who had labored in the village station for 17 years and now was on his way to a career that would put him in charge of dispatching for the entire C.N.R. and let him travel the country in a private car, living the life of Riley and loving it.

Wherever they met, villagers plugged into a network of news and nostalgia. From England, Gunner Greenberg wrote Eileen (Palmer) Sweeney's father a second letter in which he said he'd heard she'd been married and it didn't surprise him a bit, but he wondered where she was. The war was mixing people up so much that this was happening everywhere. After it was over, and her marriage had broken up, Eileen would say she got married to get to where things were happening. That's how she got to the pivotal Toronto apartment, and knew Hazen had written that he was so used to driving vehicles in the blackout that he was "like a cat in the dark." He supposed, he added, "that the old town looks awful funny in a blackout." Things kept triggering thoughts about the old town: "We had a snowstorm but there is only four inches of snow. The roads are all ice, cars and trucks sliding all over the place. It makes a fellow think of Canada." But he had not seen any of the boys for three months; "I can't find out where they are." He wanted Bill Palmer's address; he had a leave coming up and would like to see him. "Chins Up!" he said. "V for Victory."

In Africa, Bill too wondered what it was like back home. "It must be awfully dead in Dorchester," he wrote that fall, and the answer was that it was and it wasn't. It was, by and large, stripped down to people in school or past military age, yet even so the war had proved to be a liberating force, had put an overall social purpose back into life, and in this sense the old hometown was far from dead. As Ed Oulton's daughter Shirley would say, it didn't feel left out of the war, it felt very much part of it, of backing up both those in uniform and civilians in beleaguered Britain.

You take Mrs. Bob Sinclair. She had two sons overseas, and she was up to her ears in a crusade to help them and all who served with them. As "the war convener" of the

I.O.D.E., she even had some of the distinction of generals in charge of theatres of war. Every weekday people saw her going through town and up to the Anglican hall. They'd look out the store windows and they'd say, "There goes Bella," and no one found it strange that here was a Presbyterian going to a Church of England hall. The crusade just wiped out that sort of stuff and replaced it with a flood of parcels of food and cigarettes and other goods to be dispatched overseas. Then thanks would come back, and the I.O.D.E. and the Red Cross would pitch in to do more.

Yes, the I.O.D.E. and the Red Cross were both at it, and some ladies belonged to both, and both were using the Anglican Hall and smiling about it even if there was just a touch of rivalry, a feeling that the ladies of the Imperial Order Daughters of the Empire thought (at least privately) that in any social measurement they would end up preeminent. The Imperial Daughters turned up good leaders such as Mrs. Bill Hickman, and they did a heap of knitting and quilting and other things. But it was the Red Cross that had the resolute and dynamic Mrs. Colin Campbell. A nurse, she was the heart and soul of its activities. Nobody had had any doubt that she was a great organizer since she'd arrived in town in the '30s, the mature bride of a nice, quiet prison guard, and quickly pitched in to get things going and shape things up. When the war came along, she simply coalesced with it. She even used talents she didn't have: couldn't sing worth a darn but that didn't stop her from teaching kids how to sing old war songs so they could stage a concert and raise money for the Red Cross.

In this and other ways, the war was a great time for people to feel involved. You had kids in high school who had every intention, when they graduated, of enlisting, but in the meantime they had good reason for believing that the ones overseas would be impressed by what was happening at their old school. The Cadet Corps had boys drilling with pieces of wood as weapons; you had to be 16 or so to get into the reserve army and get a uniform and be trained by Robert Crosson, a guard who had two sons in the services. Boys were climbing the ladder into that dusty attic and learning how to shoot, and eventually girls were too, girls wearing boys' pants because they might otherwise be seen in an improper way from below. Nothing had prepared Mr. Reinsborrow for all this, and more; L.E. Reinsborrow, that is, the excellent principal, who taught the boys some soldiering because someone had to, drilled them, gave instructions in field craft, map reading, first aid, in handling small arms and coping with poison gas. When word came that girls were to be taught to shoot, he taught them too. Returned man Clarence Hicks, the station agent, taught boys how to send messages in morse code. Cadet Corporal John Emmerson taught how to send signals with flags. An army captain warmly praised what he saw of platoon, squad and section drills, rifle exercises, first aid, physical exercises, and John Emmerson's class.

It was typical of a small community that when Mrs. Campbell got a letter from England expressing thanks for a case of apple jelly she could pass the thanks along to the school's cadets because they had picked the apples. In the school, Mrs. Campbell was also involved in the Junior Red Cross which Mr. Reinsborrow helped get going. It was drawing an average of 50 to meetings, and it had Mrs. Campbell and others guiding groups right down to grade seven. The things it was turning out were usually sent to British families. In one school year, the members made one large quilt, 24 small ones, six turtle-neck tuck-in scarves, three bonnets, six scarves, and seven sweaters for infants and children. They also made sweaters and woollen headgear for sailors plus mitts with the trigger finger missing. A school club was knitting, working on scrapbooks for seamen, collecting comic books for children in hospitals, and there were concerts, dances and war bond drives, and cigarette-package tinsel and paper were collected and recycled. There was even an organization to cope with air raids, with returned men like Ed Oulton and Frank A. Dobson involved, and from time to time sirens or horns blew for practice blackouts; hardly a light all the way from the Elmer Lewis garage to the Micmac houses on the far side of town. If that wasn't enough to impress Gunner Greenberg and Flt. Sgt. Palmer, there also were signs warning that walls had ears, that the enemy could be anywhere, so watch what you say. Ed Oulton's daughter Shirley even began to have nightmares about German bombers setting the town on fire and her father climbing a ladder with buckets of water to save the family home.

Chapter Eight

IN THE MORNINGS, THE batmen of the Cape Breton Highlanders came to cold Nissen huts to arouse their officers for the day. Mine was Pius Hickey, an admirable young man who would do brave things after the war as a draegerman engaged in the rescuing of imperilled coal miners. Lieut. Karl Sullivan's batman was Pte. MacLean, R.H., otherwise known as Bowser, a small, chunky character with a beaked nose and ornate qualities associated with his island home. In their case, ritual became a thing of parts and layers. Picture it:

Having only recently escaped from a rifle company, Private MacLean arrives as the image of circumspection. He gently touches Lieutenant Sullivan who is hunkered down in a sleeping bag on a canvas bed. He quietly discloses that it is time to arise, and Lieutenant Sullivan as quietly agrees. Lieutenant Sullivan has a large nose. In their own process of arising, several other junior officers can just see it protruding from the sleeping bag, where in point of fact it remains. Eight to ten minutes elapse. Private MacLean returns and shakes more pointedly the sleeping bag which continues to contain Lieutenant Sullivan. He announces that both breakfast and the first parade of the day are in the immediate offing and that, in his opinion, it is definitely time for his officer to arise. More than the nose of Lieutenant Sullivan emerges, and he is heard to agree. Eight to ten minutes elapse. Private MacLean returns to find Lieutenant Sullivan in precisely the same position in which he had last perceived him. It is the third time of asking, and he finds himself yielding to the opinion that you can take the requirements of morning ritual back into the most distant stipulations of master-servant relationships, but three times are enough. He abandons army protocol. He adopts Cape Breton protocol. He descends upon Lieutenant Sullivan with a profane fury. "You son of a bitch, Sullivan," he says in part, "get out of that xxxxxxx sleeping bag or I'll xxxx your xxxx in xxx," and Lieutenant Sullivan at last arises. He is a tall, powerful man in his early 30s who after years in the militia finds it hard to understand why he is not the captain he feels he is entitled to be. He towers above Private MacLean, but does not threaten to charge him with insubordination, does not rebuke him, does not even chide or scold him, because if he did any of these things how would he get up the next day and the next and the ones after that?

On October 23, 1942, Warrant Officer Palmer — he'd had another promotion — sat down to write home, and he said, "I'm writing this in one of our sandstorms and every time the wind blows our tent jerks around with the result our table moves, thus the jerky scrawl." The intriguing thing is that even as history was being made in the immediate vicinity, he wrote the same kind of letter he'd been writing for months. For October 23 was the day the Eighth Army attacked at El Alamein and began to make it the place that would forever signify where the Western Allies started winning the war. In the sandstorm desert,

Bill Palmer was part of the backup force, the casualty-clearing force, and he must have been close enough to hear the guns or at least to know it wouldn't be long before he did. But you couldn't tell it from what he wrote. "Must close," he said. "Will write soon. All my love."

But it was November 17 before he wrote again, "I'm afraid," he confessed, "I've not kept my promise of writing once a week. This is the first letter I have been able to write for about three weeks, but I just haven't had time. As you know, things have been moving pretty briskly out here, and we all are kept fairly busy. I guess it's worth it though as things are beginning to look much better." He admitted that he had not expected Montgomery's "initial success," but things *were* looking much better in the desert, just as they were in the Soviet Union.

There, by November 17, the German Sixth Army was surrounded in the prolonged and vicious fighting for the city of Stalingrad on Russia's Volga River, and the Germans were reeling back on two North African fronts. On one, the Eighth Army had not only routed the Desert Fox at El Alamein after days of attack, it had had his Afrika Korps on the run for two weeks. Far to the west, British and American troops were fighting to exploit the first great seaborne invasion of the war, a November 8 multiple landing in Algeria and French Morocco. After more than three years of war, Germany was floundering in Russia and running out of the advantages the democracies had allowed her to acquire. In Africa, though hundreds of miles apart, the two prongs of a great pincer movement were threatening to close around her forces on the fringes of a continent where tens of thousands were still learning the facts of African life. "I sleep with four blankets over me," Bill Palmer wrote. He was wearing heavy battledress and a sweater, and they felt good.

For 267 Squadron, these *were* busy days. It was divided

into two sections, and with fighter planes guarding them their transports were leap-frogging each other to keep up with the Eighth Army advance, to keep it supplied and take out its wounded, to establish more fuel dumps behind the enemy lines. When there was no need to do so, they sat in the desert, waiting. They kept making landings on godforsaken strips of runway, putting stuff off, going back for more. Across Cyrenaica. Into Libya. While Rommel, short of tanks and fuel, fought in retreat with the skills he'd revealed in attack, and the Germans were bringing in troops to keep the vice from closing on him. While the desert lived as it had before they came and would live long after they'd gone.

"There is quite a sandstorm blowing," Bill Palmer wrote on the 17th, "and last night we had a heavy rain which is rather unusual." So were the things heavy rains could do. Douglas Appleton would remember wet, blowing sand sealing him and others in a tent for hours. He'd remember the desert for its monotony, loneliness and isolation and the way it could fray your nerves and your animosities. He had a dog he came to love, which was more orthodox than the monkey someone else had. He had a boss he came to hate. He had a squadron mate who went crazy, and he became convinced the boss did too. Bill Palmer, he'd say, would have known exactly what he felt and what it was like to fly above 10,000 feet when you could go faster but oxygen supply was iffy. But on the 17th, with a day off ("I hope," he wrote at 9.30 a.m.), Bill Palmer reported he was "getting on very well." Perhaps his morale was rising with the rising of Allied fortunes, but for one thing. His mother had written that Gerry Nugent, his pal, was missing in action. "I was terribly sorry to hear about Gerry," he wrote. "There isn't much I can say. I certainly hope they have had better news but I don't want to raise false hopes. I've seen it happen a great number of times and nothing is heard again." Those reported missing, he meant, usually were dead, and about solid Gerry Nugent he was right. He'd been killed over Denmark on October 1, aged 22, with all six others in a Lancaster crew. The R.A.F. said it was presumed they died from enemy action.

Even after Dieppe, army life seemed suspended somewhere between fundamentals and make-believe. The syllabus of the Cape Breton Highlanders called, among other things, for a period of anti-aircraft training. It consisted of the soldiers pointing their rifles or Tommy guns in the air and saying, "bang, bang, I got you" and more expressive things. I had fired a rifle and one two-inch mortar shell but not a revolver, not a Tommy gun, not a Bren gun. My only instructions for using a lieutenant's revolver came from Lieut. Tommy Lowe, an ex-Mountie. In spontaneous solicitude, he took me aside and showed me. I had never thrown a grenade, had no idea what to do in a minefield, or even what a mine looked like.

Yet being with the unit was like being in a village, even a family, again. The battalion was where you belonged and, as an outlander, you got to sense Cape Breton and/or soldier ways ranging from collective responses to imposed authority to the quickness of asserted indignation. When new Lee Enfield rifles were issued, such was the soldiers' abrupt discovery of merits in the old and replaced .303s that the orders to give them up became an act of folly and an abuse of power. But it was good to be among them. During a softball game, one said he heard I came from Dorchester and that he also had been resident there — for "a little touch of break and enter." We got to be good friends. Bowser MacLean was usually around, barking assertions, scratching his irrepressible identity into the formats of eternity. Half a century later I would remember many of their names and faces: Sam Matthews, Sandy MacDonald, Randy Steele, Gordie Serroul, Eddie McKinnon, Gordie Bell, the young and quiet corporal Don Adams, the older and quiet corporal Billy MacLeod, 17 Platoon's big able sergeant Gus MacLellan, and an older ex-miner said to play his violin best in the bathtub, loaded.

They'd tell you stories. In a group heading for Glasgow on leave was a black, and the others weren't sure what Scots would think of him wearing a balmoral; what the Scots did was buy him drinks. They had pride in a member of the pipe band who'd been in the Great War; they'd tell you that once, as a stretcher bearer, he was carrying a wounded prisoner and when the German got sassy he got dumped off a bridge to his final detriment. One favorite expression was, "Give 'em guts," which could apply to comrades in arms, particularly 48th Highlanders who suffered from the affliction of coming from Toronto; they'd "put the Cape Breton boxing gloves to them," their big army boots. The men were largely Cape Bretoners but a majority of officers came from mainland Nova Scotia and other provinces. Shaped by frictions between mine superiors and workers, the men looked upon all officers with impiety, sometimes with a vague affection as enemies they could not attack and allies they could not avoid. They knew every officer quirk. That Lieut. David MacGregor Neish had at least three different kilts associated with elements of his Scottish ancestry. That Lieut. O.J. Price had a thing about explosives and loved to blow them up. That Captain Archibald, from Truro, loved to tease Lieut. Tony MacLachlan about coming from nearby Great Village, "if you can find it behind a billboard." That Maj. Aird Nesbitt was called "the man with the tired voice." That in Lieut. Gordie Logan you saw an earthy excellence. That in Lieut. F.X. MacNeil of Iona you got the true rural Cape Bretoner. He'd tell of his grandmother's admonition when he departed for the worldiness of Halifax: "Now, F.X., ye'll be saying your prayers each night and ye'll go to confession regularly, F.X., and each Sunday to mass and mind, F.X., ye'll keep your eyes on them black Protestants."

The presence of so many officer outsiders bespoke a history that had denied Cape Breton an economy that would have bred more leaders of their own. It also may explain what happened when some of the island ones met a fellow Cape Bretoner in the uniform of an R.C.A.F. pilot. He had the Distinguished Flying Cross and when he came for a visit they were delighted to have him in the mess; Maj. Allie McSween smiled as though he'd received an unexpected legacy.

Maj. Charles Crandall and some other village soldiers spent Christmas 1942 in a cold northern place. In Labrador. After three winters of coastal patrols, the New Brunswick Rangers were involved in a new monotony as guardians of an airport being constructed at Goose Bay as a link in the movement of warplanes to Britain. Of their life there, Lieut. P.R. Robinson would write: "Here was a land destined to challenge the pioneering spirit of every man, a land of heavy forest, impenetrable muskeg and sandy soil; a land of Eskimos, rugged, wild, extreme in temperature ... No cheery billets, nothing but vast loneliness and canvas tents." Life did pivot for months on tents, and what could be done to make them liveable. "Each man," Robinson would write, "became his own architect." They dug deep holes in the sand, lined them with slabs from a sawmill run by the firm building the airport, made chimneys of tin cans, stoves of discarded oil barrels, erected the tents overhead, covered them with sand. In addition, the men eventually got their own mess building, as did the officers and sergeants. In fact, officers had a special reason for celebrating on Christmas Eve. They moved their mess out of two marquees and a hospital tent into a not-quite-finished building.

The winter would be well along before barracks were available, and by then Lieut. Richard Emmerson had his own reason for remembering it as a sequel to previous humiliations. As Doctor Emmerson, he'd had an osteopath practice in Illinois when the Japanese attacked Pearl Harbor. He'd offered his services to the U.S. forces only to be turned down because he wasn't American. Then he'd been welcomed into the Royal Canadian Army Medical Corps, only to become a private doing menial duties. So he'd transferred to the Rangers, and that's how he got to Rigolet, a tiny place some 75 miles east of Goose Bay, at the ocean end of a narrow inlet to lanky Lake Melville, at the end of which the new airport was being built. Lieutenant Emmerson was posted there as head of an outpost garrison. He had 17 men and two dated French guns to defy any enemy challenge. Sometimes, in modest moments, he would describe his detachment as a small house-keeping group. In more hilarious moments, he would readjust his status in light of the fact that Rigolet could be seen as a strategic place. For all the Germans had to do was rise above their problems in Russia, Africa and under bombing at home, cross an ocean and strike. When moved by such thoughts, he would speak of himself as the Supreme Allied Commander of Rigolet.

In England's cold weather there were complaints about the food and it was hard to keep warm. For even as the forces built up — both the Americans and the Canadians alone were there in the tens of thousands now — it got harder to get stuff to them and to the British public. For one basic reason: the Battle of the Atlantic was raging to a climax and taking a ghastly toll of Allied shipping. No one told that to the Cape Breton Highlanders or in detail to the world, but it explains why Corporal Freddie MacDonald kept asking the orderly officer of the day to examine what was in his mess tin. "Just stick your finger in there, sir," he'd say, "and see if you can find one piece of meat. Just one ... What in hell is going on?" No one really knew what was going on. What you did know was that some of it was unusual, and that it included more than meatless stew.

By this time the battalion was ensconsed on a beautiful Sussex estate pocked with round-shouldered Nissen huts ideal for letting the cold in and the heat out at a time when there was little fuel. By the time the colonel called in junior officers, the soldiers of 17 Platoon were not only threatening to slay at least one of several resident swans, they were burning any wood they could find. The colonel said he was not giving orders but would not find it amiss if the platoons were led forth in search of wood, axes having been obtained from some unstated source. Wood, someone noted, was found in trees, and trees were found in copses and forests, with which the estate was to some extent blessed. So dispatched by truck, 17 Platoon halted on a country road among numerous trees. There was only one problem. In a setting like something out of a Thomas Hardy novel, there was a humble cottage with smoke coming from the chimney, and so positioned that the householder might object to violence being done to the trees among which he dwelt. Might, indeed, be there to ensure that violence was not done.

When the lieutenant knocked, a man opened the cottage door and asked what was wanted, at first seeing only the lieutenant. Then he beheld some 25 soldiers in military formation, three abreast. "We wonder," he was told, "whether you would mind if we cut down a tiny part of this large forest to provide a warmth our huts are lacking." The countryman took a second look and said he didn't see how he could prevent it. The wood was green but it was better than nothing.

In the village, some people said one aspect of the Battle of the Atlantic was right out there in Shepody Bay, very close to Coles Point, and the reason, they said, was what Hans Klotz had done when he lived there: he'd sent Hitler information about the bay and now the submarines were using it. They had to surface frequently to store oxygen and charge their batteries, and one place they did it was in this obscure offshoot of Fundy. So it was said. So it was said in varying and erroneous versions in many places, and the rumors had only gotten worse since the submarines sank some 20 ships in Canadian coastal waters between May and late October. In some places there were even stories that German sailors came ashore to buy food and go to dances and movies. At least, however, no one reported seeing Gottfried Klotz at one of the concerts or plays organized by Mrs. Campbell or at a high school dance to raise funds for the war effort. No one could report a personal sighting of a U-boat in the bay either, but there were those who had heard someone else had.

In fact, Gottfried Klotz *was* going to occasional dances at this time — in villages some 25 miles below besieged Leningrad. Though they were not supposed to fraternize, at least not too much, sometimes at night the German soldiers of his signals unit would go to local dances and try to flirt and dance with the Russian girls. Sometimes there were fewer Russian males there than there might have been because some were out in the darkness cutting the communication lines Obergefreiter Klotz's unit had laid. In the mornings the Germans would round up the same Russians to repair or replace the very lines they had damaged or destroyed. In the cold and lengthening nights, soldiers sneaked behind the Russians' own lines and tapped into their communication nets to hear what they were saying. Some soldiers played chess and cards, and Obergefreiter Klotz worked at teaching himself trigonometry. Once he laughed as he remembered demonstrating how to do a math problem his own way and Principal March being taken aback because he'd taught it another.

Bill Palmer spent Christmas in the desert. In London a year back he'd had those two big dinners; in the desert he had one, but it was a triumph: tomato soup, roast turkey, pork sausage and onion stuffing, roast potatoes, green peas, Christmas pudding with brandy sauce, bananas, oranges and nuts, all topped off with beer and what the English called minerals. He'd been flying Christmas Eve and Christmas morning and didn't get back till 10 a.m. to his half of 267. The reason was that the squadron had to deliver the ingredients for thousands of such dinners to scattered army and air force units. Montgomery had promised them, and 267 fulfilled his promise.

By this time it was supporting two Hurricane fighter squadrons based *behind* the German lines, still had Malta as its priority destination, and Mussolini's triumphant arch in the desert — nicknamed Marble Arch — was covered with the graffiti of his foes. Montgomery had his Eighth Army heading for Tripoli behind the retreating enemy, and amid all the excitement Bill Palmer had been having a memorable time. He'd made trips from one end of Africa to the other and from one side to the other. He'd flown over Addis Ababa, Ethiopia's capital, and spent time near the equator. He spoke of the flying record of Alec Noon — more than 4,000 hours compared to his own 700 — and the implication was that for at least part of the time he'd been visiting in Kenya, where Noon's wife and child lived. He'd been in South Africa, where Nursing Sister Emily Emmerson treated casualties he may well have flown south. He also said he'd been in Algiers, headquarters of American General Dwight Eisenhower for the fighting in Northwest Africa. In fact, Alec Noon and his crew had been busy flying General Alexander and other important people to meetings about how to link up the two armies closing in on the enemy.

In a letter he wrote one day after Christmas, W.O. Palmer said that when he and the wireless operator were in a sergeants' mess in Algiers, they were so tanned they stood out like sore thumbs among the pale men just out from Britain. Unless the war ended, he didn't see any chance of getting home for a long time, but his health was very good and he liked Egypt better than England, "although I wouldn't dare tell an Englishman that." He was "very well established in the squadron," he said and, barring bad luck, he should get out of the war alive. He'd even saved $450 toward that happy day.

Far away that Christmas Private Gerald Adshade was thinking of luck and life in different terms. The two years since he'd lied about his age to enlist had turned out to be one long anti-climax, one endless series of army postings in Canada. Then this Christmas present: he'd just arrived in Fort Benning, Georgia, U.S.A. His documents said he was two years older than the 18 he finally was, but that no longer mattered. What mattered was that he was going to be trained to be a paratrooper which was just about as glamorous a job as a soldier could hope to get.

In the lines of the C.B.H. there was a big parade.

Chapter Eight

General Andy McNaughton stood on a raised position beside the colonel and other dignitaries to review one more element of the dagger that was becoming a dilemma. Parades are one way this is done: a battalion's soldiers march past a given point at which each platoon in turn salutes those on the reviewing stand by turning eyes right. It is important that they look impressive because these are ways of revealing how ready they are for battle.

On this day the leading platoon was No. 17, and there I was in front of it, in front of the entire battalion, and I was flustered and nervous and something happened. In front of General Andy and the colonel and my platoon and God knows who else, I began to twitch and stumble, my body, my face, contorted. My old problem had caught up with me. It had come close before in the three or four months I'd been with the unit, but I'd always been able to control it in time. Now I couldn't. There was too much else on my mind, and by the time I did get control we were past the reviewing stand, and I was torn, humbled, humiliated, empty.

This time there were three army doctors, three psychiatrists or psychologists, a panel, and one was the doctor I'd seen in Camp Aldershot, N.S. They started to ask questions and I said I'd like first to say one thing: that I had no desire to kill or be killed, that I certainly had doubts about my ability to lead men in battle, but I was not trying to get out of it. I was quite willing to go if they so decided. The questioning went on for what seemed like a long time, and when it was over I was so worked up that I was seized by one of the worst contortions I'd ever known. In their report, the doctors said it was undoubtedly authentic. They also said it would not be right either for my men or myself to send me into battle, and they lowered my medical category accordingly. They also said I shouldn't expect to go home, and I said that was fine by me.

Obergefreiter Klotz's signals unit was spending the winter in small, snow-draped villages south of Leningrad. It was very cold up there in the north, but he considered himself lucky. His unit had houses to live in and they had enough food and clothing to face the brute Russian climate, and he was continuing to learn the lessons that soldiers learn in the interests of comfort and survival. For one thing, he wore three pairs of socks inside high French army boots. French army boots? Yes, but when someone asked him where he got them all he said was, "In a war you can get almost anything." He had learned what rank could mean: though the soldiers were under orders not to fraternize with Russian women, their company officers found it possible to share their quarters and their lives with three Russian women who were said to be maids and cooks and housekeepers.

He learned that the farther you were from home the longer leave you got. When the time came for one, he said he came not from Saxony but from more distant Bavaria. When he got home, he heard of the harsh way Russian prisoners of war were being treated, that German girls were punished if they tried to give them things. It disturbed him. He listened to Allied radio broadcasts and learned how things were going in the National Hockey League. He learned that military production was going underground to escape Allied bombing, and he saw so many signs that Germany had its own version of what Churchill called the Tail, so many servicemen based far from the fronts, that he told an uncle it was hard to see how the war could be won. He saw and heard what the bombing raids were doing to German cities and civilians, and he felt ashamed that he had it much better than this. He heard that in bombing raids people kept documents with them so they'd be able to prove to a peacetime bureaucracy that they had, in fact, existed and were entitled to certain things. At the same time, he could only imagine what the people of Leningrad were going through under perpetual shellfire, bombing, hunger, sickness and winter's vicious cold. What they were going through was a siege that wouldn't let up and a hell they refused to quit. They were surrounded except for one thin supply line from the north. They continued to die in the thousands every week. But their city wouldn't.

To the south, in February, the Russians completed the defeat of a German Sixth Army that had been surrounded at Stalingrad for weeks and denied by Hitler's order any chance of fighting its way out. By then Obergefreiter Klotz knew Germany could not win the war, but it still wasn't something you talked about. He no longer carried a New Testament but he did read a testament of a quite different kind. He and his sergeant read Hitler's *Mein Kampf* and compared notes, and the thought came that what Hitler was doing in Russia he had planned to do all along. Including when one Gottfried Klotz was writing a Grade 10 essay which said quite different things.

They posted me to London to serve in public relations, where I first saw how valuable women soldiers could be. As advisers to the army hierarchy, the colonel and his top aide, a major, might handle matters of public policy with ease, but they were stymied by a delicate issue in their own office: a comely Scot, an unmarried civilian member of the staff, had become very obviously pregnant, and they didn't know what to do about it. Then someone suggested they seek the advice of street-smart Pte. Bea Belyea of the Canadian Women's Army Corps (C.W.A.C.) She sat for a time listening to them talk evasively about the threat to moral standards in great cities at war, the temptations to, you know, and the necessity for public relations itself, in the interests of its own reputation, to, you know. Then, with one sentence, Private Belyea brought the discussion to focus. "Are you trying to tell me," she said, "that Heather is knocked up? Everyone knows she's knocked up."

"Yes, yes, yes," the colonel sighed. "Exactly. But what do we do?"

"Make me a promise," said Private Belyea. "Promise me her job will be here when she's ready to come back, and she'll be gone tomorrow." Heather was gone the next day.

The major, Eric Gibbs, was far more certain in handling another problem. A leading American magazine writer came in keen to do a story on Andy McNaughton's sedentary dagger or "mechanized hell on wheels," and Gibbs talked him out of it. He may have done this because it was embarrassing to have writers lauding an army in its fourth year of not doing what armies are recruited to do. Or it may have been that he knew its long time of waiting was coming to an end.

Lieut. Andrew Emery was in Scotland that May of 1943 when he got a long-distance call. It was from his kid brother Joe, who knew the call would have to be pretty important to get Andy away from what he was doing. For his Ordnance Corps unit and the rest of the 1st Division were finally getting ready to go into, yes, action. But what Joe was calling about *was* important enough to make Andy say that, yes, by golly, he'd be there. So he travelled to London in his best uniform and he told Joe how proud and happy he was to go to Buckingham Palace to see this 21-year-old brother go forward on cue to have His Majesty King George VI pin the ribbon of the Distinguished Flying Cross on his chest.

He might kid about it but it didn't even bother Andy that Joe outranked him, that he had flown scores of bombing missions and been promoted to flight lieutenant, the equivalent of an army captain. The rank reflected the fact that he had become a member of a pathfinder unit, an experience that had inevitably shaped him. Someone would keep a newspaper clipping about him being interviewed right after one raid and shrugging it off as routine. Increasingly, he found, those he talked with, shared his life with, were pathfinder survivors like himself: "We became a group unto ourselves. We shared a feeling that nothing could happen to us, and we paid no attention to newcomers." The pathfinder code was that you simply went on and on, and it was for going doggedly on that he'd been awarded his medal. He had, in fact, shot down one German plane but the citation didn't mention this. This is what it said:

> This officer has taken part in many operational sorties as wireless operator/air gunner. He has always shown the greatest determination to achieve his objective and on many occasions has played a large part in locating and attacking the target successfully despite heavy opposition.

In Moncton, by opening her home in hospitality, my mother was doing a splendid job of making young British airmen feel good about Canada. My brother Jim was in British Columbia, one of thousands of soldiers sent in to guard Canada's coast from the Japanese who had no intention of attacking it. He was married to a Ukrainian-Canadian named Olga Waslyk whom he'd met out there. I was the father of a daughter born in March. Hank had arrived in England as a corporal in the air force, an armorer, which meant that he had to see that planes like those Joe Emery flew in went into action armed to be as destructive as possible.

I got word that he'd arrived and on the spur of the moment, on a weekend, I jumped on a train and headed for Bournemouth. It hadn't occurred to me that I'd arrive in a strange city in the blackout and with no idea where to go. I started to walk but it was so dark that when I saw a sliver of light in a doorway I knocked, and an R.A.F. sergeant did something in keeping with one of the ways in which the war was wonderful. He invited me in for the night. He and half a dozen others were having a party, and one sergeant got me aside and said what pleased him most about the war was that it had made the English realize they couldn't get along without the Welch. He was very serious. It did not amuse him when I laughed; laughed because England was at that moment stuffed with armed Canadians, Americans, New Zealanders, Australians, Poles, Czechs and an almost incredible variety of others. So stuffed that only recently, at a seminar at Oxford University, an elderly wisp of a lady had said something just as revealing. She was helping her professor son entertain visiting servicemen, and an American captain said she seemed reluctant to say something she'd like to say. Well, yes, she confessed, there was one aspect of the presence of hundreds of thousands of armed Americans that made her worry: were those terrible Chicago gangsters among them? The captain said he was sure President Roosevelt would not allow such a thing, and the wisp of a lady said how relieved she was to hear it.

In this crowded England, Hank was soon writing letters. He wrote one to June Hazen, a great granddaughter of Mrs. Teed, in which he said how good it had been to leave the snows of Canada and behold hills and fields bathed in green. "The tiny train that carried us south was like a toy," he said, "and puffed very hard on all grades. As we passed through the towns, children waved and cheered and shouted greetings and asked for souvenirs. In the towns every vacant lot was divided into cultivated plots and in the country most of the fields were tilled because the people over here don't want to go hungry next winter. We left the train at an almost fairyland place where the public gardens sported two miles of flowers and hotels were as plentiful as fleas on a dog's back.

This was Bournemouth, and already he had decided "I'll never understand the English. As one of our chaps put it, 'We just don't fit.'" Where they did fit was into Canada's No.6 Bomber Group which had begun operations in January and contained a dozen or so of the more than 30 Canadian squadrons now in Britain. Hank went to one of them, and found "farm girls working in the fields right on the airport. As a matter of fact, women are in evidence in every capacity, and work like Trojans." There was a nearby village "so picturesque, what with the red tile roofs blotched with the green of age, and the village church covered with vines and perched on a knoll like an overlord frowning on the subjects below, and the neat thorn hedges that serve as fences and much more pleasing to the eye. And the inevitable pub...I met the venerable gardener to the vicar, and chatted of the river tide and the number of crows and rooks about this season and the beautiful song of the lark."

"I like England," he said. As thousands would find, it grew on you.

In his mail box at the garage one day Elmer Lewis found a postcard from Bud Brian. It had been mailed to the village from Edinburgh, Scotland, and it said: "Having a swell time here. Lots of Bars! Wish you were with us." Private Brian was on leave, and George Breau and Art Black were in all likelihood with him, because they did everything they could together. In the 14th Field

Ambulance, they were known as the Three Bs, as pals who liked to do together what the postcard said they were doing in Scotland. They liked to party, and at times this didn't matter and at times it did, and in one case they were broken up, separated in the ranks, and this was part of how the Bud Brian-Len Shea thing developed.

They were, in fact, contrasts going back as far as armies go. Len Shea had been in Charlie Crandall's Dorchester Army. He took discipline seriously, and saw it as a route to advancement during the war and in his hospital career later. When he became a corporal he wanted to be a sergeant, and this he would in time become because he liked and took the responsibility that could make it possible. Bud Brian, on the other hand, had the talent necessary for a degree of the responsibility of leadership, but not the desire to grasp it. At one stage, he decided he wanted to be transferred to the air force, but it didn't work out, and for a time he just let things slide. He later became a lance corporal, was considered for an infantry officer's commission, but didn't get one. Then he went a.w.o.l. and became a private again. Friends said he just didn't want to be an officer, liked being one of the boys. An army document said he was "not accepted."

It also said he'd said he joined up "for adventure" and that he hoped to become an accountant after the war. Meanwhile, he liked to do what he and his pals did in Edinburgh, whether it made life difficult for non-commissioned officers like Len Shea or not.

One day a red-headed sergeant was sitting in a back office, looking uncomfortable, waiting for army public relations to do something about his life. I knew his name. Every Canadian sports writer knew Ralph Allen's name. When I was with the *Daily Times*, I had admired his

Toronto *Globe and Mail* columns as models of their kind. Now he was with an artillery unit, but someone said he was about to be discharged to become a war correspondent. I didn't speak to him. I guess I was in awe of him, and it was only decades later that it struck me that he may have affected me in a way I didn't realize.

In the end, after some three months, public relations found my own services no longer essential. It simply hadn't worked out for either them or me. Eric Gibbs' advice to the American writer had typified the mood, the problem of an army not doing what a wartime army is supposed to do. Never have I spent so much time drawing doodles because there was little or nothing else to do. I left feeling once more humbled and adrift, but when I got to Waterloo Station, something in me said "to hell with this." I went to a phone and called The Canadian Press office on Fleet Street. The bureau chief, Ernie Burritt, knew I'd been with CP. He asked me to meet him at a bar. There I told him what had happened and asked if there was any chance of becoming for CP what Ralph Allen had become for the *Globe and Mail*, a war correspondent. He said to leave it with him. It took a bit of time, but that's how it came about.

In the summer her flowers were beautiful and her garden was in and Mrs. Teed was in her glory. She had flowers put in each room each day. She saw, as she had for many summers, that the Anglican church brass was well and regularly shined. She directed her two Acadian maids with uninhibited French: "Bringez la broom and brossez la floor." She had with her, as always, her own family retinue and, in addition, had the armed forces as auxiliaries. She frequently had the stone house and its grounds humming with people dancing and laughing and playing croquet and charades and cards and sitting in front of the fireplace, chatting. As usual, it was by no means uncommon to have 16 or more sit down for dinners that ran like clockwork with the help of the maids — two, it was said, because one was afraid to work alone — and now, repeatedly, the guests included young men passing through a Moncton depot on their way to or from air training.

Most of them came from Britain, but some from other countries. Some came for one weekend, then were posted away. Others came more than once. They danced to music from a bulky old gramophone with a crank to make it go, or to a grand piano, danced on the stone floor, one so well that others were in awe of him, especially as they watched one of Mrs. Teed's daughters waltz with this Czechoslovakian who waltzed as one might in the most aristocratic courts of Europe. At 15, Shirley Oulton saw her own mother waltz with him too, and her face said is *that* my mother? She came to wonder at this man who was older than most of the airmen, had escaped from his German-occupied homeland, and had the graces of another world. Wondered also at his energy. He loved to walk. If he couldn't get a 22-mile lift from Moncton, he simply set out on foot. Once when Mrs. Teed had no gasoline for her car, he suggested a walk to the beach five or so miles away. He led the way on a hot summer day.

When she did have rationed gasoline, Mrs. Teed put her Dodge at the disposal of guests, and the beach was a frequent destination, for swimming, picnics, corn boils. Some of the Britons were from the upper crust, some were not, but they all behaved so properly that Miss Oulton suspected a chaplain may have selected those he felt Mrs. Teed would approve. Once, two of them almost gave up trying to hitchhike but one said they should try one last time because, he whimsically prophesied, they would be picked up by someone who knew the Teeds. A man picked them up and when they got to the stone house one of the airmen said who lived there, and the man said, "My God, I was next to one of the Teed boys when he was killed." So he and the white-haired Madgie vanished into a room and were there for a long time, talking, because this was the first time Mrs. Teed had ever met anyone who knew much about the dying of her sons.

The day Dan Hanington married Margot Wallace, Mrs. Teed made a meteorological note, "Dull in the morning but glorious later on," which the groom would say was accurate in a larger sense. Indeed, it raises the whole question of romance as an integral part of warfare which village experience alone indicates is a subject with many ramifications. For young Richard Goad, as one example, the epitome of wartime romance was an air force plane writing love letters above F.A. Dobson's house. He knew what was going on. The whole village knew that Don Hicks of the high school Class of 1939, son of returned-man Clarence, the station agent, was briding and grooming up there in the sky. He'd graduated as a pilot and was now an instructor in Moncton, and one of his ways of showing devotion to his very recent wife, F.A.'s daughter Bette, was to come whooping down the Memramcook Valley and use his two-engine Ventura to perform over her head feats of flight she could only interpret as pronouncements of the heart. Then he'd peel off and perform for a wider audience, but either way no one had a better place to watch than schoolboy Richard, son of the warden turned provost marshal, because their home on the prison hill had a magnificent view of miles of marshes, hills and valley, and especially of the Guard Row where the very recent bride would rush out to watch, giggling. At least until someone complained that her very recent groom was flying much too low, and he was ordered to desist.

By this time, Cpl. Raymond Mitton was engaged romantically under circumstances that would have demographic implications for the country as a whole. For it would be found that for roughly every Canadian killed overseas another came home with a wife. Thus Corporal Mitton's experience was typical, and began where many began. One evening he was sitting around the N.A.A.F.I. on the English airdrome where he was on guard duty with the Stormont, Dundas and Glengarry Highlanders when he saw a member of the W.A.A.F., the women's arm of the R.A.F. The N.A.A.F.I. was the Navy, Army and Air Force Institute and there were branches everywhere, selling tea and buns and other things, and providing a way for boys to meet girls and vice versa. Which was how Corporal Mitton got talking to the young W.A.A.F.— she'd recently lied about her age to enlist at 17 — and found that her name was Irene Potter. He asked if she'd like to go to the flicks, the movies, and she said she would, and in time they became lovers and got married and had a baby. They got an apartment on the south coast, and it was the first home Raymond Mitton had had in a long time and he was happy to be out of where the loneliness was.

This was the way wartime romance was: a young man met a girl he wanted to see again and who wanted to see him. People got mixed up on a massive scale. Romance blossomed. The first foundations were laid for a post-war baby boom, and the basics were simple. The young, mobile man looked handsome and brave in his uniform. A young woman's heart fluttered at the spectacle, though not always with long-range results. As when young Shirley Oulton first beheld Lieutenant Hanington leaning up against a marble fireplace in Mrs. Teed's house and looking so ... so *naval* that she could only regret the existence of the Margot Wallaces of this world. The mood could be so overpowering that some men in uniform got married even though they already were. The victims included no less than four young village women — at least two of them in uniform themselves — which suggests a phenomenon of considerable dimensions.

One of the four met an officer and they fell momentously in love. He was from another country, and his unit was in Canada temporarily, and there ensued a courtship which made people say how deeply in love they so obviously were. Her parents met the young man and were as bewitched as anyone else, and eventually a wedding was announced. A big wedding, an outstanding social occasion; the bride looked lovely and the groom splendid, and there wasn't a soul in the church who didn't feel sad because the groom and his fellow officers must leave shortly to face once more the stresses of warfare. It was after their departure that rumors grew. It was even said that the groom's fellow officers had kept silent over something they might well have disclosed but didn't, partly perhaps because they could hardly believe what was happening, partly perhaps because they couldn't find it in themselves to shatter something as beautiful as a young, attractive couple so deeply in love. Eventually, the bride's father made inquiries and was in due course informed that, yes, the groom should not have married since he already was. Not happily, it would become clear, but married. Eventually, too, he sent a postcard from a distant land. He said it was regrettable that there were times when things just didn't work out. He hoped, he added, that people didn't feel too critical of him.

Chapter Nine

IN NORTH AFRICA, THE Desert Fox kept the two great Allied pincers apart for months, but by May 12 the fighting was over and tens of thousands of Germans and Italians were prisoners. It was, Churchill said, not the beginning of the end but the end of the beginning. A year after his arrival in Egypt, Bill Palmer had seen North Africa freed of the enemy; in the closing phases of the campaign his squadron had moved large numbers of troops, and now it had been decided that Alec Noon should fly less after flying a great deal. So their days as crewmates came to an end. A reporter would eventually write of Bill's new pilot, Canadian Jack Rice, "playing tag with enemy fighter planes," write that "once in Africa German fighters strafed his grounded plane, bombed and destroyed it while he and fellow crew members burrowed furiously into the desert sand." But Bill's letters kept dwelling upon the margins of great events. Once his flight tented near Mussolini's great arch; he said he could hear the Mediterranean lapping the shore, but that was all. Back in January, he'd said he'd been trapped in Cairo for three days by "the first sandstorm that ever did me any good." Once he said he'd been in hospital in India, an occasional destination for 267. It was nothing much, he said, "just some kind of fever." He'd had other ailments, but not to worry. He'd been in Tunis; it was near there, in fact, that the entire squadron came together for the first time in months, and found various kinds of fruit a delight after a desert diet of cheese and bully beef.

He'd heard one of his observer class had won a second D.F.C., and that Bob Long was an officer in Northern Ireland. He didn't mention that once the North African campaign was over a considerable number of his squadron mates were also commissioned as officers, though their records didn't match his own. It must have hurt. It meant the sergeants' mess would be lacking familiar faces, that to the isolations and insulations the past year had brought into his life there was added a new one. Or was it? In late April he'd written, "I'm very happy out here. I've grown accustomed to everything and manage to have a lot of fun." He was going to church every Sunday, he said, yet the word in the squadron was that he, the team player, had become a bit of a loner, that he got depressed, that off-duty he was drinking quite a lot, was apt to vanish into the fleshpots of Cairo or Algiers or Tunis, and someone said he got a reputation for doing things "the rest of us would like to do but didn't dare." There was speculation that for such reasons he had not been made an officer.

As the fighting died down, he had a few days leave in Cairo — 267 still had a repair base there — but grumbled, "Every time I go in there I come back more fed up. The smell, the heat, etc., and everyone doing their best to beg, borrow, steal your money." One thing his letters inevitably missed could have been of village interest. For among the tens of thousands of enemy prisoners was the Hitler Youth cousin Gottfried Klotz had argued with on returning to Germany. He'd spend the rest of the war in a p.o.w. camp in the United States and he'd make his own peace with reality. He'd learn to speak Russian.

By that May, Dan Hanington also had a victory to celebrate. On the 22nd Germany's Grand Admiral Doenitz ordered his submarines out of the North Atlantic, admitted defeat because ships and planes had closed the mid-ocean gap where his wolf packs had destroyed hundreds of ships and thousands of lives. Lieutenant Hanington was serving in the corvette *Wetaskiwin* when he saw what this could mean: "The first of the Very Long Range (VLR) aircraft were coming into service so we could get air support, when needed, all the way across the Atlantic." In addition, it was no longer necessary to run for port when fuel ran low; escort oilers fuelled the warships at sea, and this in turn let convoys swing farther south without losing much, if any, time because the weather was so much more benign. By this time he'd been trained to be a navigational specialist, had won the Distinguished Service Cross because in one long battle he "was able to figure out where a U-boat was when we lost contact with him," and the U-boat was sunk. Winston Churchill would say they were his greatest worry, and the threat didn't vanish. But the submarines were no longer capable of major challenge to the buildup in Britain for an invasion of Western Europe.

There would be numerous times when brother Hank got bombers ready to take part in the preludes to an invasion, but it would be the first time he wrote about it in articles for the Moncton *Transcript*: "I hadn't realized bombs could be so heavy and awkward and obdurate," he said. "By the time the last kite was bombed up, I was tired and sore." But he went down to watch the takeoff, saw the bulky figures of the crew climb into one plane after another, saw the propellors race, heard the air belch sound. Then: "One after another the planes roared into the sky.

Each circled the 'drome several times, climbing ever higher. Planes from other satellites joined in the ring-around-a-rosy manoeuvres until the sky was alive with circling craft. Then, one after another, they struck a course and were soon mere specks in the blue. For a few moments there was a lull. Then like bellowing bulls the heavy bombers from farther north roared overhead. For an hour the rumble caused the hut windows to rattle. Happy Valley (Germany's industrial Ruhr) would catch hell tonight, and in a very small way I'd had a hand in the business. For the first time since enlisting, I had a feeling I was doing something to help end the war. That night I slept well."

In June, in Tunisia, a detachment of 267 Squadron, R.A.F., was set up in a place called El Aouina to prepare for further military operations, and in the village high school pupils issued a 14-page publication called *Highlights*. The war had been part of the life of that month's graduates since they were, on average, 13 years of age. They had grown up with it, and what they printed made it apparent that they thought as the village had thought from the beginning: that fighting the war was unquestionably right. The loyalty was rooted in a revealing trinity: the British Empire, Canada and the local community. The cover had a design drawn by Herbert D. "Bud" Palmer, a first cousin of Bill Palmer, and it contained a globe showing both Canada and the British Isles, and above everything a big Union Jack. The program for graduation included the singing of "There'll Always Be An England" and ended with "God Save The King." In addition, there was this quotation from a similar publication in 1910: "Since the time of Queen Elizabeth the Union Jack has bowed to no flag. It has always stood for honor, liberty and justice. Ought not the children who are going to build up Canada's future be taught to love and respect it? Let all true Canadians help Canada to a truer view of her duty, her privilege and her destiny." At the United Church in May, the school pupils had joined in an observance of Empire Day under the auspices of Imperial Order Daughters of the Empire, the service including Salutation of the Flag, a hymn "For Those Who Serve," and an inspiring address by one Dr. Tucker in which he explained "what a great and glorious union of many democratic countries our Empire really is." There also were songs in honor of Canada, the United States and Russia, and in recognition of the Soviet's massive suffering Russian Relief was to get the $19 collection.

Highlights' articles told with pride what the cadets, the Junior Red Cross and the D.H.S. club were doing to support the war effort, what graduates of the past were serving their country: an Honor Roll including 24 young men and eight young women. The figure was far short of the number of village people who were serving or would serve, one reason being that "the school record is incomplete up to 1931" and another that many did not finish school or had done so elsewhere. Cryptic notes about the graduates indicated that three of the five boys and one of the eight girls intended to join up, and at least one more boy in fact did. One item said films about the war effort were shown every month and "make us more willing to serve and lend, so that we may feel we are doing our part in this desperate struggle for freedom." The pupils' lending consisted of buying, to date, $1,323.05 of so-called War Saving Stamps. A school library was being organized and sports were thriving except for one thing: no soccer balls were available because of lack of material for making them. There were jokes: "Don't worry about butter. You can make it from grass. All you need is a cow and a churn." There were "quips": "What blonde graduate is deeply interested in her sister's boy friend?" The yearning for peace was expressed in a Bud Palmer poem:

> When we can throw aside the Sword,
> When we defeat the Nazi Horde,
> The bells will ring and all will sing
> We thank thee, gracious Lord and King.

In the meantime, there were writeups about the death of graduate Dan Stack and about Joe Emery's medal. In the latter case, however, *Highlights* had a bone to pick. It didn't like Moncton claiming Joe just because his parents had recently moved to the Moncton area.

On the 24th of June, less than a week before the 1943 graduation ceremonies at his old school, Joe Emery was in one of hundreds of bombers that became specks in the English dusk. As brother Hank had seen, they mustered over airdromes like swarms of bees, and then they headed east to lay more waste to Germany. Flight Lieutenant Emery had done this something like 70 times, so he knew all too well what was out there waiting: the steel hailstorms called flak, the terrifying fingers of searching light, the eagle pounce of night fighters steered by ever-better ground controls, the burning cities, the hurtling fall of stricken planes. With bigger planes, heavier bombs, better navigation and other tools, Bomber Harris's recipe for victory had reached a level of destruction and sophistication well beyond that first 1,000-plane raid more than a year ago, and Joe Emery had matured with it.

But there was something special about tonight. It was the first time his 7 Squadron crew was to fly in a Lancaster, the four-engine plane that would be remembered as the ultimate instrument of the Harris doctrine. That was what made Flight Lieutenant Emery wonder what flying in it would mean. In a branch of warfare in which a man was lucky indeed to live through 25 or 30 missions, he had flown so many more that he had come to think of his survival as a thing ordained. Yet the change nagged at him. There was no question that a Lanc was bigger and better than the smaller, slower, four-engine Stirlings his crew had been flying for months, but that was the rub. A Lancaster might endanger a Stirling with its falling bombs but it also was a more inviting target for night fighters. You could picture a German pilot ignoring the poor-relation Stirlings to get at those fat, fancy and more deadly planes flying thousands of feet above.

Joe Emery was a bomb aimer now; one of those designated to drop the flares and bombs later planes would use as guides. He was the lone Canadian in a crew that also included one New Zealander. The other five were Britons and, like Bill Palmer and Warren Duffy, he had proceeded from initial scepticism to something well beyond mere acceptance of some of their ways. He liked, respected and admired them. Their Lancaster had its own bureaucratic number: BIII ED595 'Q'. Five of the crew were officers, the other two were warrant officers, and nothing better exemplified their status as pathfinders than the medals, the so-called gongs, they'd won. They all had at least one. The pilot, Robert George Barrell, had three, and he was a wing commander, the equivalent of an army lieutenant-colonel who commanded a battalion of infantry.

Double daylight saving time dictated their time of departure from Waddington: 11.21 p.m. Their destination was Wuppertal in the dreaded Ruhr Valley, and Joe Emery was in an excellent position to watch as the Lancaster headed toward it. As the bomb aimer, he was filling a role introduced when four-engine planes became available in 1942 and which also made him a backup navigator and responsible for manning the front machine-gun. He looked down from a bubble up front as the North Sea fell away below, as they came in over the European coast and guns and searchlights stabbed at them. He'd made it beyond here many times, to German cities almost beyond the recalling of them.

Lancaster ED595 was near the great Belgian seaport of Antwerp, when what he had feared came true. A night fighter was directed at them from instruments far below. It closed in. Fixed them in its sights. Attacked. Made the rear gun turret unserviceable. Set one of the two port Merlin engines aflame. Riddled that great, proud and pristine Lancaster, sent it hurtling into a swamp four kilometers east of a place called Rilland. Four of the crew would be found in the wreckage; three of them dead, one mortally injured. Joe Emery was one of the three to see his parachute billow overhead, feel his heavy flying boots hit wet soil. He got out of the parachute. Hid it. Thanked God he was unhurt. He was out in the country. Alone. In the dark. He had the things they gave you to try to get away: a compass, a map, iron rations. He set out, heading south, one day after Bill Palmer wrote home that "Joe Emery has probably finished operations, and is in a cushy job."

Brother Hank was in a strange and sterile land. The Allies had decided to follow up the victory in North Africa by going after another in Sicily, and to "soften up" in advance potential sources of resistance. This is why Corporal How's squadron went to Tunisia, the country where cousin Bill Palmer was, and one of the first things that happened was marching through a village burdened with packs and singing ribald songs. "A French Canadian started singing *Alouette* and it swelled to a mighty chorus. When it ended, the French Canadians spoke to watching people in their own language. The word spread like wildfire: *Canadiens, Canadiens.* Thanks to our French Canadians, we were well received in the colonial town of Boufarik, and so noisy became the singsong that when we arrived at our billet, a girls' school, the sergeant-major had a hard time getting us to halt." After that, they were two days or more in railcars designed for "*8 chevaux ou 40 hommes,*" saw their first camel caravan, had water for their tea provided by the engineer from the train's boiler, passed through plains and precipitous mountains, encountered enemy prisoners: harum scarum Italians who went bersek over cigarettes, Germans with steely stares. For their last breakfast, the engineer refused them water because his boiler was nearly dry.

They were loaded into lorries or trucks and travelled "sardine fashion over war-scarred roads. Dust clouds enveloped us in torrid heat. You couldn't sweat, for any moisture was greedily absorbed by the thirsty air. We poured off at every stop to look for water and souvenirs: abandoned German bullets, grenades, mines. The farther we travelled the less promising the countryside. Cities where French overlords lived behind thick stone walls gave way to towns skirted by wretched mud hovels. We left the Mediterranean shoreline and turned inland. Across the plains we could see an alabaster white city dominated by the mosque's dome and high, badly chipped walls encasing the holy sanctuary. For two hours there were few signs of life. An occasional Arab herdsman watched over sheep, goats, dromedaries, burros, all desperately searching the scorched land for food. We saw people using a dromedary, a rope and a crude wooden winch to raise water from a well. At sunset, after an all-day trip, our convoy stopped at a point where the plain stretched to the east as far as the eye could see. To the west, in the distance, was a barren, choppy mountain range. Cactus lining the dirt road and a few olive trees were the only signs of vegetation. But we had arrived."

They slept that night on the hard ground, under netting, feeling a breeze from the sea and listening to "the mournful bray of the burro, the camel's noisy belch, the staccato bark of mongrel dogs." At dawn Arabs came out of nowhere to stare at them and sell things. On the 26th of June the first bombers headed across the Mediterranean to soften up Sicily. By then the men were already being softened up by Africa's own form of airpower, the house flies Bill Palmer knew too well. By then, too, Joe Emery had been on the run for a second day.

For Joe, the number of days on the run got to be a blur because he got tired and wet and hungry and discouraged. He was in polder country, on low-lying farmland the Dutch had reclaimed from the sea and protected with high dikes, and it was not easy to get through; it was not easy to get across the canals, and there seemed to be a lot of them. It might have been easier if he'd travelled by day, but he didn't. He travelled by night and, in fact, it was when he tried moving in daylight that he got into trouble. German soldiers came down a road in a truck and saw him, and when he started to run for cover they fired over his head and shouted at him to stop. He stopped. He'd been on the run for at least four days, maybe five, but he knew it was over. They took him to a place where an officer questioned him at length. Then they took him to the prison camp WW1 pilot Herman Goering, Hitler's right-hand man, had reserved for fellow airmen even if they had come uninvited into his land. It was southeast of Berlin, and it was called Stalag Luft III.

At first he was reported missing. On July 1 his picture was in the papers, and it was noted that only recently he'd received what was believed to be the first D.F.C. won by anyone from the Moncton area. Some time passed, then his picture was run again because his parents got a telegram from Ottawa saying that "the International Red Cross states that your son is a prisoner of war." So there he was behind barbed wire, in the country he had attacked so often, and he found himself looking at the guards — the ferrets, they were called — and wondering if one just might be Gottfried Klotz.

Gottfried Klotz was nowhere near. Indeed, he was the one in the cushy job, or at least in one he considered cushy. He was no longer on the static Leningrad front. He was well away from the prodigious fighting that continued to rage across miles of Russian space, and in which the Germans were being sucked deeper and deeper into a tragedy of their own making. He was in Estonia, one of the three Baltic States Stalin had forcibly absorbed into the Soviet Union as part of his 1939 deal with Hitler, and which the Germans now controlled. He was on the staff of a signals school in a city of faded Hanseatic elegance called Tallinn. It looked out on the Gulf of Finland, and he would be there for eight months, and he had a girl friend and found the whole thing so splendid that when he talked about it later he would smile.

He was there in July when great things happened both in Russia and the Mediterranean. Around Kursk, between Kharkov and Orel, the Germans and the Russians fought the greatest tank battle of the war, the Germans lost 500,000 men and from then on it would be the Russians who had the initiative in the most stupendous and ghastly war in history. The battle of Kursk raged for one week, July 5-12. It started one day after Flt. Sgt. Victor Shea was killed and it was still raging when the Allies attacked Sicily.

Victor Shea was the son of an older brother of Len and Ev Shea; he was born in the village, and was often around there after the family moved away. One year he went to the local school and was in the same class with Warren Duffy. Sometimes we'd get Ev mad by calling him Uncle Ev, which he was though he and Vic were about the same age. All Vic would do was get a shy grin on his face, but Uncle Ev would get mad even though he usually was quiet and easygoing. The strange thing was that just at the time Vic was killed with the air force Ev was getting ready to invade Sicily with the 1st Division's Hastings and Prince Edward Regiment from Ontario.

The R.C.A.F. was using bombers that summer to lay minefields in harbors under German control, and Vic Shea was given special training to do it. He'd turned 20 in May, four years after graduating from Salisbury High School, two years after graduating as a teacher, and one year after becoming an air force navigator. On July 4, his crew set out to lay mines in the harbor at the mouth of the River Ems, on the German-Dutch border. It didn't get back.

In the early morning darkness of July 10, 267 squadron crews flew out of Tunisia with strange cargoes in Dakota transport planes. Bill Palmer was navigating for Jack Rice, they were heading for Sicily, and what they'd do there, added to what had happened at the Oasis of Kuffra, would bring Rice a Distinguished Flying Cross. Actually, he would later say, 267 sold the Germans a bill of goods: "A few of us with unarmed transport planes were loaded up with dummies made to look like paratroopers. We flew to the west end of Sicily and dropped them, equipped with fireworks that sent up shots from the ground like pistol flares. The Germans believed paratroopers had landed. They diverted a division to repel the mock invasion."

The real invasion was carried out successfully elsewhere, but the 267 crews knew their trick was working when enemy guns started firing at them. But the most spectacular event of all came when a straw-filled sack somehow caught fire in one plane and the crews of others watched it plunge in flames into the sea. It was one of two planes the squadron lost as part of numerous and costly mishaps in the invasion of Sicily, and far from the greatest. But 160,000 American, British and Canadian troops landed in darkness and heaving seas from the greatest armada the world had ever seen, and what mattered most for the Canadian Army was that a lasting fighting war had finally begun. The 1st Division and the three-regiment 1st Armored Brigade went into action, and there were village-area people involved in scattered places. Ells Taylor and a young black named Adrian Howe were there with the 8th Battery, Ev Shea with the Hastypees, Andy Emery with the Ordnance Corps. Bill Palmer and others with 267 Squadron came back repeatedly in daylight to land on improvised iron runways on the beaches and take the badly wounded out; Jack Rice's D.F.C. citation would say he kept flying to the most advanced airfield. Back in Tunisia, the R.C.A.F. bomber wing saw its softening-up duties halted, at least temporarily, for a very important reason: on July 25 Benito Mussolini — the French in Africa called him Macaroni — was forced out as leader of the Italy he'd controlled for 21 years.

At this time, Nursing Sister Teresa Hickman was with No.1 Canadian General Hospital in North Africa, waiting to go on, and learning about things nursing sisters didn't do. She and another nurse decided to explore Algiers, got hopelessly lost, then rescued by an American military truck driver. He bawled them out but took them back to his unit's quarters where they were given royal treatment: a shower, a bountiful meal. Their uniforms were even pressed, and they were delivered to No.1's temporary base outside the city and became the envy of their peers.

Joe Emery wasn't in Stalag Luft III long before he realized it was engaged in a mining enterprise. Three tunnels were being directed toward destinations beyond the barbed wire. The idea was to stage a mass escape, and the gamble was that even if the German ferrets found one tunnel they might not find three. The underground operations were directed by a lanky Canadian named Wally Floody, a fighter pilot, while overhead an American millionaire's son named George Harsh directed those assigned to try to make sure that the German guards didn't find out what was going on.

Joe Emery soon was working for Harsh, but he was typical in that he had no idea that this popular, handsome and respected man had done time in a Georgia chain gang for killing a man in one of a series of holdups staged by college kids bent on proving they were smarter than police. Floody knew because Harsh had told him, but he thought Harsh was a great guy doing a great job, and what mattered was getting out of Stalag Luft III. So here was Joe Emery, the son of a prison guard, getting acquainted with a compound of prison isolation, monotony, boredom on one hand and this secret activity on the other. His experience on the run didn't make him too optimistic about the chances of making it to freedom, but he couldn't help being impressed with the elaborate efforts to make it possible: the forged documents, the improvised civilian clothes, the background information accumulated from German newspapers and hidden radios, the George Harsh vigilance system in which he and others could detect, sidetrack and/or warn about any sign the ferrets were up to no good.

Did you hear, the village grapevine said, about Florence Miller? She worked in the telephone office the summer she was 14 so when she enlisted in 1943 the army sent her to a communications post in Prince Rupert, B.C., to keep an eye on the Japanese in case they showed up. She's called a plotter-telephonist, people would say, and she's with an artillery unit at a place in the woods on the side of a mountain, a place so secret you have to have passwords to get into buildings. She tracks plots on a huge table covering a radius of 100 miles and she charts more of them that are connected to gun sites. She's out there because British Columbia panicked after Pearl Harbor and the government sent in thousands of people in uniform. Don Hicks is out there as an air force pilot, up the coast past Prince Rupert. Jim How's been out there too, with the army, and got married out there. And did you hear, villagers would say, that Ralph March, our former principal, is an officer with a communications outfit in Australia? Did you know that Doug Crosson died in Halifax and had a military funeral, and him just 20 years of age? They turned him down once as medically unfit but he made it later, this son of Bob Crosson, the guard who trains the cadets. His brother Ernie is overseas with the North Nova Scotia Highlanders but John, another brother, was discharged as medically unfit. Did you hear, they'd say, about John Robinson? When he was a kid on the family farm, he fell out of a tree and injured his back. Just before they went overseas, the 8th Hussars discovered his vertebrae was out of line and discharged him. So he joined the air force, (told them he'd been farming since '39), and got to England as an air gunner. Then his plane made a hard landing and threw his back out, and that was the end of his war.

In September, after Sicily, the Allies invaded Italy, and the Canadian government did something General Andy

McNaughton didn't like. It sent the 5th Division there to join the lst Division and the lst Armored Brigade in a new version of a lst Canadian Corps. It split the army General Andy wanted kept together, and this meant that for months there would be Canadian soldiers fighting or waiting to fight in Italy and even more Canadian soldiers still waiting in Britain, among whom was one Corporal Dube. Yes, Cpl. Leo Dube of the North Shore Regiment of New Brunswick who only recently had made perhaps the first significant architectural alteration in centuries to Westminster Abbey. Not that it had even crossed his mind till one day in London's Beaver Club he was addressed by an Anglican monk in a brown cassock. He was looking, Brother Burton said, for help, and the pioneer's insignia on Corporal Dube's sleeve made him hope he'd found it.

He was on the staff of Westminster Abbey, Brother Burton revealed, and he had a problem. A happy problem in that, in this time of food rationing, a rural benefactor had given the Abbey staff a rooster and eight hens to furnish eggs for their diet; a difficult problem in that the Abbey was not equipped to provide them a home. They were at the moment in a basement, the hens were not laying, and Brother Burton, their keeper, was being ridiculed over his plight and abused over the odors it created. But, he said in the Beaver Club, he felt he knew the solution: a chicken coop open to sun and air would encourage the production of eggs, eliminate unseemly odors and replace ridicule with praise. He had the proper place, Brother Burton said, he had nails, he had wood, he had everything but the skills of a carpenter which Corporal Dube's insignia indicated he might provide.

Corporal Dube was, yes, a carpenter, indeed, as a pioneer, a sort of odd-jobs engineer and, Roman Catholic though he was, he was intrigued by the prospects of a deal. If, he said, the monk would promise him a thorough and private guided tour through the great church, he would do what he could to help. The promise made, Brother Burton led him to the Abbey and climbed with him to his chosen place, and once there, puffing, Corporal Dube beheld a stunning sight. He was on the roof, overlooking Parliament, Big Ben, the Thames, indeed much of London and the gaps and scars of German bombing! The following morning, returned for toil, he beheld on the roof what he thought was debris from enemy attack. It turned out to be the varied wood he had to work with: cabbage cases, tea chests, orange boxes, wired slats, plus two ancient boards he suspected might date back centuries to the original Abbey construction. In addition, Brother Burton made available a shoemaker's hammer, a rusty saw with an incomplete handle, a battered hatchet, a cardboard box with a bewildering array of spikes, tacks and widely diversified nails. Thus equipped, Corporal Dube peeled off his jacket and went to work. Improvised. Made do. Wired together wood too thin to be successfully nailed. Turned the ancient boards into roosts. Made a promenade with slats and scraps of chicken wire. Stopped, once Big Ben's great clock boomed noon, to dine on the linen-covered tea, bread, cheese and biscuits Brother Burton produced as though by magic. Stopped finally that afternoon to survey a flimsy but durable coop made snow-fence fashion, into which Brother Burton proceeded to dump a rooster and eight clucking hens from burlap bags, then stood back in admiration. "Ah," he beamed, "don't they look happy." Next morning, he personally conducted Corporal Dube on a guided tour of the great church as private and thorough as even a High Anglican general could desire. All of which Leo Dube would tell about when he took up residence in the village after the war and where he lived for many years.

Indeed, even as he labored in a religious cause above the streets of London, the village continued to accumulate its own stories of wartime life, some of which contained the tinge and tang of scandal. There was, for instance, the prominent citizen who carried on a prolonged affair with the much younger wife of a soldier overseas, even had the interior of his automobile rearranged for courtship's greater comfort. Then, their husbands away, there were the women who held raucous parties to which servicemen came from out of town and from which they were sometimes cast out in an intoxicated state and lacking the money they'd had on arrival. Not infrequently, late-night calls that went through the telephone office were described as profane and picturesque to a highly pejorative degree.

Nevertheless, no equivalent of Lieutenant Goodwin emerged to record village social events. Certainly, Nursing Sister Hickman did have stories which could have qualified but they concerned events far away. In one, she told of being night supervisor in Italy, and making inspection rounds of buildings and tents. One was a building used for venereal disease patients who needed only medication, and as she and her jeep driver left it one night they spotted a large wicker container being hoisted to the second floor by twisted sheets. In it were a large container of wine and a buxom Italian. She didn't go back. "It would have been a lost cause," she'd say. "When they left for their units, many of the V.D. patients would say, 'Bye, sister, see you in a couple of months.'"

Bill Palmer wondered what Bert E. was doing. "If he has been flying," he wrote home, "he must be about through." I was in London by then, on Fleet Street, editing a weekly newspaper CP put out for Canadians serving overseas, and when Bert Emmerson and I got together things were happening to him and in him. He'd been an officer for a year and he looked great in a uniform adorned with that most charismatic of insignia, a pilot's wings. He was as quiet and unassuming as ever but he looked grown up. Dashing. As though he'd walked down London's Regent Street all his life, had become what he was meant to be. Yet once again he was frustrated. The air force had him towing gliders in anticipation of an invasion of France, but he wanted to fly a fighter plane and on at least one occasion, perhaps in rebellion, he had flown a tow plane so low it caused damage, had been admonished and fined two pounds. In short, he'd been overseas for a year and a half but hadn't seen action. He was hounding the air force for a transfer to a fighter squadron, but the training schools were turning out so many fliers that a transfer wasn't easy to get.

There was a night when we got together with Mrs. Teed's granddaughter Dolly Palmer who was in the C.W.A.C's, and Dan Hanington, her cousin, in town between convoys, and with Bert's brother Charlie who wore the black beret of the armored corps. It was Charlie who'd make me remember this night. Charlie who was different. Charlie who was paying a lifelong price for a childhood illness. Charlie who had managed to enlist in a New Brunswick regiment, only to be turfed out, then managed to enlist again. Had figured that his best hope was to get into a regiment recruited far from where he was known. Which is how he got into Manitoba's Fort Garry Horse. So there he was that night. He and Bert were on leave together. To Charlie, Bert was the beloved kid brother he'd pushed around in a baby carriage, the kid brother who'd shown him the business of flying a towing plane. They were with Dolly Palmer and Dan Hanington when I invited the four of them to come up to Fursecroft, the apartment near Marble Arch where I was living with three other CP staffers. We were heading for an underground station when I realized Charlie was walking away. I ran back and told him we wanted him to come, but he said he didn't belong, didn't fit, and he kept on going. It was sad. It was Charlie.

From the air, the Germans came back at London. They put on what some people called "a baby blitz." You'd hear sirens and see searchlights and hear the guns going, and one night an American I'd met at a sanctuary called the Churchill Club said let's go down to the east end and see what's going on. We took a bus to that battered area and in a pub near the Thames a blowsy barwoman raised a glass and said, "'Ere's to ould 'Itler, 'ooever 'e is." The real blitz had found its own sanctuary in nostalgia. People would talk about how everybody had pulled together, how great the spirit was, and to hell with Adolf Hitler.

It was a blacked-out night during the baby blitz when the air force's Betty McCabe arrived in London and it convinced her she was going to have the time of her life. The Women's Division put her to work in Records, and when the word got around the villagers started showing up to visit, to hear how she'd been virtually smuggled to Halifax after getting sick and missing her original draft: got from Montreal to Moncton hidden in a private compartment on an all-male troop train, got from the village to Halifax in a baggage car of another troop train without a seat to spare. She'd soon love London, the theatres, the sights, love roaming England and Scotland on leaves, watching for friends, learning the way things were and what happened the night a lady of the evening propositioned her companion, a cousin and army captain. "Get lost," Airwoman McCabe said, "I found him first," and it worked. But what she did most of all was help keep track in Records of what happened to people like Bert Emmerson.

On an evening late in November, Flying Officer Emmerson and Gunner Hazen Greenberg chanced upon each other at an ice rink in London and arranged to meet two evenings hence and go skating again. It didn't matter to them that Bert was an officer and Hazen wasn't, or that Bert's father was a Member of Parliament and Hazen's was the village's pre-eminent merchandiser of liquor under conditions the law considered illicit. What did matter was swapping village news and gossip.

Hazen was with a medium artillery regiment. He'd looked up the village crowd in the 14th Field Ambulance and he'd looked up Betty McCabe and he always had his eye out for more. So he looked forward to seeing Bert a second time and getting more news. By now Bert had been overseas for two years, and one piece of news he'd already passed along was that the New Brunswick Rangers had made it overseas and that he and brother Richard had met several times. Also, he said, he'd gone on leaves with Charlie and their kid brother John, 17, had graduated in June with the D.H.S. Class of 1943 and hoped to get into flight training after a year at university. Furthermore, Bert had only recently discovered a first cousin named John Deacon who came from Toronto, had had him over to an army headquarters for lunch and accepted an invitation to lunch at Bert's mess. But his biggest news was that the R.C.A.F. had finally made him a fighter pilot, that he was with a squadron, and expected to go out soon on his first mission. He'd become at last what he wanted to be.

When FO. Jack Calder came to CP's London apartment with war correspondent Ross Munro one evening, it was the only time I ever heard a Canadian serviceman say passionately what the war was all about. He was a navigator with the R.C.A.F., had been in the same graduation parade as Bill Palmer. He was a rangy and impressive man well into his 20s, the son of a minister and a former CP staff writer. In his blue uniform he looked like a Viking with flax for hair. It was fascinating to meet him because of strange letters he'd sent CP's Al Nickleson from Ireland when he was in an internment camp. His bomber had been shot up over Europe and mixed up over England and ended up in the sea off neutral Ireland. When he and others somehow got ashore, they were imprisoned. Even so, they were allowed out on occasion and Calder got permission to write articles about what he saw and did. This included eating in Dublin restaurants near interned German officers who looked straight through him. He was twice caught trying to escape, finally decided there had to be another way, and the letters started.

Each letter to Al Nickleson got more vague, dejected, morose. The consensus of those who read them was that he was going stir crazy. Then one night there was a phone call. From Calder. In hospital in Scotland. With a new problem. The letters, he said, were probably the greatest achievement of his writing career—and a fraud. He'd used them to convince the Irish doctors he *was* going crazy. But when he got to the Scottish hospital and told its doctors what he'd done, they didn't believe him. They believed the Irish doctors. It took some time to turn him loose. When he got to London and to Fursecroft, his CP friends tried to convince him he'd done his bit, that he should become an air force information officer. But that's when Calder lit up. He started talking about what the war was all about. Hitler, he said, and everything he stood for, were menaces to human freedom, decency and hope, to everything western man had done through exertion, blood and sacrifice to build democracy and civilization. His blue eyes blazed. Nazi Germany had to be defeated, he said, and there was only one way to do it: by fighting, and that's what he intended to do.

I don't know what the others felt, but he awed me. A couple of weeks later there was another phone call from Scotland. From Calder. Back in hospital. He'd gone up there on leave before going to a squadron, and in a pub he'd met a Polish bomber crew who shared his sentiments about Hitler in their entirety and beyond. He'd accepted an invitation to join them on a training flight that terminated against a mountain. He was the only survivor. This time he hobbled into Fursecroft with a prolonged cast on a leg. Surely now, it was argued, he realized that his war was over, that he had a great future, that he should be sensible. He said they could say what they wanted, he was going back to war, and out he went, grinning, with a crutch. He was posted to the R.A.F.'s 571 Squadron. He was a flight lieutenant and 29 years of age which, someone said, made him seem and feel old in messes crowded with fliers in their late teens and early 20s.

Chapter Ten

IN FLEET, HANTS, THAT November, the New Brunswick Rangers paraded in regret. Two months after arriving in Britain with 730 officers and men, the unit had been ordered to slim its numbers to 362 and to become a brigade support group with the 4th Canadian Armored Division. Among the scores cast adrift was the Lieut. Richard Emmerson who had been one of the earliest proteges of the Charlie Crandall who now, 10 years after he'd started schooling the Dorchester Army for the Rangers, was placed in charge of what the Rangers had become. He'd come overseas as second-in-command of an infantry battalion. Still as a major, he'd become commanding officer of a unit with companies designed to use heavy mortars and medium machine-guns in support of infantry attacks and anti-aircraft guns to fend off enemy air attacks.

On November 25, a day or so before he was to go skating with Hazen Greenberg, Richard Emmerson's kid brother Bert had Toronto cousin John Deacon in for lunch at the officers' mess of 430 Squadron, R.C.A.F., part of 11 Group of the Tactical Air Force which was being groomed for an invasion of Europe. Deacon, a signals officer at 2nd Canadian Corps headquarters, was what airmen called a "brown job," a soldier, an officer in khaki, so he stood out in a room full of blue uniforms, but they had more to talk about than military trivia; they came from large and linked families the war was scattering in all directions, and they had a lot of cousining to do. Bert told about his kid sister Margaret being in England driving an air force ambulance and about Emily writing home from South Africa that her hospital was getting sick or wounded patients all the way from Italy, among them Polish soldiers whose way of saying thanks for a nursing sister's kindness was to kiss her hand. Effusively, she said. She'd never seen anything like it, she said. Bert could tell about this and about young John's plans to join up and about Marion being in the air force, and that Margaret's husband and the husbands of Ruth, Barbara and Eunice were all in the forces too. Indeed, there had even been an article in the papers about the family's record, but when someone asked Marion, the family wit, why so many Emmersons enlisted she asked what else could be expected after years of being run as armies run.

Yes, and there was what had happened to first cousin Emmerson Cornell, whose mother came from the village, and who had died in the long, brutal death march of American prisoners after the fall of Bataan to the Japanese in the Phillipines. Bert Emmerson himself had complained to a doctor in recent weeks of sore eyes which got worse after flying in an enclosed cockpit, had said the sun's glare could tire him and make print blur. In October a medical specialist had said there was a possibility of fatigue and that there might be some difficulty in handling a Mustang fighter plane, and had prescribed a certain type of goggles. But all this was forgotten when, just after he and John Deacon finished lunch, someone said Bert was wanted for a briefing. This is when and how he got word that the time at last had come, that he was about to go on his first mission as a fighter pilot. Go not in one of the Spitfires or Hurricanes which had won the Battle of Britain, but in a Mustang, a bigger, heavier plane capable of flying much farther. The Americans were turning them out in great numbers mainly to protect their fleets of bombers that were being badly depleted on daylight raids deep into Germany.

Flying Officer Emmerson was in the cockpit of Mustang AM 124 when he took off from Gatwick airport at 2.35 p.m. His so-called No.1, Flt. Lt. C.D. Bricker, was flying a second Mustang as they made for the same coast Joe Emery had flown over on his last mission five months back. On a photo reconnaissance flight, they came over Holland near The Hague and flew along the coast till they had what they wanted. They were 15 miles out over the North Sea, heading home, when Bricker heard Emmerson report he was having difficulty, then saw Mustang AM 124 turn back toward Holland, climbing from some 30 feet toward some 500. Bricker asked what the trouble was. There was no reply. Instead, 45 minutes after takeoff, he saw Bert Emmerson attempt to make a landing in the sea only to have his big, heavy plane disappear the second it hit the water. Vanish like a stone.

For half an hour Bricker circled overhead, sending out calls for rescue help, keeping an eye out for enemy activity. There were no replies, no intrusions from the enemy, no signs of a rubber float on which Flying Officer Emmerson might have survived. One month short of his 23rd birthday, he was reported missing, and one of the first to hear was Trooper Emmerson of the Fort Garry Horse. Charlie had come for a visit, only to spend the night on his beloved brother's bed, very sad, very empty, very much alone. When Hazen Greenberg went to the London rink, he didn't know what to think when Bert didn't show up. As for John Deacon, he found out when he contacted 430 Squadron the following week because Bert hadn't gotten in touch again, as he'd said he would. He wrote a letter to his Uncle Henry and eventually, after the story was told numerous times, it would be said in distortion that he had listened in, on his signals network, to Bert talking to his fellow pilot before he plunged into the sea. When Richard Emmerson went to Gatwick to pick up his brother's stuff, he found a photograph of a pretty young woman, and years later someone would say she and Bert had decided not to consider marriage during the war. Eventually, his parents would receive his wings and a letter from Ottawa saying word for word what one had said to Dan Stack's mother more than two years earlier about a "young life offered on the altar of freedom." Like Dan Stack, too, his name would be chiselled into granite on Runnymede's memorial to airmen with no known grave.

Airmen would make up nearly 40% of Canada's 1939-45 war dead, and at times Betty McCabe worked late and even overnight at the job of keeping track of such things. It kept two shifts of W.Ds busy in the Records division of R.C.A.F. headquarters in London. "We had a direct open line to the Air Ministry," she'd say, "and were kept busy recording casualties during raids over enemy territory." Back in Ottawa, too young to go overseas, Betty's kid sister Margaret was doing the same kind of work and finding herself watching, as Betty did, for names of men she knew, and which would make her sad when she had to send a telegram to tell a wife or family they were dead or missing or prisoners. Now Bert Emmerson's was one of them.

Chapter Ten

In Italy, the 1st Division's long march through the mountains brought it by winter to the valley of the Moro River and violence such as it had never known. Violence in getting across the river, violence in getting into the farmlands and vineyards beyond it, violence after that. Days of it. Nights of it in a squalor of December mud and cold and repetitious death. By comparison, divisional commander Maj.-Gen. Chris Vokes would say, everything before this was a nursery tale. The losing of a war was over. On the Moro, it became evident that its winning would be brutal.

Pte. Everett Shea was there with a mortar crew in the Hastypees which paid a heavy price getting across the Moro and a heavy price once they did. He survived. Gunner Ells Taylor of Taylor Village was there with the 8th Battery, and survived too—by the same sheer chance that killed Gunner Adrian Martin Howe one day after Capt. Paul Triquet of Quebec's Royal 22nd Regiment won the Victoria Cross nearby, and while the battery's 25 pounders poured rage over the sandbags used as shields and ramparts. Someone told Ells Taylor a parcel had arrived, and he said he'd pick it up when he was relieved at his gun in a minute or so. When he left, he was replaced by Adrian Howe who, before enlisting, had been working on a farm near the farm Taylor had left in 1939.

In the village the Howes were black and the Hows white. Adrian was one of the former. He was 20 years of age, and he had led an obscure, impoverished and difficult life. His documents said his next of kin were his Aunt Sarah Howe and her husband Hance who was the janitor at the Anglican Church. He had, in fact, been born to an unmarried sister of Hance Howe and had lived for some time in an orphanage. His sergeant, Gene Hunter, and his friend John Robinson, both of whom would eventually live in the village for years, said he was a small, skinny kid proud of his muscles, happy go lucky, always ready with a helping hand, a great favorite with a strange nickname: Scottie. His comrades thought of his smile as a beam that lit their world — till he was killed almost immediately after relieving Ells Taylor. A history of the 2nd Field Regiment, R.C.A., says he was one of four men killed by the premature explosion of one of their own shells.

Pte. Gerald Ward was on the Moro too; was there by one of the incidents that posted men as reinforcements to units other than their own. He'd come overseas with the 14th Field Ambulance only to be recovering from a sickness when the lst Division needed men and drafted him. After months of battle, he was with Ontario's 5th Field Ambulance on the Moro and in what became famous as a minor Stalingrad. Which is to say that in the last week of December, at the climax of the Moro fighting, he was in Ortona, an Adriatic seaport, when two Canadian infantry battalions fought Germany's crack lst Parachute regiment. Fought a remorseless, house-to-house struggle in a city most of its 10,000 people had fled, a city of ruined buildings and shambled streets, where soldiers were served the most famous Christmas dinner of Canada's war. He was in the middle of that ravaged city by then, with guns firing behind and over the basement he and his fellow medicals had shovelled clean of debris and where they slept on bedding on the floor, and where they returned after getting the wounded back from regimental aid posts and over to medical care across a courtyard.

By now he spoke fairly good Italian and knew the ropes of warfare, such as having access in Ortona to a 10-gallon keg of wine which one reached through a hole in a roof and tapped to fill a jug. Thus he took part in one of the epics of Canada's war, though no one could be sure that Ortona's fighting made much sense for either side. But it *was* the Germans who left first.

The nursing sisters of No.1 Canadian General Hospital could have used his Italian that Christmastime. Because Teresa Hickman and friends went out looking for decorations and only succeeded in confusing an Italian shopkeeper. He wanted to know who they were, so out came their dictionaries. There, they said, pointing to the words that should explain. The shopkeeper's mouth fell open and he and his wife were still puzzled when the nursing sisters left with crepe paper in red, green and white, the colors in Italy's flag. It was only when they got back to their quarters that someone explained they'd said they were nursing mothers. They went back to the shop next day and got things straightened out, and the shopkeeper was so pleased he invited them in for wine.

On the night of the first day of 1944, Bill Palmer's crew took off from Cairo to fly 25 people hundreds of miles to Tunis. The R.A.F.'s 267 Squadron still covered a lot of familiar ground even though it now was based near the Italian city of Bari, on the Adriatic Sea and well down the coast from the Moro Valley where army violence was dying into winter's respite. Jack Rice was flying a two-engine American-built Dakota and he nearly flew it into extinction. In the worst storm Bill Palmer had ever known in the air, it tossed in violent winds and ice coated its wings and became so heavy that they couldn't make it over the mountains my brother Hank had seen. When they turned back they found they didn't have enough fuel to get to an airport. So there they were with only one thing to do: land in the best place they could find. And pray.

They came down north of Sfax, on Tunisia's Mediterranean coast, with everyone braced for the worst. Crashlanded. Survived. Climbed out into the night, in a field, with a damaged plane and an overwhelming gratitude. Not that Bill Palmer told his parents, anymore than he had told of a very close call in making it into Gibraltar in the past. They would never have known it happened if one of the passengers hadn't taken the trouble to get their address and write them. Robert Mackey said he was one of a group of American civilian aircraft technicians employed on war projects in the Middle East. They'd never met the Dakota's crew before takeoff but by the time they crashlanded Bob Mackey knew he'd never forget them. "Every passenger in that plane," he said, "owes his life to Bill and the rest of that brilliant crew," and he wanted their families to know it. When Bill's parents asked why he hadn't told them, he said he didn't want them to worry.

By New Year's Day the Italian Front had ground to a halt in the mud north of Ortona. The generals' hope had been that by this time they would be in a glittering prize called Rome, but they ended up taking what they could get, and it didn't glitter, and it was miles south of Rome. This gave the Germans a breathing spell in Italy just when they ran out of breathing spells where Obergefreiter Klotz was. By January he was in a violent storm that would last much longer than the one Bill Palmer had faced. For the Russians had turned their war entirely around. They were attacking with more men, better planes, better tanks and, yes, better generals because they kept theirs and Hitler kept firing his and running things himself. This was hard on his generals but not nearly as hard as it was on the troops he ordered to hold what they had till his genius came up with methodologies that would win the war. That winter it worked in Italy but not in Russia, and certainly not where Obergefreiter Klotz was.

He was there when the Germans began to do on a

massive scale what the French had done more than 130 years before. On the Leningrad front, they fell back from the ring they had held around most of that suffering city for nearly three years. Even as Leningrad's people rejoiced, their tormentors vanished into that torment of the ages, the Russian winter. Obergefreiter Klotz's happy months in Estonia were over, and so were the leisurely days in the village houses behind an orderly front. He was back on the Leningrad front when the great retreat began, back with his unit, his friends, but everything had changed. He found himself heading back to Estonia but in a very unhappy way, with confusion and even panic everywhere.

The world became like something wrenched from Tolstoy's *War and Peace*. His unit was attached to a frontline infantry regiment, only now there was really nothing for it to do because there was nothing to hitch communications lines to and maintain them for. When an officer found him and others stringing wires at the airport for the city of Pushkin, he told them to stop being fools and get out, get moving. The infantry regiment was decimated. Obergefreiter Klotz saw its survivors stumbling back, stumbling on, young men gray and haggard with an age beyond their own. There was no frontline, there was only chaos and shouting and the dissolutions of hope, and across his vision flowed images that would haunt him forever. The city of Luga burning, set afire by the retreating Germans. Railway tracks torn up, made useless by retreating Germans. In darkness, soothing his face with snow. Bloody snow. A sled loaded for flight, left behind in flight. Horses bolting across the bleak white landscape, men behind them, gesturing, waving, cursing, animals and men terrified, the horses dragging guns the men had fired for months, dragging the artillery of broken siege, fleeing, as fugitives flee. The regiment falling back with fewer and fewer men. The infantry and the artillery making stands, trying to check the Russians, the snow growing black from the firing of their guns. But the Russians flowing after them and around them and through them, white figures in a white world, camouflaged, merciless in the merciless cold. At times they have to fight their way through enemy soldiers who have swept on beyond them and barred their path, their retreat, their tractor-drawn guns, haunted, taunted the residue of the great and arrogant dream of quick and inevitable Aryan victory over a lesser Slavic people. In one way or another it would lurch on for weeks, and in his high French army boots Obergefreiter Klotz was like some figure out of Tolstoy. But no Tolstoy would arise to tell the enormity of it all. Perhaps not even Tolstoy could have. But one thing might have intrigued him. The officers of Obergefreiter Klotz's signals unit still had with them the three Russian women who had become part of the solace and comfort of their lives.

By strange concidence, it was just when the war became very serious for him that something quite different happened to that other human being who had also become part of the village's education in the fragilities of peace. Strange that the German-born schoolboy should become a soldier embroiled in very nasty fighting just when dedicated militiaman Charlie Crandall learned there would be no fighting for him. In January, in England, the New Brunswick Rangers were slimmed once more, their anti-aircraft company eliminated. Major Crandall was well into his 39th year, and he ceased to be commanding officer. Directly or indirectly, he was swept up in the numerous changes a new broom was making in Andy McNaughton's First Canadian Army now that Andy himself was gone. Was out after bitterly and unsuccessfully opposing its split into two parts. General Andy headed home, Major Charlie took up a staff job in Britain.

But for FO. Warren Alvin Duffy January was the happy month he was accepted into a fighting unit that took only the very best. At 21, after 15 months in a training unit, he was invited to join the elite 617 Squadron of the R.A.F. It had been formed early in 1943 for one very special reason, to smash the great Moehne and Eder dams in the Ruhr Valley with bombs invented by aircraft designer and engineer Barnes Wallis. Its success became one of the most celebrated achievements of the war, and 617 went on from there to do "special duties," to carry out many perilous attacks, refine pinpoint bombing, take pride in two Victoria Cross winners, Guy Gibson and Leonard Cheshire, win 150 other decorations and be described as "the most effective unit of its size the British forces ever had."

It was, according to FO. Don Bell, D.F.C, when 617 was looking for crews that "they heard about Duff." The record of an interview with the CBC quoted Bell as saying "it was his record and all-round ability as a low flier that interested the dam busters." In the printed version the words "as a low flier" were pencilled out, perhaps because this was the very thing that had brought Duffy two reprimands. Yet it was in all probability also what helped convince others that he belonged with the very best, and 617 got him to bring the best with him, let him pick his own crew. He chose Bell as navigator and four others with medals from previous tours of operations. With 617, the slim, spirited kid who had lived in the village for 10 years became the heart and soul of what author Paul Brickhill would call a crew made up of "a hard-boiled bunch of Canadians." He also recorded in *The Dam Busters* that within hours of their arrival on January 4 Duffy and his crew were notorious: "They could not find the toilets but, being resourceful men from the backwoods, relieved themselves out the window. In the morning they were brought before the group captain, the boss, who eyed them coldly and said: 'If you fellows do your job well you can get away with almost anything on this squadron, but one thing you can't do is piddle on the group captain.' He had been walking below at the wrong moment. As for the rest of the squadron, they thought it was wonderful that new boys should do that to a senior officer from a great height."

Even so, Warren Duffy wrote home on the 6th that "the CO seems to be a very good type," and that he himself was "really happy." But he and his crew were worked in slowly. It was January 21 before their first operational flight, against a "special target." That same day he won a commendation for a "meritorious performance" in bringing a Wellington to rest without damage when a tire burst on takeoff. Then he went on two courses before returning to 617 in late February. He approved of courses: "You can't know too much." But he was glad to be back flying "just about the biggest ships they've got over here {Lancasters}, and really lovely." Then a revealing note: "It sure is swell to get away from that instructing racket."

In March the word finally came: I was off to Italy where the front remained in a static winter quiet. I got back into a khaki uniform, this time with a war correspondent's shoulder tab, and went to the Aldershot area to wait for a call to a ship. I felt excited, very much alive, even free and exhilarated. Two nights before sailing I went to a hospital and dug the former Supreme Allied Commander of Rigolet, Labrador, out of a sick bed. After his departure from the New Brunswick Rangers, the army had sent Lieut. Richard Emmerson to a holding unit, then on one course after another (chemical warfare, radio communications, sanitation) which was what was happening when he fell ill and went to hospital. He was, however, well enough to go out so we went on a pub crawl in Aldershot, and when I woke in the morning he was in one hospital bed and I was in another. A nurse wanted to know how I got there, and I said the only way I could tell her was if she could tell me where we'd been the night before. She said to go, and I did.

It was a pleasant voyage in a troopship taking army reinforcements through the Mediterranean to Naples. I met, among others, Ross Flemington and Mike Nelligan, the army's two top chaplains, Protestant and Roman Catholic, who went everywhere as smiling buddies. I was touched when "O Canada" was sung by soldiers in English and French separately and then together. The words in French and English said — and meant — considerably different things, but I didn't know that then, and I doubt that many others did. But everybody seemed pleased and very Canadian. In stinking Naples, I passed an R.A.F. headquarters, went in and asked if they could tell me where my cousin Bill Palmer was. They said it would take time and to come in the next time I was in town. After that, three or four of us went up through the mountains to a place called San Vito, below Ortona, and when we got to where the army looked after correspondents the word was that big things would soon be happening. When I bumped into Ev Shea he didn't look very happy about this after all he'd gone through on the Moro. We had a drink and he said, rather wistfully, that being an infantry soldier didn't give you much to look forward to.

In a March of waiting for winter snow and ice to go, Warren Duffy's crew hit its stride and he entered the most exciting period of his life. On the 15th, on the 37th operation of his two tours, he recorded that they were recalled because of bad weather, got off in freezing cold to attack an aero-engine factory near Metz, France, flew through ten-tenths cloud the whole way and found the cloud just as thick over the target. "No hope of bombing," Paul Brickhill would write. "It was so cold in the rear turret that the oxygen mask studs of the gunner's helmet stuck to his face. He did not know it till he dragged his helmet off and a couple of square inches of skin came away with the studs. The medical officer consoled him with a rum."

That was also the night their Lancaster was jumped by four enemy planes, and the two gunners destroyed two of them. "Damage to rear turret. Rear gunner wounded," was all Duffy recorded. But Don Bell would later elaborate, would tell the CBC they were, as usual by then, the leading plane for, this time, a dozen Lancasters, and somewhere north of Reims the German planes attacked them: "Cannon shell came crashing through the kite from the tail, and we heard the rear gunner gasp. We thought he was stitched. In fact, his rear turret was cut to ribbons and the shells whizzed by his ear, but he got off with a wounded hand. A few moments later we heard his gun firing. Knocked the Jerry off like a duck. We had started to take evasive action and although Jerry hit us at a thousand yards he was missing at 500. The mid-upper gunner got one in his sights and gave him a burst that set him on fire. He tailed off to the rear and the rear gunner hit him again, and down he went. The third one came in and couldn't hit us; the mid-upper set fire to him too. The fourth fighter chased us for 25 minutes and didn't get a shot at us. We finally lost him. We were sitting up there taking evasive action, just like an exercise, and it was working perfectly. Except for that first burst, we weren't hit once."

Next night, Brickhill wrote, they attacked "the Michelin rubber factory at Clermont Ferrand, partly sabotaged but still making the Germans 24,000 tires a month. This was an amazing raid ..." And so it went. They were hitting specific targets in France, a factory at St. Etienne, the

Michelin rubber factory, an aero-engine factory at Lyons. Against heavy opposition, they were striking at the production of things the Germans needed to make war, and they could, Don Bell would say, "absolutely devastate an area 50 yards in diameter," about the size of three building lots.

In the darkness of March 24, 76 airmen, 76 prisoners of war, scurried out of a tunnel at Stalag Luft III and fled into Germany's night, hoping at the best to reach freedom, at the least to bedevil the enemy. This was the episode that would become famous as The Great Escape because Paul Brickhill, himself an Australian resident of Stalag Luft III, would write a book about it and then, from this, there would be a movie. Neither Wally Floody nor George Harsh was among those who crawled along the burrowed passage through the sand and came up breathing the sweet air of hope. The ferrets had discovered two tunnels, had begun to suspect more was going on, had dispatched these two and other potential ringleaders to another camp. Joe Emery was in Stalag Luft III that night, and he wished good fortune to those who went, and he saw some of the muffled excitement of their going, but he didn't go himself. He didn't draw one of the lots that would have let him try, and he was soon sobered by the statistics of those who did. Of the 76 who got out, only three made it to Britain. On Hitler's orders, 50 others were shot after recapture. Flight Lieutenant Emery, D.F.C., shared the anger and the grief when the word came through, but he also knew how lucky he'd been.

On April 6, Warrant Officer Palmer wrote home that he'd been doing some "very interesting work for three months." He was hinting about more 267 Squadron "specials." Its two sections were taking turns doing both these and regular flights. The latter went to cities in North Africa and Italy, almost like a peacetime airline. But not the specials. Some took them north, along the coast, then inland, behind the German lines, to watch for signal fires and drop supplies to the Italian partisans who set them. Some took them across the Adriatic to drop supplies to insurgents or partisans in Greece, a country that had spent some three years under German control and whose people were bitterly divided among themselves. Some took them into the mountains of Yugoslavia where Marshal Tito's partisans awaited them with the doubts of communists and the faces battle leaves.

It was Jack Rice who would eventually tell publicly what this could mean, tell the Toronto *Star* that their 400-mile flights into Yugoslavia began when they flew Maj. Randolph Churchill, son of the British prime minister, and a British and American political mission into Tito's rugged haunts. With him and Bill were six Italian transport planes carrying British and Italian paratoopers and an escort of American fighter planes: "The transports dropped their men off too high and started back with the fighters while I made three or four runs at an airfield to drop Churchill and his party. After that, we flew back alone deep in the mountain valleys, stayed right down till we got safely back to our base ... When the time came to bring the Churchill mission out, an R.A.F. plane went in on the partisan runway and reported it was a field—not 700 yards long, as we'd been told, but only 496 yards, with trees at the end. It should have been 2,000 yards. When we went in, I shut off everything and hit the ground, wondering how we were going to get out. We had 16 passengers and a crew of four and we were advised by radio that Yugoslav Chetniks, bitter rivals of Tito, had seen our landing lights and were coming after us. And we were stuck in the mud without even a shovel. While Tito's partisans dug at the mud trying to free our plane, we debated whether to destroy it and head into the hills. Finally we did make a takeoff and came home wide open, flying between the mountains."

On another flight, they brought out 49 wounded women partisans and children. "Some," said Rice, "had arms and legs off and eyes out, but they were very heroic and determined. Even the partisan children fight the Germans effectively. We saw one 12-year-old boy with a long-service decoration. He strutted around with pistols and hand grenades strapped all over him. We were told he had killed any number of Germans ... Each time we flew in partisan women appeared out of the hills carrying rifles and escorting or carrying wounded Allied airmen on litters. They danced their folk dances and sang national songs around the campfires, but they never relaxed their vigilance. Four women with rifles were assigned to guard each member of our crew against surprise attack. Every move you made, they were with you."

Bill Palmer was in on all this "very interesting work." He was also playing tennis and softball, he said, and should soon be swimming, amid "great rumors" that Canadian air crew would go home after three years overseas. He wouldn't put too much faith in them, he said, "but I will go if given the opportunity." He had become the navigator longest with the squadron and he was finding his religion "a great comfort." There were Canadian soldiers around now, though he had yet to meet one from home. But he hoped to, and he was healthy and happy. "There is nothing to worry about," he said. But there was.

On through April Warren Duffy and his crew kept hammering at industrial targets: auto repair shops at

Toulouse, a repair factory in Paris, railway marshalling yards near there, then at Brunswick, Germany, then at Munich, dropping huge bombs nicknamed cookies and 500-pound incendiaries. "Target pranged," he kept recording with satisfaction.

Obergefreiter Klotz was back in the Baltic States where he'd been so happy and felt so good, and the Russians seemed to be attacking not only up here but everywhere: in the Ukraine, the Crimea, Poland, the Balkans. In the nightmare of retreat, his unit had come to Estonia, then fled south to Latvia, with the Russians coming, threatening, and the Germans clinging to what they could hold and what hope they could find. His mind kept implanting images. In one, fleeing, exhausted, he falls asleep on a woodpile, and awakes to plunge on. In one, he comes across Germans who don't know how close the Russians are, and when he tells them they take off. In one, he takes cover under artillery attack and makes a wisecrack and someone asks what in hell there is to be funny about. In one, the Germans are going one way and through veils of snow become aware of Russians going the other. Like ghosts, they pass each other, the sound of their tanks muffled by the endless snow. When his unit reached Estonia orders came to join the headquarters of an infantry division. In Latvia it was ordered to join an anti-tank regiment, and he learned that his half-brother Walter had been killed in Russia's white wilderness, a captain once wounded in Africa, a volunteer slain trying to help contain enemy breakthroughs. Had been buried in a grave with no address. Mourned by the step-father who had called him too idealistic for his own good.

Chapter Ten

The place that became most famous in the Italy of the war was Cassino, a town at the foot of a rugged hill with a monastery at the top. Because it stood behind a river and at the entrance to a valley, it was in highly significant ways the key to how to get to Rome, and thousands of men had died and would die proving how true this was. The Germans were still holding its heights when, in early morning darkness, Nursing Sister Hickman was awakened and informed that she and her friend Ruth had just volunteered to go there. There was, she was told, a pileup of wounded at a casualty clearing station. Help was needed, and it consisted of herself and friend. Volunteers. Within a few hours, they arrived under the shadow of Monte Cassino. There was shelling as they were shown around by the all-male C.C.S. staff, and when this was completed the nursing sisters said thanks but there had been no mention of facilities. Ah, yes, the commanding officer said, and had them escorted to a small tent with a one-holer outhouse seat made of rough wood, and painted pink. Nor was that all the special attention in the weeks they were there. They were also provided with showers: a hose extended from a water truck to a hole in the top of a tent, and an armed sentry stood guard outside while they bathed.

The places Bill Palmer got to that April read like something out of a postwar tourist brochure: Tunis, Malta, Catania, Bari, Algiers, Palermo, Cairo, Mussolini's Marble Arch. On the llth he flew from Naples to Cairo, then back to Marble Arch and the next day on to memorable Malta, then back to base near Bari late the afternoon of the second day. That evening Warrant Officer Palmer played badminton, had a drink or two in 267's sergeants' mess and then went to bed in a room on the second floor of an

Italian barracks. He had seemed restless and he may well have been fatigued, someone would remember after he was found lying on the paved barracks ground some 30 feet below his room at about 0300 hours of the 13th. Found by two airmen to whom he spoke rationally though in a dazed way and who assumed he'd had too much to drink, carried him in and put him in bed. At 0630 hours he told someone he was feeling rather ill but would soon be all right. Two hours later a doctor ordered him to hospital. On the 18th he died of internal injuries.

There were two immediate inquiries which indicated he'd died as the result of a problem no one had ever reported, and he couldn't believe he had: he occasionally walked in his sleep. Two men testified that he had tried at times to get to a window and been pulled back, then remembered nothing of it when he awoke. This night he apparently did get a window open, stepped out and fell. After the testimony of numerous witnesses, no blame was attached to anyone. He had died, it was concluded, a natural death. Died two months short of his 23rd birthday and a third cable to Ruthie Lewis. Died in keeping with the tragic destiny of the 37 observers who had trained together at Fingal, Ont., and received their wings from Billy Bishop. By war's end it would be said it had claimed them all.

When I went back to the R.A.F. in Naples, they had tracked Bill Palmer down in the lost legion of Canadians. But he'd been killed since I was there before. I thought of how close our families were, and I got to Bari and out to 267 Squadron. That night, by chance, there was a banquet, and Jack Rice and I drank a lot of liquor. He gave me the story of how Bill had died, and hoped I'd understand that the party meant no disrespect. No one would have known better, he said, that there were times when you had to let your hair down. Next morning I went out to the grave in a dignified Italian cemetery, and the sun of spring was shining, and something happened that I still find hard to define. Someone has kept a clipping of my story that was published from coast to Canadian coast. It says I was struck by the names I found around the plain black cross that bore Bill Palmer's name, that I found myself writing them down: "There lay Pte. Josep Lapowsky of the Polish Lancers and Pte. Sepoy Amhed Shah of the Indian Army, Sgt. H.W.O. Pigram of the R.A.F. and Nursing Sister Anne Buckley of New Zealand. There lay Cpl. N.W. Hanlan and Pte. Richard Greig of Canada's Edmonton Regiment, Misevic Sasinovitch of the Yugoslav partisans, and Hu Ling, a Chinese merchant seaman, and scattered among all these there were graves marked unknown, and nearby there was a general grave that bore the plural of that haunting word."

It was to a large extent this way because something horrendous had happened in Bari in December: German bombers had caught its harbor packed with ships, had started great fires and hurled loose from one vessel its secret and terrible cargo, poison gas the Allies had in case the Germans used their own. No one would ever know how many lives were lost that night, how many suffered ghastly deaths from poison gas, but there were hundreds: men on ships, people in the streets, soldiers on leave, people in their homes. Bill didn't mention the disaster in his letters, perhaps because of censorship, perhaps again to protect his parents from reality or perhaps because it would take years for the truth to come out. But the graves near his were those of its victims, and they got to me in a way nothing else had. About what the war was doing to the world and what the world was doing to itself. About a civilization that had created a killing ground so vast it reached into every continent, so complex that men from some 30 nations and colonies of nations were fighting in Italy alone, so penetrating that it had plucked a kid out of an obscure New Brunswick village and laid him to rest this far from home. If it weren't some form of insanity or even death wish that had brought those names together, what in God's name was it?

As for Bill, one compensation came too late: posthumously, he'd be given the officer's commission that might have made a difference in the monotony and loneliness of his life. In difficult financial circumstances, his parents would seek something more tangible, a pension for his loss, and would be turned down. I doubt that they ever knew something else: that he had apparently been granted a leave in Canada and turned it down to stay with the unit that had become his home, his team. Personally, I can't help wondering whether standing beside his grave may have been what really started whatever this book becomes.

By May the Canadian soldiers were in the middle of Italy, below Rome, near Cassino. They had been moved there in great secrecy and in great secrecy they were preparing once more for battle, and this was when someone discovered Gallo and Letino at the end of a drunken road that wandered into isolation through the hills. They were a mile apart, with a castle in between. Gallo had 3,000 people and they tended to think of themselves as descendants of Bulgarian barbarians who had found their way here in the 7th century. Letino's 1,500 people traced their origins to Greek nomads who came hence in 1174. In both communities the people spoke Italian and had Italian blood in their veins, but thought of themselves in terms of who their ancestors were and where they came from.

For centuries, in both places, they had raised food and

livestock and drunk wine and lived a timeless peasant existence. Did ancient folk dances on festival days and married their young in blazes of color and happiness. But as communities they remained aloof and separate. They frowned on intermarriage. They had nothing to do with each other except in feuds. The feuding had finally stopped in the 19th century, and after many years they sometimes had football games, but that was about as far as it went, and even then it was said in Gallo that Gallo had always won in the feuding and in Letino it was said that Gallo had always lost. When the war came, both saw young men go away and some not come back, and in both villages they could for months hear the guns around Cassino. Also Germans came, but went so swiftly that they did nothing to make the two peoples think of themselves as potentially one, as standing together under a common adversity. When in May some Canadians came, they were told in both places that nothing much had changed, that the war had, so far, passed through their lives without brutality or bloodshed or much of anything of significance at all. Since by then it had passed over much of Italy like a storm with evil in it, and since the Canadians knew the storm was about to rage again, they went away from the two villages talking about a Shangri La, or two Shangri Las. They also said how strange it was that Gallo and Letino were the way they were, though in reality they could be seen, together, as their own country writ small.

Such was the sound and fury of distant guns on the night of May 10-11 that the people of Gallo and Letino must have known a great attack was beginning around Cassino, though no Canadian went back to find out. A great attack was beginning, in fact, from one coast of Italy to the other, beginning around Cassino alone with the thunder of hundreds of guns and with plans to, first, break past it across the Rapido river and into the Liri Valley, second, to break through a murderous defensive position that spanned the valley and was called the Hitler Line, then, third, to exploit toward Rome. Half a century later, what are left in one mind are fleeting images. A night turned white with shellfire. Morning dew on farmyard grass and the staccato voices of Calgary Regiment tank crews coming back by radio to their command post, telling of crossing the river with the magnificent little Gurkha soldiers they have a great affection for. Ducking at the sound of an exploding shell, then seeing three officers politely ignoring a novice's embarrassment.

In the ruins of Cassino, our jeep picks up a happy-go-lucky British soldier; he has his rifle and he is hitchiking to a unit that *is* in the attack. He has a pal up there, he says, and it would be nice to be with him. He might well be talking of a birthday party. A very businesslike major peers out upon a sunlit world from a big, dug hole shielded by an almost ornate pallisade of sandbags that other officers joke about. The serpentine body of an army writhing forward, stopping, starting, each regiment divided into parts scattered back for miles. The lurching by of the things that have made war mechanical: jeeps, trucks, tanks, light armored vehicles, soldiers among them, shuffling to a somewhere they are not in a hurry to get to, dust rising above them, like a banner flowing pronouncements through the sky.

In a copse, all by itself, a mortar crew from Saskatchewan fires at enemies it cannot see. The ugly snouts of 25-pounder guns fire, fire, fire, the gunners sweating around them. Behind a strapping lieutenant, a platoon from Toronto's 48th Highlanders marches toward the frontline three abreast, exactly as it would across a parade square, the officer sounding like the captain of a football team he is leading into the most important game of the year. He will, in fact, very shortly be among those surprisingly few infantrymen who constitute the "sharp end" facing the "sharp end" of the enemy.

In the mountains to the west are strange allies: French African tribesmen called Goums who wear flowing cloaks and have women with them in B Echelon and attack in their own unorthodox way, and most effectively — they terrify the Germans in the darkness — as long as they can put to their own use whatever lies in their path, be it loot or liquor or women. German prisoners keep coming back, dusty, often unkempt, silent. Among them are Poles who gladly join the Poles fighting on the other side. Or Oriental-looking people drafted from God knows where. I look at them wondering if Gottfried Klotz could be among them. Then the image vivid above all others:

I am crossing a farm field in a valley green and beautiful to behold. On both eastern and western horizons there are mountains and to the east and south, looking back, you can see the physical feature that was for months the anchor of the German line: the great hump of Monte Cassino with its controversial and now shattered monastery, destroyed by air attack because the Germans might be using it as an observation post. This is the Liri valley where military scholars have come for centuries to study how to make war, and this is where the Germans have built their Hitler Line, a mesh of guns and mines and concrete so terrible that one has to wonder that anything could smash it, and that men would have the courage to try. I am heading for the city of Pontecorvo where the streets are thick and sad with ruin. Due ahead is the Aquino airport where a squadron of Ontario Regiment tanks was trapped in the open and is still sending smoke into the bright morning air, and I see him. I see a blonde kid lying in the grass, alone, and immediately in front of his body is the ugly scar of the explosive that killed him. In one of his hands there is something white, a sheet of paper with the sun on it, shining, and I reach down and take it, and what it is is a letter. A letter home. The sort a million wartime mothers got from a million sons. Don't worry, it says. I'm doing fine. I'm healthy and I'm getting lots to eat and they're treating me good; with any luck I'll be home for Christmas. No mention of battle or death or fear or where he is or what he's about to do at the sharp end. I stand there reading it, and a terrible sense of the loneliness of death in battle comes over me. I find myself wondering why he has the letter in his hand. Did he forget to mail it before going into battle? Did he want to make sure someone saw it so his mother would get it? Did he pull it out hoping to scrawl one last message? Did he pull it out because it was, in a sense, a link with home and family? I don't know. I'll never know.

He was a private in the West Nova Scotia Regiment. The little tag he wore around his neck gave his name, Edward Drillio, and his regimental number, and years later I'd find the name in Tom Raddall's history of the regiment, find it listed among "our heroic dead" which is a tribute it deserves in a place where it belongs. And in 1994 I'd visit his grave near where he fell half a century back.

On the 23rd of May, New Brunswick's Carleton and York Regiment of the 3rd Brigade, 1st Canadian Division, first broke through the Hitler Line in their greatest day of the war and as part of a vital victory in the march on Rome. But to their right the 2nd Brigade, the western brigade, took a terrible pounding because its own right flank was open when it shouldn't have been, and the Germans kept pouring shells into it. This is why Lt. Col. Cameron Ware of the Princess Patricia's Canadian Light Infantry was the way he was. An image: he is in a deep, precise slit trench. He is one of those battalion commanders who "fight" the army, who have men both below and above them but on whom the immediately decisive share of battle descends The Canadians take lawyers, engineers, stock brokers and other civilians and turn them into good ones. Cameron Ware is one of the best, but he is a professional soldier. War is what he's been trained for since his teens, and he has just passed through as sad an experience as a battalion commander can know. His Princess Patricias have been slain and sacrificed in futility. Decimated. Their bodies are scattered due ahead, among torn trees and smoking tanks and abandoned guns, and his eyes are like no eyes I've ever seen. Glazed. Exhausted. Glassy. As though the hospital of the human body has treated them for the temporary and merciful containment of disaster.

He talks in an inordinately measured voice, a polite and courteous voice schooled by the chivalries of the officers' mess, but it is when he looks out and sees a soldier lying on the grass that something more comes through. The ring of command is gone. The bark and bite of rank are gone. When he calls out to the soldier that he is in the open and should take cover because shells are still coming down, his voice is like that of a father speaking quietly to a son. Like that of a man made gentle by loss, by seeing war expose the frail and precious quality of human life by its terrible capacity for destroying it. The soldier hears him, but doesn't move. He says he's too tired to move, but what he may well mean, and what Cameron Ware may well accept he means, is that he is immersed in his own gentleness of grief for the friends he's lost and the beloved battalion that's lost them. He wants to be left alone, the voice implies, and his colonel understands and respects his wish. His glazed eyes look away.

That night the Germans tried to contain the breakthrough a few miles north of the Hitler Line by taking a stand on an unpretentious river called the Melfa. They failed to do so primarily because of Maj. Jack Mahony of the Westminster Regiment. A gentle man with a core of steel, he won a V.C. when his company gained and kept a Melfa bridgehead, so the attack could go on. Even as Mahony was doing this immediately ahead and above, it was the considerable height and sandy character of the Melfa's banks which became of importance to a soldier who had known the summer of 1933 in all its glory. Lieut. Douglas MacKean, a minister's red-headed son, was sent forward by the Cape Breton Highlanders on a reconnaissance mission to report on where and how to get the battalion across the river. He was evacuated hours later from a cave in the Melfa's bank, where he'd been put, unconscious, after being wounded. Three days later Pte. Patrick de Varennes, out of that picture of Ina Breen's class in 1925, out of Labrador and the diminishment of the New Brunswick Rangers, joined the Westminsters as a reinforcement. They were a very good outfit indeed, and he'd be with them for some seven months and through some rough moments, he who had once hoped to be a priest.

Even as the Allies headed for Rome — it fell on June 4 — L. Cpl. Gerald Adshade had every expectation of sharing in further exciting events. For the village's one paratrooper could see all around him signs that there would very shortly be an invasion of France in which his outfit, the 1st Canadian Parachute Battalion of the 6th British Parachute Division, would be eminently involved. There were so many tanks and vehicles and guns being crowded into certain parts of southern England, so many soldiers hiding under trees near crucial seaports, so many officers being busy, so many people spreading rumors that there could be no doubt that dramatic and quite possibly disastrous history was about to be made. Most of them would make it by crossing the Channel by ship, but Lance Corporal Adshade would not. He wore the maroon beret, the high, shining brown boots, the paratroop wings that signified that he'd be one of thousands of Allied soldiers who'd jump out of planes in darkness and come down by parachute to take out key German positions just before the main invasion. He looked the part: compact, tough, ready, a strapping specimen as keen as ever to do what he'd been waiting years to do. Twenty-two years of age, his documents said, still telling the lie he'd told at 16. Then he made one last practice jump and landed in a tree. His leg was caught in a strap, and by the time he was cut loose it was badly mangled. Off he went to hospital for an operation, and as he lay there he knew the whole vast company of Canadians, Americans and Britons would set forth without him for their rendezvous with history.

Even as he grieved over this, entrepreneurial Pte. Herman "Newt" Cooke of the 14th Field Ambulance, 3rd Canadian Division, ran a crown and anchor board and gathered in considerable sums from his fellow soldiers under the trees of England. Also experienced an urge to make one last visit to London, to his favorite pub, the Elephant and Castle, even though he would have to violate orders to do so and even though the invasion camps were sealed. He found a willing accomplice in George Breau and together they slipped away to the great metropolis and got back only with great difficulty because there were military policemen everywhere.

On the 5th of June Warren Duffy went on his 46th operation. Without elaboration, he recorded it as "special tactical cooperation with second front invasion force." At last the preliminaries were over and the 6th of June arrived, and for the rest of their lives people would recall where they were on that fabled day. What brother Hank would recall was being sent, by chance, to London and the strange way London was. As with Gerald Adshade, injuries had sidetracked his military career; one leg was shorter than the other because of an accident in Africa. He got to London by train that day, and it was on the way down from an air force station in the Midlands that he began to notice how different things were. "To my surprise," he'd write, "the train was not crowded, and I got a double seat all by myself. At the first stop, at one of the largest railway junctions in the country, the platforms appeared almost deserted and the porters weren't shouting as loudly as usual, and when they did shout their voices reverberated eerily through the practically empty building. In London, the Picadilly commandos (prostitutes) who ordinarily lined the Circus by the hundreds were conspicious by their absence. At the Service Club, there were only three of us for dinner. In Hyde Park, the traditional orators were fewer than usual, and their chatter less vehement. Their audiences were small, and for the most part comprised of civilians. The largest gathering was singing the old popular hymns."

He went to a canteen a short distance away. "It too was practically deserted. At nine o'clock the King spoke to his people. The dozen or so British soldiers in the canteen, the two bobbies and the elderly lady behind the counter listened and stared pensively into space. Through a window I could see the Hyde Park orators flailing the air and a grounded barrage balloon tugging half-heartedly at its moorings, as though aware its (anti-aircraft) job was nearly done, and it was glad it was. At the end of His Majesty's speech, the national anthem was played and the soldiers jumped to their feet and stood rigidly to attention.

There was no trace of a smile on their faces, or on the faces of anyone else I met in London that day. There was no laughter, no visible sign of emotional stress. It was as though England were holding its breath, and collectively praying." About the invasion of France.

Chapter Eleven

OF THE TENS OF thousands of people who saw something of that momentous event it's doubtful that any had a better seat than Harry Ison's boy Edgar. On the night in which June 5 became June 6 he flew out of England as a mid-upper gunner in a bomber of 432 Squadron, the so-called Leaside Squadron of 6 Group, R.C.A.F. They crossed the Channel and ran north along the coast of France dropping bombs on gun batteries and other targets. He'd been at this sort of thing since April and there had been some very rough times. His plane had made it back to England twice after being badly mauled by enemy fire. Once the crew had counted 36 holes. Once, on a daylight mission, they'd been hit and he'd been sure they were going into the sea. On the other hand, he had been officially credited with shooting down one German plane, a Junkers 88, and was personally convinced he'd shot down another, a Messerschmidt 109. As a mid-upper gunner, he sat on top of the plane and, one might say, on top of the world, and he could see better than anyone else in the crew, but never would this advantage be as vivid as in the early morning of this 6th of June 1944. They were heading home and he was keeping alert for enemy action, and dawn's light was coming across the Channel when he beheld below a quite incredible spectacle, that vaulted into memory and would remain forever there. The pilot was under orders to stay a bit away from what was happening but it was plainly visible. The Channel was alive with ships. Miles of ships under clouds of warplanes. A stunning sweep and pageantry of ships in choppy waters. Big ships. Little ships. Ships with guns raging. Ships with tens of thousands of men with guns. Ships heading for the coast of France, for where the Germans were. Invasion ships. Second-front ships. Ships in such overwhelming numbers and ordered and even stately ranks that Edgar Ison knew at once what they meant and could find just one word to describe it: "Fantastic." He'd still be using it half a century later.

At the time, he'd have been impressed if he'd known that some 20,000 Canadians were involved in what he beheld , and that some 19 of them came from the village where he lived. When six Allied divisions started landing early in the morning, there were 14th Field Ambulance men in assault sections attached to the three battalions of the 7th Brigade, 3rd Division, and there were others elsewhere. All told, the unit was divided into seven groups called serials and assigned to get the wounded back and to give them frontline treatment or send them on. The tank landing craft Earl Stiles and Frank Tracy were on had two three-ton lorries and two heavy ambulances and one smaller one. By the time it anchored a few hundred yards offshore, waiting, there had been landings and fighting for nearly four hours, and the men could see fires burning, warships firing, small, stubby landing craft all over the place. Yet things seemed surprisingly peaceful.

Sgt. Ernie Crosson and L. Cpl. Arnold Tower were there with the North Nova Scotia Highlanders that day. Cpl. Raymond Mitton was there with the Stormont,

Dundas and Glengarry Highlanders. His village neighbors Walter "Mousie" and Victor Amisson were there with the 3rd Anti-Tank Regiment, an outfit with both self-propelled and truck-drawn guns. Lieut. Dan Hanington had hoped to be there in the *New Waterford*, one of the R.C.N.'s new frigates, only to be disappointed because she needed repairs. Amid all the confusions, the traffic jams, the tensions, Sgt. Paul Whalen was there with the Signals Corps and came upon entrepreneurial Pte. Newt Cooke at his post with the 14th Field. Private Cooke's recollection would be that Sergeant Whalen was less than optimistic that the landing could survive and that it was fortunate that he (Private Cooke) had already exchanged with a Frenchman a quantity of cigarettes for a quantity of calvados, the trenchant wine of the Norman countryside. By the time Sergeant Whalen left, he'd say, he was ready to take on the entire German Army.

It was dark when one landing craft lowered its ramp onto a motorized raft and Earl Stiles, Frank Tracy and other soldiers and their vehicles started going ashore on it. Earl perched on a vehicle beside his friend Percy Fletcher, the one black in the 14th Field, awed as rocket ships fired multiple tracers into the night. Then a nearby craft hit a mine and blew up and they could see chaos and, very close, another mine. They fled to the back of the raft, screaming a warning, and the raft stopped just in time. When they got ashore, the 14th had an advanced dressing station set up and was treating wounded soldiers, most of them Germans. One sergeant had been wounded and seven men were missing, presumably drowned while in support of the Canadian Scottish Regiment from Victoria, B.C. They would, in fact, eventually show up after surviving a terrifying immersion in the Channel, and Percy and Lloyd Atkinson would be among them.

By nightfall, the Canadians had had 359 men killed and

made the deepest penetration inland, could see the city of Caen, and had learned lessons no training could impart. Al Tower would remember one: a rough, tough soldier, a fighting hellcat in England, going to pieces almost immediately after landing. The three-regiment 2nd Canadian Armored Brigade would remember another: in losing a considerable number of tanks, they learned what infernos they could be. All in all, the greatest invasion in history had not achieved all its objectives, but it had breached the Germans' vaunted Atlantic Wall and gained a great victory. Sergeant Whalen's fears had not been fulfilled; the Canadians and their allies were in France to stay.

Off the coast of Normandy in the frigate *New Waterford*, Lieut. Dan Hanington had his own ringside seat as navigation officer for the navy's 6th Escort Group. Their job was to fend off attacks by any German submarines and small surface raiders trying to interfere with the flow of things to support the invasion: "The battleships and monitors were lying at anchor off the beaches and bombarding the roads and rail lines up to 25 or 30 miles inland; at night the explosions lit the horizon and the roar was continuous. Then there was the extraordinary sight of hundreds of DC3 aircraft, Dakotas, each towing a glider full of airborne troops to be released and land in the general vicinity of an enemy-held objective."

Within one day of the landings, Ernie Crosson and Al Tower were involved in the North Nova Scotia Highlanders' brutal encounter with fanatic elements of the 12th S.S-Hitler Youth Division commanded by one Kurt Meyer, soon to be a general. The Highlanders were trying to get to Carpiquet airport. The Germans were trying to drive them into the sea. It was their first encounter; it would not be the last. Caught too far forward, lacking artillery support, two North Nova companies were riddled by infantry and tanks, the remnants forced back, but Meyer didn't get to the sea. Sergeant Crosson of the mortar platoon was involved in the wild fighting to stem the tide. Al Tower found himself departing battalion headquarters for temporary frontline duty, then helping the chaplain round up the dead.

Within days of the landing, the ingredients for quite a tale about Back Road boys would be available for old Bill O'Blenis, the storyteller. Two were the Atkinsons, Percy and Lloyd, who couldn't swim but whose lifejackets saved them from the Channel that claimed a colleague who could swim very well. One was Raymond Mitton who on the 8th of June became the first village boy to be killed in Normandy. He died of wounds around Les Buissons, a hamlet the soldiers called Hell's Corners. Died because there were so many wounded help didn't get to him till too late. Died fighting the German who had driven the North Novas back with a devastating counter-attack. Died not far from where New Brunswick's 105th anti-tank battery supported the infantry, and Sgt. Walter Amisson did so well as a troop sergeant that he would eventually be awarded a mention in despatches.

Then there was old Bill's grandson, the Billy Manship who had wept because the forces wouldn't take him. He had stuffed himself with food while working on the extra gangs for the C.N.R., built himself up to 150 pounds, and finally heard the army say that would do. It made old Bill O'Blenis weep, and he himself found that the prospect of going to war was not as appealing as it had been. He'd quit school after Grade 8, been a cobbler, worked in lumber mills, gone west for prairie harvest, hoboed on freight trains; it was only after he got the job with the railway that he reached out for a happy home life with a wife and family. He'd become the father of two children, and now the weeping in him was over the thought of leaving them.

This was the way it had been in the long army wait in Britain: even in uniform, men reached out for certainties the Depression had denied. That's how it had been with Raymond Mitton who found there his first home in years, had given his wife papers to fill out so she could greet him in Canada when the war was over; what he didn't know was that she was pregnant for a second time. After his own long wait, the stunning thing for Billy Manship was how quickly the army could act. It sent him out of Halifax with the first big batch of reinforcements for a Normandy where battle was already congealing into the shape it would hold for weeks. Sent him off within 24 hours of Raymond Mitton's death, which he didn't even know had happened. But the newspapers were full of stories about what he was heading for, and when he said goodbye to his mother he said he felt he would never see her again, and she felt the same way although she didn't tell him.

In Normandy, his guitar-playing friend Earl Stiles learned something Nursing Sister Hickman learned in Italy: that the wounded did things to those who cared for them. Teresa Hickman learned it especially through a young soldier brought to No.1 General with his eyes bandaged and who, once she knew he was from New Brunswick, "got lots of T.L.C. (tender, loving care)." Eventually, because the boy seemed to depend on her, she was asked by a doctor to tell him he'd never see again. "It was," she'd say, "one of the hardest things I've ever done, but it was made bearable by the boy himself. I sat on his bed and talked and then he groped for my hand. 'It's O.K.,' he said, 'you don't have to tell me I'm blind; I've known it all along.' All I could do was give him a big hug and go for a walk."

In Normandy, the wounded came back from fighting

which became a very ghastly thing. The Germans were, many of them, very young and they fought with a terrible, indoctrinated hate and dedication, and they killed prisoners in cold blood, some at Kurt Meyer's headquarters, and the Canadians retaliated in seething anger. The fighting lasted for weeks, in green fields and among trees and hedges and gentle beauty, and the men of the 14th Field Ambulance kept picking the wounded up at infantry regimental aid posts and taking them back in jeep ambulances, and Lance Corporal Stiles saw the way they came. Sometimes there were Canadians and Germans in the same ambulance, mutilated, limbs gone, bloody, groaning. Sometimes weeping. Often just sitting there, quiet, waiting in or near the great tents because there were others with greater needs. Sometimes silent in what he'd call "the compassion of shock."

Years later he'd sit down and write that phrase and the scenes would come surging back. "You were," he'd write, "often only for minutes, as intensely close to them as men ever get, and then they were gone. But part of them had become part of you." The Canadian who would never again know a sex life became part of him. The German who walked into the great tent with grenade fragments peppering his body and everything in his face missing from the nose down, teeth, mouth, chin all gone, yet both his jugular veins untouched as by some miracle. The German of 16 or so, blonde, Teutonic, who came in with a leg wound and could speak English so that what the Hitler Youth were fanatic about came out of him. "It's strange," Earl Stiles told him, hurrying, "that you're going where I'd like to go and I'm going where you'd like to go," and when the boy frowned and asked what he meant he said, "You're going to Canada as a prisoner of war and I'm going to Berlin." The boy soldier sat bolt upright on a stretcher, fury on his face. "You'll never get to Berlin," he snarled. "Yes, we will," said soldier Stiles, "and we'll be there in a year," and he gave the stretcher a jolt, and saw the boy wince, then vanish for more elaborate help.

Half a century later he'd remember. Half a century later Teresa Hickman would regret that she couldn't remember the blind soldier's name or home town because he was as vivid to her as he'd ever been.

If things had worked out differently, Uli Klotz might have heard George Goad's daughter Jean sing a solo at the village's 1944 school closing. But it would probably have been a different solo. Hers was entitled "The world is waiting for the sunrise," and no one present could have known how relevant it would have been for the Klotz family. Because Uli was one of the thousands of soldiers slain that murderous June. He'd lived near the village for more than four years but many of its people didn't know he existed. Those who had known him at the Dorchester Cape school said he was popular enough and quite comical. He and Gottfried used to walk up the long hill together, play together on the rocks and sand at Coles Point. He became a teenager in a military organization originally established by Hitler as a counter-balance to the Wehrmacht, the Waffen S.S., the million-strong combat branch of the highly political *Schutzstaffeln* (S.S.). It included men from other countries. In Uli's case, recruiters had come to Mulda's school and said things that led him to join up.

The month he died the Russians ended a pause in their massive movement west and attacked in the Baltic States and south of them. One German Army Group was destroyed within two weeks while trying to defend Lithuania, East Prussia and northern Poland. To the north, another defending Latvia and Estonia was cut off and forced into a broad peninsula as the Russians advanced to the sea west of Riga. This was where Gottfried Klotz was, with the Gulf of Riga on one side and the Baltic Sea on the other, when he heard Uli had been killed. At 18. In Poland. So that now the war had taken both sons whose idealism Hans Klotz had feared would do them in.

In Normandy, the top German general was asked what Germany should do now that she was besieged from west, east and south, her naval forces were dying and city after city was being bombed into ruin. Surrender, he said, and Hitler fired him. It was obvious that Germany could not win, yet she was producing more war materials than ever, striking deadly blows at Britain with unmanned missiles, and thousands of boys like Uli Klotz continued to die for the Feuhrer in forces that would fight resolutely to the end. Uli's brother felt they fought that way now not so much for Hitler as because his enemies were demanding unconditional surrender. From what he could see on a trapped, narrowed Baltic front, they felt that meant either being killed by the Russians or taken prisoner and sent to a living death in Siberia. For them, what Hitler was doing in concentration camps was not something they talked about and not something whose veiled dimensions many may have fully grasped. But one jest indicated they were not unaware of it. "Look out," they'd kid, "or you'll be floating soap," a statement linked to rumors that in concentration camps human flesh was turned into just that. Sometimes they went to farewell parties for Latvians being sent off to become guards at such camps or drafted into the Wehrmacht. They'd see the family tears and they'd have their own reactions when they heard of Latvian guerrillas hiding boys in the hills so they wouldn't have to go. When a rumor spread that the Germans were going to smash free of that Latvian peninsula, strike at the Russians from the rear and rout them, the soldiers laughed as hardened soldiers laugh. When orders were issued that July that Wehrmacht soldiers should salute with the Nazis' extended arm, two months would pass before Obergerfeiter Klotz's officers would pass the orders on.

While the battle for Normandy raged below, the weeks after D-Day brought Warren Duffy's war to a fever of their own, and he exulted in it. On June 10 he wrote home, "Things are the very best here, lots and lots of work to do & I love it. Great news eh? Lots of second front and plenty of bombing, that's where we come in, and, boy, it's great." His Lancaster winged across the English Channel to strike at targets particularly vital to Germany's ability to strike back, at bases for missile attacks on England, at the thick concrete hiding U-boats and the quick little E-boats that waged coastal warfare. Because the targets were so hard to pierce, he dropped enormous "penetration" bombs nicknamed tallboys, one to a plane. He could see Spitfires protecting his formation against tough defences. Yet he still tried to perfect his skills. On June 13, he carried out one of many high-level bombing practices: "Error of 42 yards at 20,000 feet, 6 bombs." His log recorded his attacks: June 8, 47th operation, railway tunnel at Saumer, 1 12,000-lb. bomb. June 14, submarine and E-boat pens at Le Havre, 1 bomb. Squadron went over in formation at daylight. Many hits on target. June 15, submarine and E-boat pens at Boulogne. Could not identify aiming point from 7,000 feet. Brought bomb back. June 19, rocket-bomb installation near Gravelines. Formation effort, 1 tallboy. Fighter cover. June 20, formation ordered to return to base, 10/10 cloud over target. Fighter cover. June 22, Pas de Calais area, ordered to return, 10/10 cloud cover over target. 51st op; last two tries count one complete op. July 4, rocket bomb storage depot near Paris, 1 tallboy, attack appeared successful. July 6, rocket bomb installation in Pas de Calais area,1 tallboy. Several hits seen on target.

His letters, even more than Bill Palmer's, were usually limited by a double censorship, the military's and his own concern for his parents. But the July 6 attack made him do something unusual. At a time when the Germans were already hitting England with so-called flying bombs, were preparing to hit it with even more devastating unmanned missiles, his parents got a front page torn from the London *Daily Express*. The headline: ROCKET LAIR BLASTED. The story: "Earthquake bombs — the heaviest in existence — have been dropped on German rocket emplacements in the Pas de Calais. The attack was made by Lancasters, and an official announcement tells what happened: 'One of the large concrete structures which appear to be connected with the enemy's threatened long-range rocket assaults on England was attacked with 12,000 lb. bombs. Reconnaisance confirms their great accuracy. These structures are of immense strength and so the heaviest bombs in existence were used. One of the first exploded inside, leaving a great hole. A number were seen to explode well inside the target area. The enemy did not put up fighters but there was heavy ground fire. All aircraft returned though the first over the target was hit in all four engines and its crew had narrow escapes from shell splinters."

For "young Duff," that 53rd operation completed a second tour. In his log, his squadron commander called it distinguished, and no one was better qualified to say so than this legendary Wing Commander Leonard Cheshire, VC. Yet Duffy just kept going. At his own request, he went on more raids because, a statement said, he saw "their vital importance." On July 17 his Lancaster attacked a rocket-bomb installation at Wizernes, France, and he won an immediate Distinguished Flying Cross: "This pilot was detailed to attack a target which required high resolution and great accuracy. In the face of considerable anti-aircraft fire, he made three runs over his target and released his bomb within a foot of the centre of his objective. He displayed great courage and devotion to duty, setting a very fine example." Three days later Mrs. Sydney Smith of Woodhall Spa, Lincolnshire, posted a letter telling how his crew had come through all this, and what he meant to the others. She wrote his parents that she'd had them in for supper; "gave them strawberry shortcake, knowing that is one of the things they'd get at home. I am afraid the cream was not as it might have been!....Have you had the news that your son has been awarded the D.F.C.? He is well & jolly, and they are all happy in the crew & and have the greatest confidence in him." In fact, their days together were virtually over. On the 20th, they made one last attack, against that same deadly Wizernes. But three days earlier he had been up to familiarize himself with the new, swift, light, all-wooden Mosquito fighter-bombers. Liked them "even better than the Lancs." With Don Bell as his navigator and lone companion, he'd fly them from now on, and he began with days of dive-bombing practice.

It was the same type of plane Flt. Lt. Jack Calder was navigating on the 21st of July when he and his R.A.F. pilot set out to attack Hamburg. The Jack Calder who'd freed himself by literary fraudulence, had passionately pictured Hitler as an evil who must go, and the 21st was, by great irony, the very day Hitler proclaimed that his survival from an assassination attempt by high army officers was "a sign from Providence that I must continue my work." He had on the 20th had a miraculous escape Calder would have greeted with eloquent regret — if he and his pilot hadn't died even as Hitler reasserted his control.

Since completing his second tour of operations, Warren Duffy had at his own request flown four more, the last on August 4, one day before he was told he'd be going on to other things. But he was still around on the 7th and took a Mosquito up to practise dive-bombing. This time his navigator was an Englishman named Phil Ingleby who needed the experience, and they both died when the plane completed a dive, started to climb, then plunged.Crashed, Don Bell wrote the Duffy family, because of a mechanical failure. The story author Paul Brickhill told was that Duffy took up a Mosquito Leonard Cheshire may have damaged in a mad dive in a raid on Munich; a wing folded and "at about 400 m.p.h. they went deep into the mud of a bombing range." He was 18 days short of his 22nd birthday, and his promotion to flight lieutenant, in the works for months, would come through later. The five members of his Lancaster crew still in England conducted his casket to a Canadian air force cemetery near Harrogate where he was buried with full military honors. Wing Commander J.B. Tait wrote his parents that his "cheerfulness under all circumstances, and his skill and enthusiasm were unsurpassed and an inspiration to all."

No one thought more of young Duff than the Don Bell who wrote that they'd planned to go home on leave that fall, that their Lancaster crew had been "very happy in this lovely spot with fine lawns, hedges, golf course, rose garden and swimming pool." Only the day before he died, Warren had spent hours in the pool and sun–bathing. Bell himself had fought over Norway, Africa, the Mediterranean and Western Europe, and he would tell the CBC he welcomed the opportunity to "pay tribute to a wonderful flier."

CBC: "He was good?" Bell: "The best. You haven't heard much about him, but his log book shows his record, plus excellent in everything. He was just getting into his stride when he was killed."

"You say the Dam Busters heard about him when they were looking for crews." "Yes. He was red hot....."

"Did they have a crew for him?" "No, they let him pick his own. He got quite a lineup of second-tour men, five with medals."

"You were all experienced on Lancasters, I presume." "We took a conversion course one afternoon."

"One afternoon! I thought it took weeks." "Duff converted to Mosquitoes in half an hour."

"That's remarkable." "Duff was the best pilot I've ever seen."

He never got to Buckingham Palace to receive his medal, but in time Canada would name a northern lake in his honor. The day he died, Don Bell said, "he was most happy. He had no regrets in life, and now he is at peace."

What killed young Duff was not the fighting but his love for what Charles Lindbergh loved, for flight itself. And just one day later young men he'd known in the village beheld a grotesque example of what man had done with Lindbergh's gift of "the continent of the sky," beheld a wrath imposed upon the German people by a Hitler Lindbergh had admired. It became a memory like an umbrella covering a common horror: Leo Fabien LeBlanc's horror on seeing a field thickly carpeted with the dead; the terrible price of a strategy that drew most German armor to the British-Canadian front so the Americans could break out elsewhere; the toll that took almost as many Canadian lives in 2 1/2 months as Italy in 18, that wounded Maj. Ed McManus, the Dieppe M.C., just after he'd become one of four officers to command his unit in two days. Statistics like those Al Tower and Ernie Crosson saw with the North Novas, a turnover of 150% in officers. The bloody 18-mile march to Falaise after the July 9 fall of Caen, through a countryside glorious with bounty. The historic introduction to battle of the First Canadian Army with British, Polish, Dutch and Belgian troops under command.

But what above all would remain in villagers' remembering concerned what man had done with aviation. They knew airpower was reducing Germany to ruins; some with awe had seen it reduce Caen to ruins. But never would it mean more than it did on August 8 when something went wrong with plans to carpet-bomb immediately ahead of attack, and hundreds of bombs fell upon soldiers they were supposed to help. Al Tower was playing poker in a truck when he saw the planes overhead, bombs coming down. Pte. Tom Pickles, attached to the infantry as a fixer of damaged anti-tank guns, saw bombs making holes big enough to put a truck in, a terrified soldier running, running, running through webs of dust. Sgt. Frank Tracy saw planes emerging through smoke and soldiers running and a small artillery-spotter plane madly trying to signal the bombers that something was radically wrong. He didn't know Lt.-Gen. H.D.G. Crerar was in it, horrified at what was happening to his First Canadian Army. Cpl. Vic Amisson, with his anti-tank outfit, was wounded that day and friends would say he was never the same again; he of whom it had been said that he could smoke, chew gum and square dance all at the same time. For Pte. Tom Lowerison, fishing pal of Bill Palmer, now a machine-gunner with the New Brunswick Rangers, it became part of a patchwork of things that didn't connect, a crazy, mixed-up and destabilizing mental scramble that ended his war in Normandy and would haunt him for years. Gunner Hazen Greenberg would say, "I think I shit myself," when bombs struck his artillery regiment. Tom Pickles would say there were, in all, three such erroneous Allied air attacks, "and I saw them all." Sgt. Paul Whalen managed to get through that day and most of Normandy before a wound ended his war. Pte. Roy Tower of the medical corps got through too, only to have shell concussions end his war. Pte. Billy Manship survived the first mistaken air raid, only to die in a later one, die with the South Saskatchewan Regiment as a stretcher bearer carrying wounded from the field two months or so after arriving overseas. Die after rejoicing in reunions with14th Field friends, after reminiscing with Earl Stiles about playing their guitars together, and only shortly after meeting by chance on the battlefield a Newt Cooke who thought he was still in Canada.

At this time someone in Rome said there was to be another invasion of France which I could go on if I wished, which I did. One reason was that the Canadian divisions were at rest, another was that I could go with a Canadian ship and report a bit about the navy's war, a third was that invasions were rare things, and this one was complicated more than usual by collisions of national interest. The Americans wanted to cut down in Italy and build up in France. The British didn't, but Churchill no longer had the clout to get his way. As some seven divisions headed for the south coast of France to broaden the advance on Germany, General Alexander was left in Italy with just enough troops to keep the pressure on the Germans who kept just enough there to keep the pressure on him.

The invasion was on August 14-15, the island of Corsica was where you went to get in it, and memory has pictures of rugged mountains, lush forests, magnificent beaches, sunny days. There was no hiding as in England's June. Hundreds of soldiers stripped and swam in the blue Mediterranean, packaged energy, laughing, golden humanity. When I think of them, I think of what someone wrote about twice seeing a New Zealand division, once when its men were keen amateurs, once after they'd become cold professional killers. The war was nearly five years old that August, and had changed many things. Hundreds of the soldiers were Canadians in a Canadian-American Special Service Force, and they'd done a lot of fighting in Italy. The *Prince David,* the Canadian navy ship I joined, was a former peacetime steamer that had been on several invasions. The war had become a highly efficient instrument in the pedagogy of annihilation.

We sailed in style toward the Riviera, toward a 15-mile front between Toulon and Cannes, eating and living well. In all directions there were ships, some 800 of them, aircraft carriers, cruisers, destroyers, torpedo boats, troopships, the works. I asked Lieut. George Allin if I could go ashore in his small landing craft. He said he didn't mind, so I made sure I got his name right for his home-town paper. On the last night out, a British naval officer briefed a room full of officers, said the landings could be met with heavy resistance or none at all or something in between; it was impossible to be sure because the situation in France was changing so fast. The Canadians were, in fact, closing in on Normandy's Falaise. Still, the British officer said to a very quiet audience, this new invasion must be prepared for the worst. In fact, according to Joseph Schull's navy history, the best German divisions had been withdrawn north but the ports and coastal areas were heavily garrisoned.

The landing craft hung like lanterns along the deck, and when the time came they were lowered into the sea and people got in, soldiers and two British nurses who'd been popular in the officers' wardroom. The 25 or so soldiers in my craft came from French colonies in North Africa, so they were going in to help liberate a country that ruled their lives. It was very dark and everybody was very quiet and, when I got in, the long, low, open steel boat was loaded and George Allin had forgotten our arrangement. I asked him, whispering, where I should go and he whispered that there was only one place left: up front where the ramp would go down. I went there through soldiers making room for me, and wondering, not for the first time, what might happen in this exposed and tiny space if my old problem took over. The budding greatness of war artist Alex Colville was in another landing craft, and he'd paint my memory of thin light creating silhouettes of crowded heads against a dark and quiet sea, implications of anticipation and doubt and mystery. Were "they" waiting? You heard a plane. A rifle shot. Saw a flare. Airborne and commando attacks had gone in first, and somewhere the Special Service Force was meeting opposition on an island, but here it was so quiet you could hear the boat nudge the shore, and the ramp go down, and I steeled my legs and got out and stood on a fabled coast. The soldiers vanished with hardly a sound, and we went back to the ship. It was daylight before enemy fire descended on the shore, and by then it didn't matter much.

Falaise fell a few days later, and Newt Cooke would have his own salient memory of an Allied trap closing even as more divisions moved up from the Riviera, German dead and wounded everywhere, S.S. troops firing on comrades who tried to surrender. Would remember bringing out Germans badly in need of care for stinking wounds. Just as Earl Stiles would remember the stench when they reached a dressing station; by the end it could even sicken pilots overhead. Yet a lot of Germans got away, among them Maj.-Gen. Kurt Meyer, he who at one crucial stage of the fighting had come upon German troops in panic and led them back to battle. He got away with an estimated 300 from an original 20,000 in his division. After that, Raymond Mitton and Billy Manship became neighbors once more, in a military cemetery. Left their wives with four children to raise without the fathers they had lost.

There was a theory that if you made life hell for civilians, they would eventually force peace upon those who governed their lives. The Germans were testing it again with unmanned missiles or flying bombs. Sergeant Betty McCabe was living among London civilians, in one of the thousands of places damaged or ruined by these so-called V-1s and V-2s, Hitler's *Vergeltungswaffen* (reprisal weapons). In Italy, war lurched through civilian lives like some monster feasting on destruction and despair. By September a year had passed since its surrender had created a land divided, some supporting the Fascists or under the control of the Germans, others taking up arms against them, millions standing back, watching. The Germans scorned them as allies and savaged them as enemies. The Canadians, for their part, saw them and didn't see them through priorities of their own. Sometimes saw them as fugitives with animals, carts, packs of things they carried in files of sadness and fear. Often, as peasants, they clung to their land and hovels as though they feared that if they left they'd never get them back. Sometimes, if the enemy might be using them, the gunners destroyed the houses with the peasants in them.

What mattered primarily was not them or their lives but what the soldiers were trying to do for lives of their own. But sometimes there were happier endings. Once a few Canadian soldiers were smuggled ashore to spy behind German lines, were landed from a boat in darkness, and in the wrong place. A humble Italian became their salvation. Guided them to an attic overlooking a main highway where they could see what was going on. Brought food. Brought information they passed on with wireless equipment. Guided them, when the time came, back to the coast, from where they reached Allied lines along the beach, though some were wounded by soldiers who didn't know they were coming. Once his village was overrun, the healthy ones found the Italian, and asked what they could do for him in gratitude. He said he hadn't expected anything but, since they'd asked, he *would* like to be the doorman at the municipal building. So it was arranged, and what pleased him most was that a handsome uniform went with the job.

Off the coast of Western Europe, navigation expert Hanington found life difficult because powerful Channel tidal streams made it hard to avoid minefields, and convoys kept blundering into one another in heavy fogs. From his frigate, he watched what he called the bumbling of V-1 buzz bombs making for England. They bumbled "till they ran out of fuel and fell heavily to earth and exploded thunderously. If you happened to be in the Straits of Dover or north of them during an attack on London, you were in serious danger of being wounded by falling shrapnel from anti-aircraft guns and clusters of rockets. The steel shards pattered all around and occasionally clanged on the deck and richocheted." Eventually the air force found a way to have planes tip the bombs with a wing and send them crashing out of control. Eventually, too, Lieutenant Hanington would find his ship patrolling the Irish Sea and England's Bristol Channel to keep an eye on U-boats trying to sneak by in "a last desperate attempt" to hold up the Allied advance beyond Normandy. One problem: the submarines now had equipment that let them hide better, move faster and stay immersed much longer. Another: it was hard to tell from the surface what was a submarine and what was a sunken ship. He once saw a warship lifted completely out of the water — and the war — when it exploded a sunken ammunition ship.

On September 29, one day before Calais fell after one more siege in a long, Canadian march up the coast of France, 14th Field Ambulance soldiers began making pilgrimages to the Vimy Ridge memorial. Three lorries took the first batch, and two more batches would follow, and when they and thousands of other Canadians got there the magnificent memorial did things to them. It had survived intact, and when someone in CP Toronto phoned its designer, 68-year-old Walter S. Allward, and read a despatch that said so he was so moved he had it read three times.

The soldiers saw it as what it would remain: the ultimate statement of Canada's literature of stone. Perhaps of Canada's existence, as they themselves had come to indicate. They resented being called British troops. They believed, as both Sir Arthur Currie and Andy McNaughton had believed, that they fought best as Canadians together. In Italy, if they felt affection for any allied troops in particular it was the magnificent little Gurkha mercenaries. There were no American divisions in the Eighth Army, but there were elsewhere in Italy and it was these they compared themselves to. Felt better than. Agreed with the opinion that the best division in Italy was the 1st Canadian and that the 5th kept getting better all the time. Though they wore British-style uniforms, High Commissioner Vincent Massey once said something many agreed with, that something in the way a Canadian soldier carried himself said what he was. If the typical soldier found it hard to say why he was far from home, he sensed, felt, knew that what had crystallized in 1914-18 was true of him as well; that in this sense, deeply, the two wars were one. This, he felt at Vimy. Especially at Vimy.

But the pilgrimages were followed by dismal months. In September there was widespread hope that the war with Germany was near its end. After September, there wasn't. On two fronts Canadians were condemned to months of bitter fighting, and at home to the greatest political crisis of the war. In Italy, the Canadians broke through the vicious Gothic Line on slopes behind the river Foglia, well north of Rome, and in jubilation fancied they could be in Vienna by Christmas. Instead they spent costly weeks fighting through a coastal corridor and ended up in a frustrating land of canals, dikes, vineyards and rivers turned into torrents by merciless rain. In Western Europe, while the British and Americans swept forward amid great acclaim, the Canadians had harsh fighting for six French and Belgian ports. They took 30,000 prisoners and became the toast of London by overrunning V-l sites, only to get locked in a grim campaign to clear Germans from the 45-mile-long Scheldt estuary between the crucial port of Antwerp and the sea.

Richard Emmerson would remember it for a "bird's eye view" of what war could be. On D-Day, he'd been halfway through one more course. He volunteered to join the 2nd Division's Essex Scottish and caught up with it in time for fighting in what the Dutch called "land God had no hand in," diked polder land reclaimed from the sea, rain-sodden land. When the Scottish struck north beyond Antwerp, he was in the area brother Bert had flown over the day he died. It was the first week of October, and within days they fought across the Netherlands border and made for the narrow neck of land opening into the South Beveland peninsula where the Germans held the north side of the Scheldt gateway to the sea. The 2nd Division got close to it by the 7th, but it took more than another two weeks to break into the ham-shaped peninsula itself. Amid this, Lieutenant Emmerson was far from being the only officer to face battle for the first time, and by no means the only rookie in his own platoon. In a world of drenching rain, sucking mud and vicious shellfire, he found himself in the thick of conditions forcing the Canadian government into the crisis it had tried to avoid since 1939: whether trained conscripted men, so-called zombies, should be ordered overseas to meet an urgent need for reinforcements. The Essex battalion had been riddled at Dieppe in 1942, rebuilt, riddled in Normandy, and was trying again to restore its *esprit de corps* , to rebuild with poorly trained men from non-combatant units, wounded men sent back into action too soon, green soldiers from Canada. The problems, Richard Emmerson soon found, were far beyond anything he'd known in Rigolet, Labrador. He was his platoon's 10th officer since July, a stranger commanding strangers. During the fighting, he got six reinforcements who'd been conscripted, then volunteered to go overseas. He found them "unseasoned." In action, two became demoralized and afraid to move. One begged to be shot in the midst of heavy mortar fire. On paper, a platoon was supposed to have some 30 men. Frontline platoons rarely did. His fell well below 30 in what he would remember as "a series of static bivouacs in vacant houses in Belgian villages, then short forward moves, then getting tied down again." The regimental history would call them "a series of well-executed operations." They took the Scottish to within sight of Bergen-op-Zoom, only to be tied down once more, then move in darkness west into flooded South Beveland. There, on October 30, Lieutenant Emmerson's platoon was on a dike, water on both sides, when there was an exchange of hand grenades. "I threw one and got two back." Several men got minor wounds. He was wounded in an arm and leg; one foot dropped when he walked. He and the 12 men left swam and hobbled back to a casualty clearing station just as the fighting on South Beveland neared its end. At 18, he'd been part of the happiest of summers. At 21 he'd qualified as an officer. At 29, after roughly a month in action, he left his platoon to its 11th leader since July.

This was the fall Mrs. Teed got from the same area news she'd hoped she'd never get again. Her grandson Lionel Palmer was too young to have shared with Richard Emmerson and Doug MacKean in the happiest of summers, though for weeks he'd been around the great stone house. He was the one who'd been turfed out of the army for being too young, and because his political pull helped do it, it must have seemed sadly strange to H. R. Emmerson, M.P., that Lieutenant Palmer was killed in Holland within a few days of his own son being wounded. The boy had become an officer with the Governor General's Foot Guards of Ottawa, and the 4th Canadian Armored Division. By October he'd been in action for some time, been mentioned in despatches, even as sister Dolly served with the army in London and older brother John as an officer with the Cameron Highlanders of Ottawa, a 3rd Division support unit.

The Foot Guards had been fighting in the Scheldt battle and its preludes for weeks, and Lieutenant Palmer had already distinguished himself. Cooperating with infantry on a patrol, his tank had received a direct hit from one of the Germans' dreaded 88 guns. Oil was leaking from the transmission when he climbed out under fire, plugged the hole, climbed back in and pressed on with his four-tank troop into what the regimental history calls "a sizable enemy pocket." The pocket was eliminated, 17 Germans taken prisoner. By the last week of October, the regiment was meeting fanatical resistance amid sand dunes, marshes and flooded land in the Bergen-op-Zoom area, was on the right flank of the First Canadian Army and trying to help block the one escape route for German withdrawal from the Scheldt campaign. The regimental history: "The troop of No.2 Squadron under Lieut. Palmer was committed to the main attack (on the town of Wousche Plantage) from the south. Fighting its way forward to the outskirts, Lieut. Palmer's troop had one tank bogged down in treacherous ground while a second had its turret jammed by a shell. The remaining two tanks pressed on and came under sniper fire as well as increased mortaring and shelling. Gallantly leading his depleted force into the teeth of the enemy defences, Lieut. Palmer was instantly killed by sniper fire."

When the news came, Connie (Teed) McMackin thought of seeing her brothers cheer the beginning of the war that took their lives, of having sensed, as a child, the ramifications of a grief that had no language. She could remember her father coming in once and asking where her mother was and finding her in a closet, upstairs, alone, and the bedroom door being closed. Memory said it must have had to do with the death of one of her brothers, but she couldn't be sure because there were things words were not allowed to say. Yet in the death of a second Lionel her mother seemed to find one consolation. At 79, she became not so much a grandmother bereaved as a mother to her daughter Emily who had lost a son and been devastated by the loss. "She was strong, you know," said Connie McMackin.

Lionel Palmer's death and Richard Emmerson's wound were part of the price of opening Antwerp to shipping, two of 13,000 casualties in five weeks of battle on both sides of the Scheldt, half of them Canadians. What happened to a village private that same autumn was part of the price of the reinforcement crisis that had bedevilled Richard in action and immersed Ottawa in controversy.

But the conjecture that still would linger in village minds years later involved not the convulsive political issue but what happened to a single individual. To the Bud Brian who didn't like being called Francis, had joked with Bill Palmer and Gerry Nugent about what might happen overseas, and knew now that both had died there. Who sent a postcard exulting in Edinburgh's bars. Had gone to school and church with the Len Shea who, in the 14th Field Ambulance, had taken the road to promotion he himself had avoided as one of the inseparable Three B's.

What did happen came to a head in a time of celebration. The great Belgian city of Ghent threw open its homes and hearts to the 3rd Division which had been heavily involved south of the Scheldt, and when the 14th Field arrived on November 3 it was greeted with cheers, flowers and acclaim. There was much visiting and partying, and the Three B's were among those who partied most. Then on the 6th, as the revelry went on, it was revealed that Bud Brian and Art Black were among six other ranks being transferred to the beleaguered infantry, to the Canadian Scottish, and there were those who associated their departure in particular with two recent events. On October 14 Len Shea had been promoted acting regimental sergeant major, which made him the unit's top N.C.O. and responsible to a large degree for discipline. Three days later a diary of unit activities said, "It is intended to move personnel to different parts of unit in order to avoid cliques." Just that. No elaboration. But the sequel on November 6 would eventually be seen as part of the elaboration. After what happened.

In Italian dusk, an infantry file was passing our jeep on the way into battle when a soldier came bursting at me, his face one vast smile. All we did was touch hands and speak a few words, and then he was gone, but it was the sort of thing village people passed along. He was Weldon Adshade. Did you hear what happened to Weldon Adshade, village people would say; the army converted his anti-aircraft unit to infantry. Did you hear, they'd say, what happened to his kid brother Gerald after he missed D-Day? The army discharged him after his accident and within 24 hours he joined the air force in England, hoping to make it as air crew. On July 31, 1944, the army recorded that he was 22 years old, 5 feet-9 1/2 inches tall, had a medium complexion, blue eyes and dark brown hair. On August 1, the air force recorded that he was 23 years old, 5 feet-11 1/2 inches tall, had a fair complexion, gray eyes and brown hair. Four months later, he'd be discharged again. Did you hear, people would say, about Tom Pickles getting into a crap game and cleaning out Newt Cooke and his two kitbags full of Dutch guilders? Did you hear about Everett Terris, the guard who told so many stories about dramatic careers? Who said that enroute overseas he fell overboard and swam all night till someone hauled him in. Well, damned if he didn't prove he was every bit as good as he said he was, got a mention in despatches for outstanding service in action with the army engineers. Did you hear, they'd say, about another guard, Herb Harris, getting mentioned in despatches for the way he kept his warship's engines running, especially with speed in emergencies? Did you hear about Walter "Mousie" Amisson getting a mention in despatches too, as a sergeant in Northwest Europe, the same Mousie I'd helped hitchhike home just as the war started, he and Harold Forsythe. Well Harold had been training to be an air gunner when he got seriously hurt in a rugby game in 1942. The air force eventually discharged him, village people would say when they met.

By late 1944 the Cape Breton Highlanders were known by higher-ups as the most difficult of their brigade's three battalions out of the line and the best in it. They had changed a great deal; 17 Platoon had not one face I recognized. Among many others, Pte. MacLean, R.H.,had gone; Eddie MacKinnon and Gordie Serroul told of his dying in voices that knew more would die — Gordie among them. Gordie Logan and Tony MacLachlan had both been wounded three times. One officer had been captured with his pants down, caught relieving himself and borne away by an enemy patrol. David MacGregor Neish had refused to accept a parcel because it spelled his middle name McGregor; there was, he said, no such person in the regiment. Battalion headquarters was at one stage in the sandbagged basement of a big barn in sodden land near a river too wild and wide to cross, and Capt. Harold Frizzell lamented the dying that would not die. In the Gothic Line, the Highlanders had attacked a German strongpoint three times and two privates had died on its edge in brutal darkness, giving their lives to let others withdraw. The next day, the 8th Hussars and infantry took the strongpoint from the rear after a breakthrough elsewhere. In a deep concrete well, beside a great gun, there lay two Germans with bodies like textbooks of mutilation. Nearby, a young Canadian sought a friend among bodies piled like cordwood, and wept himself into incoherence when he found it. Soldiers advanced up a slope, one carrying a bayonet and looking like a church elder with a bible. Soon after that the Highlanders fought their most vicious battle on Coriano Ridge.

In a broken village, there stood that fall a broken church. Gunfire had carved away its front quite precisely so that the inside stood naked to the storms, and above it the tower still stood and in it a bell, and at times the bell would toll in the wind, toll a voice of grotesque and timeless calm amid the ruin of battle going nowhere except to more of what it was already. Tolled as peasants moved past in melancholy procession, as jeeps went by with soldiers huddling behind canvas sides under driving rains. The guns helped create and shape such scenes, in many ways dominated the fighting. Even in the frontline, soldiers often rarely saw the enemy because the guns, the artillery, kept them apart, and in a strange way the gunners paid tributes to one another. Waged duels. They couldn't see one another but they could figure out exactly where the guns were that were firing at them. Once I talked to officers of the 8th Hussars in a big trench they'd dug under a tank, and when I climbed out German shells were landing just down the slope. One exploded directly under a 25 pounder surrounded by sandbags, and the gun's steel snout jumped as though it had been goosed. The Canadians had plenty of guns, but nothing to match the superb 88 the Germans used against tanks and planes and human flesh. They talked of the whistling of its shells with recollected terror.

Then one night I saw the guns in a different way. There was a motor torpedo boat operating out of Ancona, and its commander was one of a number of Canadian naval officers who had made big reputations in coastal warfare in the Adriatic. His name was Cornelius Burke, and he took two of us out on a patrol. We cruised north well behind the German lines, snooping around, and Burke and his small crew were ready in case they chanced upon enemy ships. So there we were out on the dark flowing sea, moving slowly, quietly, and what got to you was what you could see of what was happening on the land. At that distance, the guns made no sound, became two thin, tiny lines of bubbling light, as artillery firing at artillery firing back, and in your mind they dominated the night and the sea as, in quite another way, they dominated the day and the land. The world consisted of multitudes of stars and the darkness around them and us moving on the water and those sparkling jewels of madness. In a curious way they became a consolation because, apart from our one small boat, they alone certified the existence of the human species. Yet what struck you even more was the pathos of man's divisive rage when he was so small and so very much alone in a dark and overwhelming universe.

In late November, the village held its annual meeting of ratepayers. There was no council because the community was not incorporated, but there was a three-man board of elected commissioners who looked after things for the Town and who, by chance, bespoke the links between two generations of warriors. One of the three was Ed Oulton who had a son-in-law in Italy. Another was Edward LeBlanc who had a son in Italy, and a third was elected in the person of Q.E. Campbell who had a son in Northwest Europe. C.R. Dooe, the postmaster, was on hand as secretary-treasurer and reported that the Town had purchased 27 carloads of hardwood during the past season to ensure a supply of fuel, hadn't made any money on it but hadn't lost any either. But the big news lay in evidence of economic boon: the Town, Call Dooe said, was in the best financial condition it had ever known. Thus encouraged, the ratepayers gave prompt approval to the hiring of two extra part-time firemen.

Immediately after the meeting ended, another began, a citizens meeting to discuss the Canadian Legion's urgent nation-wide call for the use of trained conscripted soldiers, "zombies," to reinforce the army overseas whether they wanted to go or not. It didn't take long to back the Legion unanimously. Nevertheless, for H.R. Emmerson the meeting was one more part of an issue that had become the curse of political life, and more so for him than for most

MPs. One of his sons had been killed, another wounded, daughter Margaret was driving an ambulance overseas, and though son Charles had come home it was not a happy coming. The army had discharged him again, and when the family met him at the station he was weeping inconsolably because he felt, felt they all felt, it would have been better if he'd died instead of Bert. It was sad. It was Charlie.

For Bud Brian, his village's decision was basically irrelevant. Thousands of miles away, and for other reasons, he was just becoming an infantry reinforcement anyway. On November 23, Parliament ended the weeks of political turmoil by approving a government proposal to send 16,000 "zombies" overseas. Politically, the conscription crisis was over after dividing the nation and poisoning English-French relations. But for Private Brian the results had just begun. Two days before the proposal passed, he joined the Canadian Scottish. Two days after it passed, he went into his first action with them on a static front near both the German border and Nijmegen, Holland. Because of a massive and ultimately unsuccessful German counter-attack to the south, that was where they would remain for three months of shellfire, trenches and patrols.

Bud Brian joined one patrol shortly before it set off, went as a stranger, with men he didn't know. Went as a stretcher bearer, in a new meaning of the term. He was experienced in getting the wounded from a regimental aid post back to an advanced dressing station. But now he was up where the wounding was — and no one would ever know for sure what happened to him. In answer to queries from his parents, the Defence Department in Ottawa would say in March 1945: "Pte. Brian was last seen by the Company Commander being detailed for a fighting patrol at approximately 2100 hours, 25th November. The task of this patrol was to obtain a prisoner. The patrol moved up to within a short distance of an enemy position and lay quiet for some time. At this time the patrol was complete, and Pte. Brian must have been there. The patrol was unsuccessful and started back. They were fired on by the enemy, and grenades were thrown in their midst. The platoon commander ordered one section to attack, and Pte. Brian was with this section. This was the last seen of these five men. It is believed by the patrol commander that all five were taken prisoner, with the possibility of one being wounded. A search was impossible at the time, and all five were evacuated quickly by the enemy."

The platoon commander's runner, Private J. Nimcan, reported that the section sent to take on the opposition "had gone only a few steps when stopped by grenades. We saw the bursts and could hear at least one man moaning." He was quite certain none of the five got back but "we had little time to check because we had considerable difficulty in getting away ourselves." In fact, it would only be after they were freed from prisoner-of-war camps that three of them would tell officials what they knew about the stretcher bearer none of them seemed to know. Pte. J.W. Harris said he was captured about 2.30 a.m., added, "There was a fellow killed behind me and I believe it was the stretcher bearer. I didn't know him because he just came into the unit." Pte. J.L. Ryan: "One of the patrol, whose name I did not know, was killed and four of us were captured. I do not know what happened to the rest of the patrol and I do not remember the name of Pte. Brian. I had been with the company less than one month." Pte. E.J. Brooks said he didn't know Bud Brian either. In fact, none of those who did get back the night of Nov 25-26 knew Brian, Ryan or Brooks. In short, one patrol indicated what battle had done to Canada's infantry.

On December 4, 1944, Ottawa wired the Brians that their son was reported missing. On March 9, 1945, it would say that an intercepted German wireless message had said on February 4 that he was killed in action. This, the Defence Department added, "cannot be accepted as official, but it appears that there is little hope of your son's being a prisoner of war." The International Red Cross never had any record of him being one. His pal George Breau took his own steps to try to find the truth. He and a friend went out from the Canadian Scottish lines into the area where Bud Brian had recently disappeared. They found nothing. Two months later Pte. Art Black died in a way suggesting he'd been shot as a prisoner. Thus ended the story of the Three B's, but not the conjecture it inspired. Bud Brian's only brother Percy was a wartime army company sergeant major in Canada and later both a judge and a senior militia officer. He'd say the conjecture about the role of Len Shea became a legend but that he attached no importance to it. George Breau would say he felt there was no bad blood between Len and Bud, that Len "had a job to do." Leo Fabien LeBlanc would work with Len for years in a veterans hospital in Saint John, and he'd say the subject was never discussed, that Len never talked about it.

Bud Brian's body was never found. Forty years later I'd find his name on a memorial near Nijmegen which listed soldiers who had no known grave. It did him one last favor. It didn't spell out the name he'd hated all his life. It called him F.E. Brian. As for the controversy about his death, his brother, the judge, ultimately delivered what may well be the final verdict. "You'll never," he said, "get the whole thing clear."

Pte. Florence Miller of the C.W.A.C. kept a scrapbook of press items like the one that said Bud Brian was missing.

Her sister Edna sent her clippings while Florence was on that secret mountain near Prince Rupert, B.C., and later when she was posted to Victoria and could look out a seventh-storey hotel window and admire the harbor. In Oriskany, N.Y., half a century later she would dig out the scrapbook and she'd note that it was a sort of fading chronicle of the village and the war in 1943 and 1944. She had the deaths of Bill Palmer and Bert Emmerson and Victor Shea recorded there, and Edgar Ison's picture, and Richard Emmerson's wound and Hazen Greenberg's marriage to an English woman. She kept the local social notes too, and they alone disclosed that a lot of what happened to people in the services happened in Canada: visits, homecomings, marriages. Examples: LAC. Aubrey Card, P.E.I., is visiting his wife. Pte. Bernice LeBlanc, Saint John, was a visitor to her home. Dorcas Petchey has joined the C.W.A.C. Stoker Clifford MacNeil has completed his naval training course with an exceptionally high standing. PO. and Mrs. John MacNeil and infant son of Greenwood, N.S., are visiting Mrs. MacNeil's parents, Mr. and Mrs. Harry Ison. LAW. Marion Emmerson of Summerside is spending a few days with her parents. Allan Bishop was honored by friends before joining the navy. LAC. Glenn Dobson of Dartmouth., N.S., visited home. Navy Sub. Lieut. George Cook, the banker' son, was married in Halifax. May Aderine Mitton (Raymond's sister) married LAC. William George Perrement who is stationed at No. 4 Repair Depot, Scoudouc, N.B. The wife and child of Captain Douglas Chapman, Halifax, are visiting his parents. LAC. Ted Palmer of Vancouver spent a furlough with his parents, Mr. and Mrs. H.G. Palmer. Able Seaman Peter Hanington spent a weekend with his aunt, Mrs. M.G. Teed. PO. Keith Dobson has reported for duty in Calgary. Edward Gaudet's mother and sister visited him in Charlottetown where he is with the navy.

Other items linked home and overseas: Sgt. James Innis, formerly of Dorchester, has returned from England where he was injured on active duty with the R.C.A.F. Kathleen Cole married Sgt. Frank Belliveau who has returned after four years with the air force in Britain and Africa. Nursing Sister Ruth Belliveau was married in England. FO. Bayne MacKelvie, formerly of Taylor Village, has been awarded a mention in despatches. Three sons of Mr. and Mrs. Fred DeVarennes are in uniform: Trooper Laurie was injured in Italy and had a serious operation, Leonard was invalided home from overseas, and Joe saw a lot of service on a navy minesweeper. There also were non-military items. The bear Ward's tourist cabins kept on display for years escaped and was shot in the woods; it is being replaced by a cub Russell Ward captured near Turtle Creek. Ed Oulton and two friends came home from a hunting trip with two fine deer and a couple of brace of partridge. Mrs. Dean Mason held her fall party as Supt. of the Baby Band of the United Church. Despite inclement weather, 13 babies and mothers were present. A dainty lunch was served, the babies using their own small tables and chairs.

Chapter Twelve

IN DECEMBER I MET some *Prince David* officers in Rome. They had received tumultuous welcomes in a stricken but liberated Greece and they said they were going back on a relief mission, and why not come along. So I did, and in Athens a Red Cross woman told me how very much it had meant to the Greeks to get Canadian food during the war, and on an island in the Aegean I saw children who had hunger in their bodies and their eyes. But, what strikes me now is a parallel. I came away from Greece convinced that a people that had fought enemies for five years was on the verge of fighting a tragic civil war, as they would. I got back to Canada soon after that and saw within hours a spontaneous drama straight out of the bloodless civil war that is the ultimate curse of national life.

I got home just before Christmas, Naples to New York on a U.S. Navy troopship. The food was terrific and when we went past the Statue of Liberty I was surprised at how emotional it made me. On the ship were wounded, sick and decorated Americans, but the ones many of them regarded with amazement and awe were a few dozen Canadians: the first Canadian soldiers to be sent home solely because of how long they'd been overseas. They'd arrived in England in December 1939 with the 1st Division, and the government had finally decided they'd been away long enough. The Americans would ask if it was possible any country would keep soldiers away from home for five years, and go away shaking their heads.

We went from New York to Montreal by train, and that night the few going east left Montreal on the C.N.R's Ocean Limited, and somewhere in the St. Lawrence Valley we saw, crystallized, what the conscription crisis had done to the country. No playwright could have imagined a more evocative setting. No historian could have called forth from our history a more telling revelation of the implacable factor at its core. Picture the scene. A passenger car shabby, worn from years of war. Outside, brute Canadian winter. Inside, a cast slimmed by sheer chance to dramatic basics, to theatrical essentials, to just eight men singularly fitted for the roles they are about to play. I sit with three of the soldiers who have been overseas for five years, French Canadians from the Royal 22nd Regiment, the celebrated Van Dos. One sergeant, one corporal, one private. We are nearing home. We are happy. We have a bottle, and we get happier. They are good guys. They talk about Italy and how, to their surprise, they liked Britain. The sergeant is from Mont Joli, and somewhere in him there is what turned many frontier French Canadians into *coureurs de bois*. The private is from northern New Brunswick, and only 22. The corporal is from the Gaspe. We engage in an archetypical Canadian conversation: that is to say, we speak English because I can't speak French. It embarrasses me but I don't say so. What it does to them they don't say either. It's just the way things are.

We don't speak about the history the country has just made, about the 16,000 conscripted soldiers ordered overseas. By no means all of them, and by no means all the other so-called zombies are French Canadians; figures will eventually show that the percentage of French Canadians who are is not much out of line with their share of the population. But they have become *the* zombies to millions outside Quebec.

The four of us don't talk about this. It would make us uncomfortable, and we don't know too much about the details. But its essence is in our blood and bones. It comes with being Canadian, and suddenly it begins to beat in on us. The four others in that shabby car are across the aisle. Two sit together well down from us, two together well up from us. The first two are sailors with ribbons on their uniforms. The other two are soldiers. There are many seats separating them, but suddenly communication springs up. One-way communication. The two sailors belong to a force that is said to tell French Canadian volunteers to "talk white." They are drinking and their voices begin to rise. Become taunts, and even though their shouts have nothing to do with us, the four of us stop laughing. Stop talking. Our eyes stop meeting as the taunts go on, the abuse, the profanity, the vocabulary of Canadian division. In English, the sailors are calling the two soldiers, among other things, zombies and yellow bastards, and the two soldiers keep talking as though none of this is happening. They are speaking French, and when they keep ignoring the shouts the sailors get up and start toward them.

They pass us without a word. They stop beside the two soldiers. From what is or isn't on their uniforms, they assume or know they are zombies. French. *The* zombies. The sailors keep haranguing them and when the soldiers reply it is in broken English. They sound young and not tough. They say little, none of it vehement or challenging, and what they do say is shouted down. They are outmatched, defensive. They sit there, and the distilled essence of centuries of Canadian rancor pours over them, but I am fascinated above all with what this is doing to the three men with me. We are all silent, empty, sober. I suspect some form of sickness is in all of us. I try to imagine what's in their minds. They went overseas in that first flush of national unity when Ottawa planned a limited war and promised Quebec there would be no conscription. They have come home to a country split as only conscription could split it. Are they torn between two gut sympathies? One for comrades they've left behind, needing reinforcements, one for two boys who share a heritage they understand in the very depths of their knowing? Do the sailors personify, to them, the chronic shadow of an implacable majority, with an immemorial right to sit in judgment on French Canada? Do the two soldiers personify, to them, that Quebec remembering that sees Britain as a conqueror and blood shed in her behalf as subservience? Do they feel robbed of all belonging?

There is no telling. It's as though the four of us are watching a play in which we have no part. The three Van Doos sit without a word, inscrutable, and the sailors tire of what they're doing and come teetering down the aisle. They pass us with scarcely a glance. They have condemned, in the two soldiers, the French Canada they feel has let the country down. They ignore, in the three soldiers with the red patch of the 1st Division, the French Canada which manifestly has not let the country down. The irony, the contrast, the reality escapes them, or maybe they don't choose to see it. They go back to their seats and fall asleep, and we try to sleep too, and that's all that happens. Or is it?

For when I think of that night I think of might-have-beens, of flowers that never bloomed. Of soldiers enroute to Italy singing "O Canada" in both languages, separately and together. Of what one Ontario soldier once said about having the Van Doos next to them in the line: "We felt secure." Of brother Hank and his English and French comrades roaring "Alouette" in arid Africa. Of what happened to a sparkling Quebec lieutenant I met on the troopship: he'd gone first to an English-speaking battalion because of the need for reinforcements and one of its officers later said things hadn't worked out too well — until they went into action and language ceased to matter; after that he'd gone to the Van Doos and, my friends on the train told me, died in battle. Of Rowland Frazee saying he had both English and French-language New Brunswickers in his Carleton and York company and that it made a good mixture. Yet in two wars Maritime battalions had been brigaded with the Van Doos and somehow it left no profound imprint. And somehow in time you could see that Canada's 31-year-war did not help bring her English and French-speaking peoples together, it drove them further apart.

Meanwhile, in that December of 1944, it was wonderful to get home to my wife and daughter Patricia.

That was the winter Obergerfeiter Klotz's German unit escaped from the trap it was in. Its soldiers and thousands of others got away from the Latvian sector where they had been penned in by the Russians north of the mainstream of their relentless drive toward the German heartland. Got away not by breaking out and hurling themselves upon the enemy's rear, but by ships. Got aboard with the weapons and equipment they could salvage, and it was surprisingly easy. They went without interference some 125 miles across the Baltic Sea and into the Gulf of Danzig and then into a place with the thrust and bruise of irony: the very area Hitler had used as the ultimate provocation for his 1939 invasion of Poland. Were back where the Poles had had a corridor to the seaport of Danzig (now Gdansk) which the Germans had owned before 1918 and which Hitler was determined to have back. They got to Danzig itself and then thousands were ordered to go through a barren countryside to a new front, indeed to part of the former corridor, and the only reason they could get their tanks and anti-tank guns there was that they had brought with them from Latvia gasoline they'd been ordered not to bring. Then their destination turned out to be one more place of chaos and bewilderment from which they retreated once again.

They were caught in a circus of catastrophe. Klotz would remember wondering at times if the war would go on forever, and yet he'd also remember being happy, as he had seemed to be through it all. His one regret when he thought about being killed was the grief it would bring to his family, after Walter, after Uli. He had become what danger made him; had slept with shells falling on a roof above his head, been wounded by an exploding bomb or shell, only to have more trouble with the medical treatment than with the wound itself. He would remember being on a train with soldiers waving from open windows like kids going to summer camp. By now, they knew Hitler was using boys and old men to help hold off his multiple enemies until the Third Reich could be rescued — rescued, he said, by secret weapons. Obergefreiter Klotz saw some of the boy soldiers acting as though the disasters in Russia, Africa and France had never occurred, or the defeat of the submarines or the decimation of countless cities. Saw them full of a willingness and even an anxiety to fight for the Feuhrer, to protect and project his magic; and the others, the older soldiers, like his 22-year-old self, exhausted, prematurely aged men with little or no faith left in the Feuhrer's secret weapons or in the Feuhrer himself, and with, in their beings, the conviction that what lay ahead was in all probability death or Siberia. And for the officers in his unit there was an extra melancholy. The three

Russian women they'd had with them for many weeks had vanished. Slipped away. Had, it was finally realized, been Russian spies all along.

Even as this happened, Germany's more deadly, more elusive U-boats were still attacking with "reckless daring," says Joseph Schull. Four days before Christmas 1944 one of them sank a ship off Halifax even as a convoy was forming up. On Christmas Eve, Obergefreiter Klotz's former neighbor and wrestling affiliate Melvin Sollows was in the minesweeper *Ungava* in the area when a U-boat sent the minesweeper *Clayoquot* to the bottom with the loss of eight lives. He was a Leading Seaman and he looked after the pistols that sent depth charges into the sea which was what he did after the *Clayoquot* went down.

Lieutenant Hanington spent some of that winter between Norway and the Faeroe islands, in waters so unkind that the Germans called them The Rosegarden. His frigate was screening an escort carrier hoping to assail U-boats with her Swordfish aircraft. When it proved impossible to get a single plane airborne in a week, the carrier gave up and her escorting ships headed for Scotland's Scapa Flow, a home-away-from-home so bleak "that even the presence of Wrens could do nothing for it." Enroute, they came upon a submarine making for Norway. It put up a great fight but was sunk, and into *New Waterford's* wardroom, as one of a number of prisoners, came a young cadet who said "Heil Hitler" in a loud voice. He was greeted with cries of "Shut up and sit down," which he did. "I don't think," Dan Hanington would record, "he said another word while he was aboard." Nevertheless, the prisoners were treated so well that it renewed their confidence and made them hard to interrogate when they got ashore.

Obergefreiter Klotz and his mates knew that tens of thousands of German civilians were trying to flee west before the Russian advance, that Hitler's orders were not to let them, and that as a result thousands were being killed by shellfire and raped by Russian soldiers and desperate for food and shelter. They heard a soldier was shot for refusing to blow up a bridge on which refugees crossed. They heard it was this way now. Whether they knew it or not, Hitler's orders had also caused tens of thousands of military refugees to do what the civilian refugees were not allowed to do. Hence when the Russian advance into Germany was reported within 100 miles or so of Sagan on January 19, things began to happen in Stalag Luft III. Joe Emery was one of 10,500 airmen prisoners-of-war who began to prepare to head west, away from the Russian advance the Germans feared they'd help. In the web of compounds, men began to figure out what they could take; made packsacks from kitbags, picked clothing, overhauled boots, built sleighs, listened for news. In a country reduced in many ways to the primitive, they knew they'd have to walk, but it's doubtful that many foresaw what the walking would become. For when it finally did start Joe Emery, like his classmate of 1938, found himself caught up in the ultimate convulsions of the Third Reich.

It started on the 27th day of the January of the Reich's 12th year — Hitler had said it would last 1,000 — when the 10,500 p.o.w.'s walked out of Stalag Luft III group by group, walked away from abandoned cigarettes, Red Cross parcels, thousands of books and other possessions, from the barbed wire and the guard towers and into something far worse: their own equivalent of Napoleon's retreat from Moscow. It was dark when they left and it would be bitterly cold for five days, through what Joe Emery's old escape-team boss George Harsh would call "a pastiche of cold, hunger, human misery and frostbite." Harsh and

Wally Floody weren't with the Stalag Luft III contingent, of course, but they also were on the march. From the p.o.w. camp to which they'd been expelled, they became part of the spectacle of tens of thousands of men shuffling west in ragged, gaunt and increasingly famished ranks, through a country peopled by enemies and exhausted by war. For Flight Lieutenant Emery, it was an experience quite different from his flight through Holland . Now he was part of a multitude being conducted on its way under a guard made up of older, often elderly, men ill fitted for marching winter miles let alone for controlling thousands of men. There were stories of them shooting prisoners who got out of line, who couldn't keep up, stories of them becoming webbed into the processions themselves, being helped by men they were supposed to guard. And, as Joe Emery noted, they had one extra disadvantage: they had to lug weapons.

The whole thing eventually became a study in the dimensions of misery. There were six inches of snow to walk through when Joe's group started out, there were the five days of cold, then an abrupt thaw, snow storms, rain storms, slush, sodden bodies and sodden feet, even in some cases men walking in their socks because frostbite made it too painful to wear boots. There were nights in packed barns, nights with men billeted in a cinema, a factory, a riding school, a laundry. Endless hours of marching in silence, hours of waiting. Sick men, vomiting men, barely surviving men, scant medical help or none at all. There was never enough food or water or heat or shelter, and eternal scrambles for what there was. There were dickerings with German civilians for food and shelter, in one case for a baby carriage (100 cigarettes) to carry things, kindnesses from Germans who gave what help they could. There was the sound of guns far to the north, the sight of German refugees fleeing not from east to west but from west to farther west, a night when prisoners shared life and conversation with a German panzer regiment just out of battle and destined for more. There was at last, on February 2, a train waiting, and then two nights and days cramped into stinking cattle cars and finally, after one last march, arrival at a camp in far northwestern Germany. It was dark and raining and after an eight-day ordeal the men were exhausted, hungry, sick, sometimes close to collapse, and there was more to come. In the rain, for hours, they were searched.

They were out in the country in the Bremen-Lubeck area. It was, Joe Emery remembered, an area that had inspired groans when airmen were told this was where they were going, because it was far away and hard and dangerous to get to. By early February 1945 he'd reached there both by air and foot, and neither had been easy.

As they had for months, the village's Mr. and Mrs. Edward LeBlanc were worrying about their son Leo in Italy. He'd arrived there the previous summer, just after the battle for Rome, and in the intervening months his Carleton and York Regiment had played a vital role in the Gothic Line, again in a line shielding the city of Rimini which involved crossing the Marano and Ausa rivers and the ugly capturing of a ridge called San Fortunato, then once in the plains of the Romagna making assaults across the Lamone River and the Naviglio Canal.

It was in the September fighting on the Marano that the village's Pte. Homer Lane had been wounded. On the 25th of January, 1945, Private LeBlanc was wounded too. Homer Lane was in his late 20s. Leo LeBlanc was 19. He'd been working in the C.N.R. shops in Moncton before enlisting, and his fighting career had ended where the Canadians' offensive had ended for the winter after weeks of struggling through a flat and promised land that had become a nightmare of reclaimed marshlands, high dykes, canals, drainage ditches, bloated streams, orchards, orange groves, vineyards and farmhouses. When he was wounded, seriously, the army reported, by bomb splinters which lodged in his chest, the lst Division was in defensive positions along the Senio River, in close contact with Germans who harassed them with shelling, mortaring and machine-gun fire. It was, as things turned out, the last chapter for the Canadians in what had become a sullen, dismal and deadly war fought far from where decisive things were happening. Indeed, Leo LeBlanc was recovering in hospital during the mass February movement of the lst Canadian Corps from Italy to rejoin the First Canadian Army in decisive Western Europe.

He bespoke things beyond himself. He served in a regiment that bore two very English names yet reflected the bilingual character of New Brunswick. He was, according to the regimental history, one of 18 casualties who bore the LeBlanc name, 17 of them wounded, one killed. He was representative of the fact that the war had gone on so long that he'd grown up with it. He'd been 13 when Joe Emery, Bill Palmer and Gottfried Klotz graduated from high school. He'd been 14 in 1939, and 16 when Dan Stack was killed and the woman across the street was worrying about her brother in Hong Kong, 17 when neighbor Bert Emmerson was killed, 18 and overseas when that other Leo LeBlanc, Leo Fabien, looked with horror upon a carpet of the dead.

In time, he'd go home minus one lung, and over the years it would strike people that it was with him as with others maimed and marked by one brief, searing period in their lives; that the war had changed him, left a sort of pensive sadness in him. He would be injured in a motorcycle accident and spend another year in hospital. Would become known as a kind and gentle man, but seem to people to be a sort of victim for which there was no name, as though the war had corrupted for him the integrity of peace. He got a pension and he would from time to time drive a taxi in Saint John, and he would die of heart failure at the age of 52.

    Late in the winter of 1944-45, Gottfried Klotz's unit was among those that retreated into a long, narrow peninsula north of Danzig. It stretched out into the Gulf of Danzig like a skinny finger, and there was just one way out of the disaster that was gathering around it. This was to get lucky, which is what happened to Obergefreiter Klotz. He volunteered one night for guard duty and was wounded a second time. It was not a severe wound, but his officer ordered him out, to be evacuated. Obergefreiter Klotz told him he had no need for serious medical care, that he wished to remain with his unit. He had great pride in his unit. He would, years later, say his comrades were 100 per cent and there would be pride and defiance in his eyes when he said it. For there had happened to him what happened to many soldiers; in the final analysis, they fought not for nations or flags or ideologies but for those who fought beside them.
    But the officer said to go, to get out. He had seen enough of Hitler's fantasies, enough of his orders to fight to the last man and last bullet, enough carnage and catastrophe. It was time to think of the survival and the future of Germany herself. Go, he ordered, and Obergefreiter Klotz went. He found his way to a ship that came to take wounded out. There were, he found, more wounded waiting to go than the ship could take, partly because officers insisted on having the cabin space they felt entitled to. So not all the wounded were taken, and among those who weren't were those with the worst wounds. The fortunate ones left on what turned out to be another

unmolested voyage that took them west through the Baltic Sea, away from that looming horror of Russian retribution and revenge. On board, Obergerfeiter Klotz saw medical officers who showed scant interest in the wounded, saw officers demand that a generator be brought up from the hold so they could have light. He met a senior officer from his own signals corps who said bitter things about what was happening to Germany and what was still to happen. He had lost an arm, but what embittered him most was that he had brought a daughter into the world to be raped by enemy soldiers.

They landed in Denmark, Germany's tiny neighbor and 1940 victim. Germany itself lay due south but it quickly became obvious to Gottfried Klotz that much of its ordered life was over, that he would have to get home as best he could through a country besieged from both east and west and, day and night, from the air. As he set out, he knew Mulda was several hundred miles away as the crow flies, and considerably farther than that the way he had to travel. The varied way. By hitchiking thumb, by train, by truck. He passed through the ruins of a great nation, saw for the first time Jews being herded like cattle toward extermination. Even now, even as Americans, Britons and Canadians moved closer and closer to a rendezvous with Russians, even as tens of thousands of Allied prisoners of war awaited liberation. By chance, he passed not far away from where Joe Emery was one of them.

In a March 2 news item, at a time when the army was locked in a vicious struggle to force the Germans across the Rhine, it was stated that the village's Walter Amisson had been informed that his son Walter, Jr., "Mousie," had been slightly wounded. Just that. There was no mention of the unit he was with, no details whatever, and this, scrapbooks indicate, was largely the way things had come to be. Early in the war, I had done a big front-page story on a Moncton airman who had joined the R.A.F. in peacetime and had just become a prisoner of war. By the sixth year, it was vastly different. What was happening in Europe and the Pacific was simply too overwhelming to make it otherwise, given the limited facilities of local newspapers. Or put it another way: it was assumed that the war was an aberration that would eventually go away. A meeting of the I.O.D.E or a juvenile championship hockey game were covered much more amply than items like those about Sergeant Amisson. Scrapbooks kept by both Florence Miller and Mary Catherine LeBlanc reveal that it took one brief paragraph to cover the news that Pte. Homer Lane had been wounded. It took another brief paragraph to record that Ottawa had informed Mrs. Walter Briggs that her husband, a lieutenant, had been wounded in Italy, but was staying with his unit.

No Maritime Provinces newspaper had its own correspondent overseas. They relied very largely on CP and otherwise covered the war as best they could. It was typical that a Salisbury memorial service for Vic Shea was covered at length, the fact of his death just briefly. Trooper Barry Chapman did get attention in a dispatch from Italy that said he claimed the army's speed record because he had unwittingly driven the 8th Hussars paymaster into Faenza before it was captured, had made a hasty retreat. It was indicative that it was a 1944 despatch. By then, the army was sending newspapers items about home-town boys dug up mainly by officers travelling with correspondents. They were called "little joes." This was a "little joe." Ultimately, what did appear in the the press unwittingly hinted at something else: the war was far away, in some ways, as once before, it would always seem far away.

The Germany through which Gottfried Klotz passed suggested both the wrath and the promise of God: gutted buildings, streets, cities, a massive geography of melancholy and destruction, but around them the budding pledge, the eternal hope and implications of another spring. Once he got on a train and saw what Allied air attacks were doing to German transportation. He was congratulating himself on his luck when he heard planes coming and the sound of bombs and with hundreds of others he fled to a ditch until the danger passed. Once he got a long lift from a happy-go-lucky truck driver, but when he came to the last miles he was walking. It was April and the hardwood trees were leafing out and he could smell the spring, and he saw its miracle as a farmer does. He came to a forest and walked through it and knew he was nearing Mulda, nearing home. In the earliness of morning, he heard birds singing and a silence that made a glory of the world. When he got to Mulda, he called home by phone because the family didn't know he was coming and he thought it best to tell them. He was puzzled because there was no one in the streets, and learned why only when he got to the farm and to the joy and laughter and tears because he was back.

The Russians were coming, the family said. A German division had suggested that it defend the village, but the village had said it would be a bloody and useless thing to do, and this was what things had come to. Only recently Hans Klotz had looked up into a sky black with Allied planes enroute to Dresden, and had growled "stupid war." Now the Russians were very near. The word, the warning, had come just last evening and the reason people were not in the streets in the morning was because they had spent the night destroying or hiding the things that would link them to the Nazi regime: flags and banners and pictures, documents and uniforms and newspaper clippings and scrapbooks. This had happened at the farm home of Hans Klotz, and there was just one major consideration left when his son got home: what to do about daughters Erika, 13, and Margaret, 12. In the end, they were hidden, and when the Russians came they took some things but they didn't find the girls. Meanwhile, in a Berlin under Russian siege, Adolf Hitler prepared to commit suicide, though he felt it would not have been necessary if the German people hadn't let him down.

Chapter Thirteen

HITLER WAS DEAD WHEN Ruthie Lewis saw village people celebrate over something she only partly understood. But church warden Ed Oulton, understanding fully, climbed the steps in the Anglican Church on his war-ravaged legs, climbed to the bell and rang it for a very long time. Because the war with Germany at last was over. In Halifax, Lieutenant Hanington got back from a picnic to find himself ordered back to his ship because there was rioting in the streets. He had to walk and he saw "a happy crowd of sailors shambling out of Oland's Brewery carrying whole cases of beer, which they drank on the spot." The rioters, he became convinced, were very largely "barrack stanchions," sailors waiting to go to sea for the first time and "who hated Halifax." Far away, the 14th Field Ambulance was in Leer, just inside northwestern Germany, when Germany surrendered on May 7 and the formal end of the war in Europe, VE Day, came one day later. There had been a ceasefire in this area since the 5th, and a few of the boys even took over a tug and whooped it up on the Ems River, and people got talking about home and things they had to take back. S/Sgt. Frank Tracy, for one, had his steel helmet with a piece of shrapnel embedded in it from the Scheldt campaign; it would end up in a museum. He'd already sent home a toy horse he'd come across near the Rhine; two generations of Tracy kids would play with that in the village, where he'd live for years. In 11 months, his unit had seen amazing sights: the carpets of the dead, the exultation of the liberated, the skeletons of ruined cities. They had worked in fields, in remnant basements, a German naval hospital, a monastery, a former headquarters of the dreaded Gestapo where 10 Dutch civilians had been murdered only hours before they took over. They had cared for 11,350 people, of whom 1,917 were Germans, 320 civilians, and one of the 8,218 Canadians was the angry Maj. Connie Smythe of Toronto Maple Leaf fame who went home and provoked the reinforcement situation into crisis. They had survived shellfire, bombs and sniper fire, and even before peace formally came they were preparing for a signal honor: to march through Berlin as part of a select Brigade Group. In the end, the plan was cancelled, but their selection capped their war.

On the 8th, a diary said, "it is amusing to see German soldiers walking around unarmed." In the same area, on the eve of release, Joe Emery had been watching German soldiers pile their arms in surrender and wondering if Gottfried Klotz was among them. Hundreds of miles to the east, Gottfried Klotz was under notice to report for infantry service but knew he'd never have to go. Thousands of miles to the west that night there was unbridled celebration in the packed lobby of Toronto's Royal York Hotel, and off to one side, alone, stood one of the 1st Division soldiers who had come back on the same ship as I had. He had his uniform on, with the red badge, and he kept looking at the celebration, at the many people in civilian clothes, but he didn't join in. It was as though he felt that what he saw had very little to do with what he'd known.

Thousands of Canadians had volunteered to fight against Japan after fighting against Germany. But on August 14 Japan surrendered, still reeling from atomic bombs that had ravaged two of her cities and proclaimed a terrifying new age. When the word came, Able Seaman Doug Johnson was in the frigate *Eastview* in Vancouver, waiting to go. Flt. Sgt. Edgar Ison had finished 33 bombing operations in September 1944 and he was waiting to go too. Lieut. Dan Hanington was in Scotland waiting for a new destroyer not quite ready to go. His aunt, Mrs. Teed, died within a few weeks, and the way the family put it was that she got the war over and then, at 80, she died. On the Vimy Memorial there is the figure of a woman representing Canada, representing a mother with her head bowed in grief. When, years later, I saw a photograph of it, I thought of a saying from the golden days of Maritime shipping: "the sea is made of mothers' tears," of tears for those it claimed; I thought of people saying Mrs. Teed had died with a broken heart, and Billy Manship's mother had, and Raymond Mitton's mother and Dan Stack's mother and Bill Palmers's mother, and that for years Bud Brian's mother kept his things exactly as he'd left them because his body had never been found and he might yet come back. That Harry Ison's wife died while their son Edgar was having a rough time in the air war, and the family felt it killed her. I thought of Mrs. Teed seeing the beginning of the 31-year war, and its agony, and its end, and of her being buried in the village cemetery with the names of two lost sons on her tombstone and the name of a lost grandson in her heart.

And that, on the other hand, at least 16 of those in this story were officially recognized for their gallantry and their contributions, 10 with medals and the others with mentions in despatches. And that when the 25 names on the village monument became 41, 11 of them would be

French. And that all this is part of the literature of stone, and of the emergence of a thing called Canada.

After the 31-year war ended, it was as though a great circle had been made. The country became like it had been until shortly before it began: prosperous, optimistic, confident, on the march. It had more than twice as many people, and they lived in a Canada quite different in major ways from the Canada of 1914; far more industrial, more urban, more almost everything. One massive outpouring of energy and blood and treasure had made her independent and given her international recognition. A second had made her what Mackenzie King liked to call a middle power. The first had crystallized among her overseas forces a soul sense of national pride and being and belonging epitomized by Vimy Ridge. The second had confirmed and corroborated it. People said it, writers said it: Canada had come of age.

For this reason, it would surprise me years later to read what 1943 village students wrote about the importance of "the Empire." It sounded archaic, compared to what I remembered of 1943, but never more so than when in 1994 I returned to Italy with some 60 veterans and a color party of 20 or so young servicemen, all from coast to coast. Because something beautiful happened. The veterans became affectionate grandparents and the young men became their affectionate grandkids. When one young soldier heard an Italian say they were Americanos, their bus absolutely bloomed with Canadian flags. When they all roared out "O Canada" together on Coriano Ridge I thought my hair would stand on end. It was an experience profound with "identity."

Yet it not only said something about what students wrote in 1943, it said something about what was happening to modern Canada. To a country that seemed to be divided in too many ways, to have a vacuum where a nation's heart is supposed to be. That was like some equivalent writ large of Italy's Gallo and Lentini, two communities with visions locked and blocked in the past. The wartime sense of national being and belonging seemed to have given way to forces that drove its people apart, and you wondered if what Canadians had achieved in battle had drifted away in peace. And why. In the village itself its own part in the 3l-year-war has never been taught, is very largely unknown, and this is typical of Canada, and you wonder whether in her determination not to glorify war she missed an opportunity to build a nation with a deeper sense of having done momentous things together. If it could speak for the fallen, you wonder what the granite soldier, what the literature of stone, might say to the troubled Canada of the '90s. Just remember, it might say, that they wore upon their sleeves a rectangle that bore one word: Canada. It wasn't very big, but they'd have felt naked without it.

I first went back to the village soon after getting home, and it looked beautiful to me. Wherever you looked there was snow, snow on the marshes, up the Memramcook Valley, a magnificence, a white and perishable innocence of snow. Soon the veterans began coming back. Some joined aging returned men on the prison staff. Some had grown up in the village, others came in from elsewhere as they always had. They merged at work, in the Legion branch, in the Masonic Lodge, in the churches and elsewhere. Many others didn't come back, chose to live in the wide world of elsewheres the war had revealed. The veterans got a good deal from the government and by and large they settled down gratefully and helped raise the most permissive and assertive generation in history, one that said war was bad and was not much interested in the literature of stone. The veterans vanished quickly into the general population, couldn't be bothered, many of them, even to apply for their medals. By and large, except among themselves, they didn't talk about their war anymore than the returned men had, partly perhaps because they fitted into a mold the returned men had created. Indeed, in some ways they helped define what the war had done to them and to the village by reaction to two men who'd been enemies, one a dedicated Nazi, one a member of the Class of 1938.

The veterans were barely home before a convicted war criminal came to town, to the prison. Maj. Gen. Kurt Meyer, leader of Germany's fanatical 12th S.S. Division, had first been sentenced to death, then to life imprisonment because his men had murdered Canadian prisoners in Normandy. Potentially, the penitentiary was a dangerous place to put him because all too many of those prisoners of war had come from the North Nova Scotia Highlanders whose headquarters were just 18 miles away. Indeed, for some time, Meyer was kept in protective isolation, and there were fears that he might commit suicide. Both on the staff and in the cells there were ex-soldiers. George Goad came back as warden. Charlie Crandall came back and eventually became deputy warden. They accepted orders that Meyer be treated like any other inmate. But the scope for reaction went far beyond any two men. Among other vetererans, Al Tower joined the staff after being wounded in Holland, and what he would say about Meyer seemed to be what others felt: the war was over, prisoners had been murdered by both sides, so leave it at that.

Years later, Meyer's son would come to express thanks for the way his father was treated. No one had molested him. No one harassed him. He eventually went to work in the prison library, perfected his English and became friends with a defrocked lawyer and others. The one time he erupted was when he was carrying on a long-range chess game with another prisoner through written messages, was discovered and ordered to stop. When one veteran asked this former member of Hitler's bodyguard what he thought of Hitler, Meyer put his hand on his heart and said his feelings were in there, private. When Tom Lowerison said some of the murdered p.o.w's had been his friends, Meyer said it was not he who had murdered them, nor had he ordered it.

He behaved correctly, and would say he was treated fairly and well. He wrote about the war, said Canada produced good soldiers but not very good generals. From time to time, he took physical exercise under Everett Terris, that decorated sergeant who was still telling stories; after one, he turned to George Smith and asked "How old does that make me, George?" Everett was a good man, George Smith would say, and Kurt Meyer added a tribute of his own: he couldn't imagine why the Allies had needed Generals Eisenhower and Montgomery when they had a Sergeant Terris.

From time to time, too, Meyer had visits from a Moncton man who said he was his Uncle Fritz. German-born building contractor Fred Lichtenberg was not his uncle, but said he was to get around prison regulations. He also sent things to Meyer's family in Germany, kept a picture of Meyer in his home, and was a link to the second German who helped define the village. Lichtenberg had been a visitor to the home of Hans Klotz, had hired his son Gottfried, then fired him over a minor misdemeanor, thus helping set the stage for the boy's return to Germany.

Kurt Meyer was transferred to a German prison in 1951 and eventually released, but he was still in the penitentiary when Gottfried Klotz addressed a letter to any one of three former schoolmates, saying he'd been wounded on the

Russian Front and asking if they could help him get back to Canada. Of the three, Bill Palmer was dead, Joe Emery was elsewhere and having his own difficulties in getting over the war, Murray Dobson was still in the village but not much for correspondence. Thus Gottfried Klotz's letter was never answered.

In 1986, in the German edition of the *Reader's Digest*, he read an article I'd written, got my address and wrote another letter. We began to correspond and he invited me to visit him in Bremen, Germany, and in 1987 I did. But before I left I had a long talk with Joe Emery. I knew he didn't much like to talk about the war, felt a sense of guilt that he'd survived when so many good men hadn't: "Who was rolling the dice?" Nor had he found it easy when he emerged from the war at 23 without any special job training. Restless, even lost, he tried university and didn't like it, had trouble with the bottle, vanished for a time into the lumber woods, tried other things before he found his niche. For 29 years he was on the editorial staff of the Montreal *Gazette* , then retired to a small Quebec village. Then his wife died unexpectedly and he lost part of a leg in an accident. But he remained the solid, decent human being he'd always been. When I told him I was going to visit Gottfried, he asked me to extend his best wishes, said he'd be happy to see him.

Gottfried was pleased when I told him. I spent two weeks with him and Else, was warmly received. They were retired and living in a modest apartment where they insisted I be their guest. Gottfried was white-haired now. Else spoke no English, but day after day he and I talked for hours. Talked, stuffed ourselves with Else's good food, went for long bicycle rides, came back and talked again. Talked so much of the past that Else wondered why we did. But, to us, the past was like some fabled land crying out for discovery. Gottfried told things woven into this story. He had, in the village school, been an unwitting link with the follies of our time. Once the war was over, he'd become a link with the follies of the West's so-called Cold War with Russia. For three years he worked with his father, but by 1948 Hans Klotz was fed up with trying to meet quotas set by communist authorities in East Germany. He sold the farm, the sixth he'd lost. At 60, he also lost his wife to illness and went to work in a zoo and later as a school janitor. His son took off, came in darkness to the Iron Curtain, that forbidding mesh of guns and wire that barred the way to freedom. He found that smugglers went through nightly with black market goods, and he went as they did. At 3 a.m. he knocked on a door and asked someone if he had truly reached West Germany. For the rest of the night he sat in a railway station, feeling good, and then went on.

Into more trouble. He had little money and no profession, couldn't be employed because he had no identity card. Then his rusty English got him a civilian job with the British occupying forces. Cold War tensions were at their height and Germany was again in the frontline as he worked in Lubeck through the months of the airlift of supplies to prevent Berlin from being starved into Russian control. Later, he spent years as a military clerk in the Middle East. From 1957 to 1983, he held supervisory jobs in German industry, then retired on a state pension.

He had come to know a lot about the war, not by reading German books — losers don't write much about wars they lose — but by reading British and American books that impressed him with their objectivity. He was candid about the impact of Nazi propaganda on his youth, still felt that in war it is your country right or wrong, but now felt too that it was a stupid Germany that had started his war. Hitler, he said, was both a bandit and a madman, and far too many Nazis were still embedded in German government. He dismissed the village stories about his father being a spy, asked "How was he going to spy when we lived out in the country, had no car and no radio and didn't even get a Canadian newspaper?" He told about the fate of the mates he'd left behind near Danzig: they had, he'd heard, surrendered after peace returned and only after all their wounded were shipped away. He had never seen or heard of any of them since, but had no doubt that the survivors had gone to what they'd feared: Siberia.

In the war, Else had been bombed out of one home, survived years of it. She and Gottfried were in their 40s when they met, and it was touching to see their devotion, to hear about the long vacation trips they enjoy each year. One of his sisters was living in East Germany, the other in West Germany. His half-brother Arndt had been captured in Western Europe late in the the war, now had a West German farm, and still believed in the cause for which he'd fought. The Hitler Youth cousin with whom Gottfried had argued now had an East German farm, and wished for politics and politicians a pox upon them all. Gottfried was obviously saddened when we talked about Bill Palmer, Bud Brian, Bert Emmerson and others killed in the war, obviously pleased to get maple syrup sent by Harvey Smith's daughter Joy Johns. Shortly before dying of cancer in 1956, he said, his father wrote him that returning to Germany was the worst mistake he'd ever made. Gottfried wouldn't say he agreed, but he told a story that had a message of its own. It was about a dream he'd had again and again. He was walking down the dirt road to the farm at Coles Point. When he came to the home of neighbor Elmer Buck, he dropped in to say hello, and then he went on, and each time he hoped the dream would last till he got to the house where he'd been young, but it never did. When I reminded him that 1988 would mark the 50th anniversary of his high school graduation and suggested a class reunion, he at first seemed hesitant. I think he was wondering what sort of reception he'd get, but then he said he'd much like to see Joe Emery again; he'd like to see the village again. Yes, he said, he'd come, and his face lit up. "You know," he said, "your schooldays are your utopia."

It was surely a cause for celebration when men wanted to meet again in friendship after seeing war at its worst on opposite sides. Perhaps that helped what happened. Anyway, the reunion idea outgrew one for the Class of 1938, grew into a tribute to the village itself, into a celebration of remembered happiness. By the time it took place on July 1-2, 1988, it was for anyone who'd gone to school in the village and was at least 50 years of age. They came from six American states, from eight Canadian provinces, and for two wonderful days they talked and laughed and reminisced. They included numerous people who hadn't been back in 50 years, and when they sat down for the climactic banquet there were some 320 of them. The village itself wasn't what it once had been but it didn't seem to matter. The reunion was a magnificent success.

Six of the 27 people in the 1925 picture with Ina Brien came. Six members of the Class of 1938 came, Joe Emery among them. He had only recently been in hospital and was not feeling well, but he came. Gottfried Klotz and Joe met and they didn't get emotional — "I didn't know what to say," Joe would say — but each knew why the other was there. In fact, Gottfried and Else were overwhelmed by the warmth of the reception they got. They tramped across the Coles Point farm, now almost unrecognizable; abortive efforts to turn it into a chemical park had bullozed both house and land. For a week they and my sister Peg and her husband George Sibley, brother Jim and I were guests in my cousin Frances (Turner) Matheson's big white farmhouse, and when it was all over and Stanley Bateman was there to whisk them off to Fredericton for another visit, Else Klotz wept and Gottfried told someone it had been the happiest time he'd ever known. Within days, Joe Emery wrote that it had marvelously exceeded all his expectations.

Through it all, the stone soldier in the square had watched, and everyone present had known the war in one way or another, and a layer of grief was in them all. But no one talked much about the war. No one said anything to Gottfried Klotz about Hitler or the Nazis or his father being a spy. On the contrary, Frances (Turner) Matheson said, marvelling, that for a week her big white farmhouse was filled with love, and I suspect this was true of the village too.

Yet mystery remained. For people still asked the sort of question a boy had asked at the national war memorial some 40 years earlier. And none had a better answer than the one his mother gave.

Appendix

The 41 names on the village war memorial:

1914-18
George Bishop, William C. Bowser, Lester Buck, William Burns, Arnold Chambers, Raymond Cormier, Lloyd Crossman, Charles Elsdon, Laurier Emmerson, John F. Hickman, Ira King, Edward Landry, Edward LeBlanc, Frank LeBlanc, Pascal LeBlanc, J. Allen Milligan, Howard (really Harvard) McAllister, Lemuel McDowell, Ernest McFadden, Clove Saulnier, Albert V. Starratt, Robert Sutherland, Harry Taterie (really Tattrie), Hugh M. Teed, Lionel Teed.

1939-45
F.E. Brian, L. Bourgeois, D. Crosson, A. Cormier, B. Emmerson, A.M. Howe, U. LeBlanc, W. McManus, W. Manship, A.R. Mitton, G. Nugent, W. Palmer, C. Richard, D.E. Stack, V.H. Shea, A. Cormier.

To these might well be added three others: Warren Duffy who lived in the village for 10 years, Lionel Palmer who spent the summers of his youth there, and Gerald

Grant, goalie of that legendary 1927 high school hockey team who was, according to a history of the North Nova Scotia Highlanders, killed in an accident in England. Several attempts were made to get information about a number of French-speaking soldiers whose names are on the memorial and who came from the Dorchester parish area, but no replies ever came.